Saucers, Spooks and Kooks

UFO Disinformation in the Age of Aquarius

Adam Gorightly

Daily Grail Publishing

Contents

Foreword

David Perkins

"I cannot confirm or deny that we lied."

"The Air Force is committed to providing accurate and timely information within the confines of national security."

- Brigadier General Ronald Sconyers' statement at a press conference when asked if the Air Force purposely misled the public by promoting "UFO explanations" to cover up sightings of top secret U.S. spy planes.

Have you ever considered starting your own religion? If that's not your cup of tea, how about settling for creating a modern myth that will permanently imbed itself in world culture? If that's the case, Adam Gorightly has just the recipe for you.

Adam goes forthrightly where few have dared to tread. Never one to shy away from the tough stories in his books and articles, he has tackled such twilight subjects as the Manson family, the Kennedy assassination and just about every fringe topic in-between. An admitted "kook whisperer" and avowed "crackpot historian", Adam is the adult in the room, not the crackpot. Like any good cultural historian, he knows that the fringe has a way of gravitating to the center. He is a one-man expeditionary force with a canny ability to navigate the shadowy borderlands and come back safely with "the goods".

In this mighty tome, Gorightly takes on arguably the most intractable and enduring myth of modern times - the UFO. Specifically he's targeting one particularly tenacious tenet of the UFO myth - Dulce Base.

Most saucer enthusiasts are familiar with this piece of UFO lore. In a nutshell, Dulce Base proponents claim that the Dulce area in New Mexico is home to an underground base which is populated by humans and space aliens working in collaboration. Allegedly, the U.S. government and the aliens made a deal in which extraterrestrial technology would be given to the government in exchange for allowing the aliens to operate an on-going alien/human breeding program. At some point, a misunderstanding or disagreement triggered a massive shoot-out between workers and the ETs in which 66 humans were killed. Let that sink in for a moment.

Dulce is a sleepy village within the Jicarilla Apache reservation in a remote area of northwestern New Mexico. Rumors had begun to seep out of Dulce in the mid-1970s. Unidentified craft of all descriptions as well as helicopters were zipping around. Strangely surgerized "mutilated" cows were said to be falling from the sky.

As word got out, more and more investigators (including me) made the journey to Dulce to see what was going on and to talk with New Mexico State Policeman Gabe Valdez, who was the unofficial point-man on the ground in Dulce. Most investigators left Dulce feeling more perplexed than ever. After my first Dulce trip I recall thinking that whatever/whoever was behind the Dulce follies had a good sense of theater.

With his characteristic acerbic wit and amused ironic detachment, Gorightly builds on the ground-breaking reporting of Greg Bishop (*Project Beta: The Story of Paul Bennewitz, National Security and the Creation of a Modern American myth*) and Christian Lambright's book *X Descending*. Both books tell the story of a hapless Albuquerque scientist/businessman, Paul Bennewitz, who was driven to the brink of insanity and an early grave by a highly-focused military disinformation operation directed against him. Bennewitz's only "crime" was being a concerned citizen who was curious about the unusual nocturnal phenomena that he witnessed at Kirtland Air Force Base.

Gorightly takes this tawdry tale to the next level with his granular reporting of the workings of every wheel and cog in the government's disinformation and myth-making machinery. In the process Adam details the motives and machinations of all involved - both spook and kook. What he finds is the perfect storm of converging vectors — zealous UFO true believers collide with hardened military manipulators, a deceivers vs. believers combustible amalgamation.

In this "hot mess" there was bound to be collateral damage as all parties involved connived to bend the Dulce myth to their own purposes. Careers were ruined, lives were shattered and many innocent bystander cows met their premature demise. What began as an operation to steer the inquisitive Mr. Bennewitz away from the action at Kirtland AFB and redirect his focus to Dulce, ended up developing a life of its own. Dulce became a "strange attractor", luring into its gravitational field virtually anyone with an interest in the subject and who had an agenda, either personal or institutional.

As Gorightly hints, perhaps the government was attempting to kill several birds with one stone. Not only did they hope to destabilize Bennewitz and fragment the UFO research community, but they recognized that the UFO mania surrounding Dulce would provide the perfect cover to run several clandestine programs. These might have included weapons testing, covert operations training, and perhaps a read-out of nuclear contamination caused by the Project Gasbuggy nuclear detonation near Dulce in 1967.

In the late 1970s I advanced the theory that the cattle mutilations were part of a secret test program to determine the extent of environmental nuclear contamination, specifically at Dulce and also nationwide. Time may tell how much truth there is to that theory, but it has yet to be either definitely debunked or confirmed.

So why does any of this matter now? In his Intro, Adam asks if the Dulce myth was "spun out of whole cloth by opportunistic myth-makers" or "even more bizarrely, was the U.S. government involved in helping to create these myths?" Was the Dulce Project so successful from the military's perspective that they kicked out the stops and cultivated Dulce as a kind of paranormal playground and laboratory for developing exotic technologies, prototype false flag operations, PSI OP (psychological warfare) exercises and advanced social/mythological engineering techniques? Yes we should be shocked, shocked that our government could possibly be engaged in such nefarious activity.

Consider if you will, one possible scenario provoked by Gorightly's elucidation of the facts of the matter. In the years after Kenneth Arnold's famous 1947 "flying saucer" sighting, the U.S. military tried its best to figure out what the heck was going on with UFOs. Two major studies (Project Bluebook and the Condon Report) set out to debunk the notion of ET-manned craft, which had steadily been gaining traction in public awareness.

Privately the military men came to the conclusion that they couldn't figure out the true nature of UFOs, but since they didn't seem to pose a serious threat, it would be best to sweep the subject under the rug. They then set about debunking reports and discrediting the UFO believers.

Since the military's primary function is to protect and defend the country, they couldn't very well say "we don't know what these 'things' are, but since they're not blowing up the White House or anything, don't worry about it. We'll keep an eye on 'em." Then "somebody" looked at public opinion polls which showed that about half of the American public believed that "UFOs are real." The social engineers in the government realized that this was a myth that needed to be "managed", hopefully in a way that would work to the advantage of the established power structure.

Then maybe some fancy think tank came up with a brilliant Machiavellian solution: How about this? On one hand we vigorously deny the reality of UFOs, and on the other hand we discreetly float suggestions and "evidence" suggesting that we are fully aware of the ET presence. Let people think that we have recovered craft and bodies from saucer crashes and maybe even leak stories to indicate that we're actively working with the aliens. Yeah that's it, they've given us technology which will guarantee U.S. world supremacy and permanent hegemony. So don't worry about it people. We've got this. It's complicated but trust us, it's all for your own good.

The degree to which the components of the UFO myth were manufactured, as opposed to manifesting spontaneously, is difficult to gauge. The major memes or building blocks of the myth included: crashed saucers, abductions and cattle mutilations. Over time, the myth came to include missing time, implants, intrusive medical procedures on abductees and alien-induced mind control.

The Dulce Base miasma marked the full flowering of what has been called The Dark Side Hypothesis, a paranoid, conspiratorial vision which still holds considerable sway. Was the Dulce Base turn of events in some way a catalyst for this shift in the perception of UFOs, or merely a symptom of a society that was veering toward an Orwellian dystopia?

Gone were the Golden Days of the 1950s colorful "contactees" with their fanciful tales of visits to other worlds on flying saucers with gorgeous space babes and hunky alien dudes. In return for the guided tours, the contactees were obliged to listen to gently scolding lectures from the aliens about the dangers of pollution and nuclear weapons. Keep in mind that this was almost 20 years before the rise of the modern environmentalist movement.

Was the decline of the Space Brother era due to a natural devolution toward malignancy inherent in "feel good" utopian movements? Or was the shift to the Dark Side engineered because the social controllers knew that, in terms of societal control systems, fear provided substantially more leverage than utopian dreams as a tool to move the populace to the desired level of pliability and "compliance".

If the population felt generally content and not threatened, we wouldn't have to spend about half of our yearly federal discretionary spending budget on military-related expenditures, now would we? With fear and apprehension as prime motivators, it was much easier to condition the population and have a strategic impact in shaping the culture to suit the needs of the ruling elite. With little regard for the citizenry, the "world beater" social engineers manipulated the UFO myth solely to address the needs of the ever-increasing alignment of business, politics and military/defense industry interests.

In his prescient 1980 book *Friendly Fascism*, former government policy-maker Bertram Gross addresses the issue of the "mysterious establishment" and their "tremendously sophisticated methodology of technological and political manipulation". Gross points out the need for myth in this process: "Without myths, the rulers and their aides cannot maintain support... and the legitimacy of empire may decay."

In his 1976 paper "Democracy vs. the National Security State", noted philosopher and social critic Marcus Raskin echoes Gross's observations: "The National Security State has been the actualizing mechanism of ruling elites to implant their imperial schemes and misplaced ideals ... which poses a danger to world civilization and menaces the well-being of its citizens."

Sure, this might sound like some pointy-headed intellectuals flapping their lips about civilization and its discontents. Still... the dynamic described by Gross and Raskin is alive and well as illustrated by recent comments from an administration official. Asked to describe America's current doctrine, the official replied: "We're America bitch. No friends. No enemies. Permanent destabilization creates American advantage."

Although the official was apparently talking about Middle East policy, the same principle of destabilization/fragmentation could readily be employed to "manage" American society and undermine ufology. If an unlimited number of conspiracy theories were amplified and allowed to "flood the zone", the result would be cacophony, atomization and permanent destabilization. So much for those pesky researchers who were constantly poking and prodding officialdom for

The Truth about the National Security State and its secrets. This tactic would also have the bonus effect of neutralizing the Russians, who had become increasingly interested in whatever the ufologists could expose. As Harry Truman used to say: "If you can't convince them, confuse them."

It's well known that a "coverup" can conceal either ignorance or knowledge. In a 2014 interview with Open Minds, the seasoned French UFO researcher/author Jacques Vallee said: "To my mind, the phenomenon has probably resisted all analysis, classified or not." He goes on to say that field study is more useful than "speculating on inaccessible, hypothetic secrets in the drawers of governments." In other words, the government is bluffing it. They don't know substantially more about UFOs than the researchers.

The social engineer-types must have taken heart in a 2019 Gallup poll showing that 68% of American adults think that "the government knows more about UFOs than it is telling us." Apparently the Big Bluff is still working. The same poll found that 33% of adults believe that "some UFOs are alien spacecraft." That is roughly 100 million Americans!

Any way you look at it, that's a lot of belief to be "managed". On a positive note, lately there appears to be a reevaluation of the permanent destabilization school of thought among the culture crafters. Some have come to question the idea that the tactic of destabilization is appropriate to the actual existential threats at hand.

Some of you might remember the days when President Reagan was fond of "ad-libbing" his kumbaya remarks paraphrased as: "I've often wondered what would happen if the earth was under attack by hostile aliens. Our differences world-wide would vanish and we would all unite to save mankind." It appears that Reagan was trying to have it both ways by promoting the globalization agenda while simultaneously fanning the hostile alien myth. If General Colin Powell was within earshot, he would roll his eyes and whisper to his staff: "Oh no, here come the little green men again."

With looming climate change threatening civilization, the myth-makers might see the value in substituting "climate catastrophe" for "hostile aliens" in Reagan's sentiments. With everything on the line "for reals", some policy-makers have entertained the notion that a stabilized and unified world would be necessary for survival. Some may have even reached the conclusion that a secular UFO "religion" is less destabilizing than traditional religions. To fight the common climate change enemy and avoid total environmental and societal collapse, at least some form of "globalization" would be required.

Hard-line conspiracy enthusiasts aren't buying any of the talk about "peace dividends" and world union. According to this scrambled school of thought, humans are hard-wired for aggression and domination. For the U.S. to abandon its bellicose strategic posture would be opening the gates to the barbarians. Any move toward New World Order globalization would be suicidal. UFOs are the instruments of "the cabal", part of the plot by the Rothchilds, the Bavarian Illuminati, etc. to direct even more wealth and power into the hands of the ruling elites.

It will be interesting to see how it all turns out. Meanwhile, the "alien threat" card would be handy to have in the social engineering portfolio if it ever became necessary to launch the ultimate false flag operation. For starters, about 100 million Americans would be potentially dupable almost instantly.

Life is filled with uncertainties, but one thing is certain — Adam Gorightly has given me much food for thought in *Saucers, Spooks and Kooks*. It is an impressive piece of research which is destined to be the "go to" book on the Dulce Base era for years to come.

Adam doesn't spoon-feed the reader with pre-digested pablum fit for consumer consumption. He lays out the dots and leaves it for you to connect them in a meaningful way. He is not big on polemics or hectoring screeds.

As someone who was present at several of the events that Adam describes and who knew many of the major characters in this saga, I can attest to his impeccable reporting.

A special treat for the reader is Adam's chapter "Adventures in Chapel Perilous". It is, hands down, the funniest and most poignant description of the life of a UFO and conspiracy researcher that I've ever read.

Adam Gorightly's book may rattle some cages and rock some boats, but he is willing to let the chips fall where they may. His tale of lunacy and deceit will hopefully be a reminder to truth-seekers everywhere to use extreme discernment in choosing their sources of information. Don't be a dupe or a shill or anybody's "useful idiot" and above all ... refuse to be managed.

David Perkins
Santa Fe, New Mexico
September 23, 2019

Introduction

A curious set of stories

In the 1980s, a curious set of stories simultaneously emerged in the field of UFO research. One involved crashed flying saucers, from which the dead bodies of aliens had been recovered. These claims of crash saucers were further amplified in the mid 80s by a series of documents that surfaced alleging that a secret government group had been established in 1947 to address the "extraterrestrial problem." The name of this group was Majestic-12 (MJ-12), and the release of these documents—known thereafter as the MJ-12 Papers—would shape the face of ufology in the years to come.

Another of these overlapping stories concerned a secret underground base in Dulce, New Mexico, where—it was alleged—aliens in collaboration with the U.S. government had agreed to a secret treaty in which ET technology would be exchanged in return for test subjects to be used for an alien-human hybrid breeding program.

According to legend, a group of Dulce base security workers became outraged over the breeding program and decided to revolt against their ET overlords, which led to the massacre of sixty-six workers in a firefight. One of the security workers, a fellow named Thomas Castello, was able to escape the carnage, taking along with him photos, documents, and other evidence that would ostensibly blow the lid off what was going down in Dulce. Castello, before disappearing for good, was said to have passed this information on to a number of UFO researchers, and these revelations later appeared in a five-page document called *The Dulce Papers*. From there the legend grew of vast breeding chambers filled with alien-human fetuses poised to conquer humanity. These images, in time, oozed their way into our homes courtesy of *The X-Files*, and other films and TV programs of the 1990s.

The Dulce Base story emerged around the same time that a self-described "nuclear physicist" named Bob Lazar surfaced claiming he had worked at a secret base on the outskirts of Las Vegas, Nevada, called Area 51 where alien craft were being reverse-engineered. As with MJ-12 and the Dulce Papers, these Area 51 revelations likewise set ufology on its pointed ears, and the mythology that grew out of this period has since become ingrained in popular culture.

But were these stories based on the truth, or half-truths, or were they spun out of whole cloth by opportunistic myth-makers? And, even more bizarrely, was the U.S. government involved in helping to create these myths?

Chapter I
Crash go the saucers!

The flying saucer crash mythos flew into contemporary culture in 1950 with the publication of Frank Scully's *Behind the Flying Saucers*. Scully's account expanded upon an article he had written for *Variety* magazine based on a lecture delivered at the University of Denver by self-proclaimed millionaire oilman Silas M. Newton. In his lecture, Newton claimed that a flying saucer piloted by otherworldly midgets had crashed in Aztec, New Mexico, in 1948. The source of Newton's saucer revelations was a mysterious "Dr. Gee", who had purportedly examined the remains of these interplanetary travelers and viewed pieces of the saucer debris.

Behind the Flying Saucers was later exposed as a hoax based on bogus information provided by Newton and his partner in crime, Leo Gebauer (aka Dr. Gee), who—when they weren't gas-lighting as saucer experts—peddled phony oil leases and "magnetic oil-detecting machines."

Former CIA officer Karl Pflock discovered records indicating that after Silas Newton had been outed as a hoaxer, he was visited by agents from "a highly secret U.S. Government entity" who informed Newton that they knew his saucer story was false, but nonetheless encouraged him to keep pushing it out to the public. Pflock later wondered: "Did the U.S. Government or someone associated with it use Newton to discredit the idea of crashed flying saucers so a real captured saucer or saucers could be more easily kept under wraps? Was this actually nothing to do with real saucers but instead some sort of psychological warfare operation?"[1]

The flying saucer crash-retrieval legend took a back seat in ufology until the late 1970s when researcher Leonard Stringfield helped revive interest in the subject during a presentation at the 1978 Mutual

UFO Network (MUFON) Symposium in Dayton, Ohio. Although Stringfield didn't cite Roswell among the crash-retrieval incidents he spoke about, certain details in his presentation would later be replicated in the Roswell crash story, including accounts of dead aliens transported to Wright-Patterson Air Force Base.

One of Stringfield's cases concerned a flying saucer crash-retrieval that allegedly occurred in 1948 along the Texas-Mexico border referred to as the El Indio-Guerrero Incident. The source for this story was a retired Air Force Colonel who claimed that a dead alien was recovered from the wreckage, a story first reported by ufologist Todd Zechel. UFO researcher Kevin Randle later discovered that Zechel never bothered to vet the "retired" Colonel, who wasn't exactly a retired Colonel after all but had simply served as a Civil Air Patrol squadron leader, and hadn't actually seen a crashed saucer—or dead aliens, for that matter. Nonetheless, these cases planted seeds that later sprouted into what is now regarded as the flying saucer crash to end all others.[2]

Per a Freedom of Information Act (FOIA) request, a five-page National Security Agency (NSA) memo surfaced concerning this very same MUFON Symposium featuring Leonard Stringfield's crashed saucer presentation. The memo, dated August 29, 1978, was written by an unidentified NSA "assignee" who commented on what he suspected to be a number of fraudulent "CIA memos" presented at the symposium.

It was later revealed that the "assignee" in question was a former NSA employee and MUFON board member, Tom Deuley. As Jack Brewer wrote at The UFO Trail:

> The memo author/NSA assignee indicated he suspected the letters to be fraudulent, and proceeded to interact with the researchers in order to investigate the authenticity of the docs. He went on to explain he contacted CIA personnel who verified the letters to be frauds.

The memo author described his suspicions of the origin of the purported CIA letters, as well as his concerns about the activities of researchers involved, including Todd Zechel (who founded Citizens Against UFO Secrecy, or CAUS.)

The memo author describes a nearly hour long telephone conversation with Zechel in which the NSA man clearly developed a sense of responsibility to inform the Agency of its contents. The author explained Zechel was requesting he "watch out for UFO related information within NSA" and "that I pass on what I could." The NSA assignee added he had "to some degree" checked on Zechel's character "with some people who have worked with him more closely."

"There is some thought," he continued, "that he would be capable of being behind the CIA letter fraud and that he is apt to go to most any length to collect information or to bend facts to fit his needs."[3]

Todd Zechel formed the Citizens Against UFO Secrecy (CAUS) in 1977 with fellow researcher Brad Sparks and attorney Peter Gersten. That same year, Gersten filed an FOIA request with the CIA concerning UFOs, and in response CAUS received over nine hundred documents from the agency in 1979. However, missing from this massive tranche were fifty-seven documents that had been held back under the advisement of the NSA due to "national security considerations." Subsequently, Peter Gersten filed a lawsuit in an attempt to shake loose these withheld files, but the judge overseeing the case ultimately upheld the NSA's decision. Due to these legal battles, it's quite possible Zechel's UFO activism was a factor that brought him to the attention of the NSA assignee, Tom Deuley, who was monitoring his activities at the '78 MUFON Symposium.

Also in 1978—which appeared to be a very busy year in ufology with FOIA requests flying left and right amid tales of crashed saucers spinning around—up and coming ufologist Stanton "Stan" Friedman tracked down a witness to one such flying saucer crash that purportedly occurred near Roswell, New Mexico. The witness in this case was retired Air Force Major Jesse Marcel, who on the morning of July 7, 1947, responded to a reported crash of some sort that had occurred at the Foster Ranch located thirty miles north of Roswell. The bare bones of the original report simply stated that a "disc was picked up at the rancher's home" by Marcel "and it was inspected at the Roswell Army Air Field..."[4] Speculation soon began to spread that the Air Force had recovered a genuine flying saucer. As the story developed over the next few days, it was soon after reported that the mystery object was actually a weather balloon, which many later grew to suspect was a cover story to conceal the recovery of an alien craft.

When Friedman interviewed Marcel there was no mention of aliens (dead or living) discovered in the wreckage. The alien angle would only surface after Friedman happened upon the second-hand account of another alleged witness to the event, a government surveyor named Barney Barnett, who was on assignment when he encountered the remains of a metallic disc-shaped object that included several dead alien bodies. While Barnett was taking in the scene, a military convoy rolled-in, cordoned off the area, then collected the remains and hauled them away.

Friedman joined forces with another up-and-coming ufologist, William "Bill" Moore, and during the months of 1979 the duo would dig ever deeper into the Roswell wreckage. Their investigations led to the publication of *Incident at Roswell* (1980) authored by Moore and Charles Berlitz, a book that almost singlehandedly ushered into popular consciousness a story that, until then, had been not much more than an obscure footnote in UFO history.

Incident at Roswell would include similar details found in the phony Aztec story, such as hieroglyphic writing discovered on pieces of the saucer debris, and the transport of dead aliens to a secret government hangar where they were put on ice. Due to the success of *Incident at Roswell*, crashed saucers became a sudden craze, and Bill Moore a rising star in ufology.

What goes up must come down.

Chapter 2
Bait and switch

The term 'UFO Disclosure' has become a popular mantra for those who believe that the powers-that-be are sitting on evidence that would at last reveal the existence of ETs visiting our planet. To this end, UFO Disclosure is a movement within ufology petitioning the keepers of these secrets—often presumed to be high level government officials—to disclose what they are hiding; to lift the lid on the secrets of crashed saucers and the entities who pilot them.

UFO Disclosure, in many instances, is akin to the old 'bait and switch' routine, as one hand diverts attention while the other, unnoticed, slips into the mark's pocket. Such sleight of hand has been attributed to the rash of cattle mutilations (aka 'cattle mutes') that occurred in the Dulce area starting in the mid 1970s. The 'bait' in this case being UFOs, and the 'switch' as a means of creating a false narrative concerning cattle mutilations. In this regard, rumors have long circulated that cattle mutes were part of a bio-genetic experiment program—such as the one reportedly going on at the Dulce underground base—the ultimate goal of which was to create human-alien hybrids to preserve a dying ET race.

In the early 1970s—when the first wave of cattle mutilations began—these incidents became associated with flying saucers and/or satanic cults. Although in subsequent years nothing substantive surfaced connecting saucers or Satan to cattle mutilations, these memes continue to haunt UFO lore, conjuring images of ETs with surgical laser beams—or witches poised under a full moon with ritual daggers—dissecting hapless heifers for unfathomable reasons.

As the years pass and the cosmic dust settles, a more prosaic answer may rest at the heart of this enigma of excised bovine bungholes. As sexy as saucers or satanic cults sound, perhaps the mystery swirling around cattle mutes (and Dulce Base) have more to do with a certain subterranean nuclear detonation known as Project Gasbuggy that occurred in 1967, twenty-one miles southwest of Dulce. Part of the Atomic Energy Commission's "Plowshare Program" intended for the peaceful use of nukes, Gasbuggy was designed to release natural gas reserves from the subterranean environment—in essence an early attempt at fracking. When all was said and done, the explosion created a massive cavity, 80 feet wide and 335 feet deep, filled with radioactive gas which became unusable and potentially life threatening as it was dispersed into the atmosphere. Those of a conspiratorial bent contend that Gasbuggy was intentionally designed to create an underground cavity and facilitate the excavation and clandestine construction of the Dulce underground base.

A theory that dovetails with Project Gasbuggy suggests that a certain alphabet soup agency conducted cattle mutilations as a method to measure radiation levels in the greater Dulce area. In this respect, cows make perfect test subjects: dumb, docile, slow moving targets, whose cattle colleagues tell no tales. All of this smacks (to your humble author) of a sophisticated Psy Op (Psychological Operation)orchestrated to conceal the true nature of what was going on, and then to run these rumors through the UFO research treadmill and observe how they spread like so many mind-bending mushrooms, sprouting from steaming cow pies. In the decade following Project Gasbuggy, reports surfaced of radiation leaking into the Jicarilla Apache Indian Reservation, which ostensibly contributed to a rise in cancer rates in and around Dulce.

New Mexico state trooper Gabe Valdez investigated a series of Dulce area cattle mutilations, which began on June 13, 1976, on the ranch of Manuel Gomez located in the Jicarilla Reservation. Valdez's police report noted that two sets of tripod prints were discovered in the vicinity of the mute, and a third set of smaller tripod prints appeared to have followed the cow to the spot where it was discovered, thus leading to speculation that alien craft had been involved in the mutilation.

Although a number of the Dulce area cattle mutes were linked to unexplained lights in the sky, it soon became evident that there was a distinctly human component to be found in many of the cases. In one case, a high dose of atropine was found in the test samples suggesting that the cow had been drugged prior to the mutilation. Another mutilation, that occurred on June 12, 1982 on the Gomez ranch, included the discovery of what was referred to as "radar chaff." Radar chaff, typically comprised of aluminum shavings, was used during this period by the air force to conceal experimental test flights by dispersing the chaff into the air as a method to block radar tracking. Two weeks after the discovery of the radar chaff, a high-altitude temperature/pressure sensor device, used for collecting chemical and biological samples in the atmosphere, was discovered in the same general location as the chaff. Gabe Valdez speculated that this device had been accidentally ejected from an aircraft involved in the mutilation, and during that same mishap a larger than intended quantity of the radar chaff had also been released.[5] In another incident, a gas mask was discovered at one of the cattle mute sites, and all of these pieces of evidence, stacked one on top of the other, suggested to Valdez that a government agency was behind a secret cattle testing program targeting the Dulce area.

In contrast to the theory that cattle mutes were part of a clandestine government project, *The Tao News* reporter Phaedra Greenwood recalled a conversation with Edmund Gomez (son of rancher Manual Gomez) which concerned:

> ...an artifact that looked like a mask of some kind, just the front plate like a Halloween mask, with a wide forehead, big eyes, a narrow chin and two spigots that emerged right and left from the mouth piece that might attach to hoses and/or gas tanks. He let me try it on. It was too wide at the forehead and narrow at the jaw; it wouldn't have fit a human being. Gabe [Valdez] had mentioned this mask to me. (Phaedra Greenwood email to David Perkins 12/6/19)

Gomez said he usually kept the mask and other evidence stashed away in a safe place. His voice dropped. 'My house was broken into and many of my photos and records of the mutilations were stolen. My mother received threatening phone calls. It was always a man's voice. If they got me, they'd hang up. When they got my mother they'd say, 'Tell your son to stop investigating these cattle mutilations or you're going to lose him.'"

He flipped the cover of the album closed. "That's why now I keep all my own records. I make four copies of everything and send them all over the country."

In the majority of the cases he investigated, Valdez observed that the lymph nodes had been removedfrom the cows, in contrast to the removal of sex organs and other body parts that varied from case to case. This led Valdez to conclude that the removal of the lymph nodes were due to the fact that they provided specific medical information as an internal organ that could be tested for cancer. In Valdez's opinion, everything else removed from the mutes served as possible obfuscation or misdirection.[6]

There were even accounts of UFOs and helicopters working in tandem, which led to speculation that the military was in cahoots with the space people to abduct the cattle and then slice and dice them in clandestine labs. These stories sprouted like some weird fungus, fueled in part by Linda Moulton Howe's documentary *A Strange Harvest* (1980) which further propelled cattle mutes into pop culture.

In *A Strange Harvest*, Gabe Valdez appears in his police cruiser with Howe riding shotgun, traveling the dusty roads around Dulce, attempting to unravel the cattle mute mystery. When Valdez was asked who or what was behind the cattle mutes, he replied: "It has to be a highly sophisticated agency that has total secrecy and the money and technology...or *something* else...As far as an occult group being involved, I think [the case] would have been broken a long time ago."

Howe: "So what's left?"

"Either the government or extraterrestrials," Gabe answered, followed by his signature trademark chuckle, which wasn't meant as a complete dismissal of ETs as the possible perps, but more a nervous tic about how ludicrous this whole scenario must have sounded back in 1980—or even today, for that matter—that ET's are traveling across the cosmos to carve up cows. Ultimately, Valdez grew less convinced of the ET angle and eventually came to believe that the hidden hand behind cattle mutes possessed all too human characteristics, and that UFOs had been inserted into the narrative to intentionally obscure the facts.

Apparently Linda Howe arrived at a different conclusion than her friend Gabe Valdez. During the 2003 "Majestic Documents Crash Retrieval Conference" in Las Vegas, Nevada, researcher Greg Bishop asked Howe her thoughts regarding the theory that a clandestine government operation was responsible for the mutilations. In response, Howe dismissed the idea, stating that ETs had most likely planted the evidence (radar chaff and gas masks found at the scene of the Dulce cattle mutilations) as a means to throw investigators off track and make it appear that humans were actually the perpetrators. On occasion, Howe has used a similar tack in regards to UFOs. According to film maker Mark Pilkington:

We put forward the theory in *Mirage Men* that UFO mythology was encouraged at various points by the U.S. Air Force and other military and intelligence organizations as a useful cover for all manner of technologies related to aviation. We were suggesting that the UFO story can be used to disguise accidental sightings of these things. And we suggested such to Linda Howe, who basically said the opposite was true: that extraterrestrial spacecraft were being disguised as classified human military projects.[7]

Chapter 3
The strangest collection of weirdos ever assembled

In 1969, physicist Paul Bennewitz launched Thunder Scientific Corporation, a company specializing in "Humidity Generation, Calibration and Measurement Instruments." Thunder Scientific headquarters were based out of Bennewitz's home located adjacent to Kirtland Air Force Base in Albuquerque, New Mexico.

During the 1970s, Bennewitz became a card-carrying member of the Aerial Phenomenon Research Association (APRO), a civilian UFO research organization that was headed-up by the husband and wife team of Jim and Coral Lorenzen in Tucson, Arizona. In 1979, Bennewitz's interest in UFOs significantly spiked at the same time cattle mutilations were going through the roof in the Dulce area.

On April 20, 1979, Bennewitz participated in a cattle mutilation conference organized by former moon-walking Apollo astronaut Sen. Harrison Schmitt (R-New Mexico) held at the Albuquerque Public Library. Schmitt opened the conference by telling the attendees:

There are few activities more dangerous than an unsolved pattern of crime. There is always the potential for such crimes to escalate in frequency and severity if allowed to go unsolved and unpunished. Such a dangerous pattern of crime is the mutila-tion killings of thousands of cattle, horses, and other animals over the past several years throughout many states...In the last five years - and probably longer - in at least fifteen states animals have been killed and systematically mutilated for no apparent purpose, by persons unknown.

This now legendary and somewhat controversial conference included in attendance: "…FBI agents, state police, sheriffs and local police from around the country, Indian pueblo governors, tribal police chiefs, Los Alamos scientists, veterinarians, New Agers in robes, hippies, news media, politicians, spooky agent types, dusty ranchers in beat-up cowboy hats, independent researchers and, of course, ufologists of all stripes and colors"[8]—not to mention a growing legion of cattle mute sleuths, among them Tom Adams, Gary Massey and David Perkins, as well as the enigmatic Thomas Allen Levesque (aka Tal), who will later loom large in our saga.

In January 1978, Tom Adams began publishing the newsletter *Stigmata*, which soon became the central clearinghouse for a growing cattle mute subculture. Adams—along with his cow-curious colleagues, Massey and Perkins—referred to themselves self-deprecatingly as "mutologists." According to Perkins, "We thought that being professional 'mutologists' sounded a little classier than 'weird people who get a kick out of looking at dead cows.'"[9] As Perkins recalled:

Tom Adams (left) and Gary Massey in 1980 with "Thang"
(Photo credit: David Perkins).

"I first met Gary Massey and his partner Tom Adams in the mid-1970s in Colorado. They were a dynamic investigative duo, hot on the trail of the elusive cattle mutilators. The three of us quickly formed a close bond. Over the next several years we spent endless hours traveling together in Gary's big van 'Thang', investigating mutilation cases, attending conferences and scanning the skies from my mountain top home in Colorado. We were the Three Musketeers of 'mutology', although at times, we seemed a bit more like the Three Stooges."

A Yale trained sociologist, Perkins ventured westward in the late 1960s to study non-traditional communities, and during his research became part of one such counterculture experiment, joining the Libre commune in Southern Colorado in 1970. Perkins (known by the name of Izzy Zane to his cattle mute coterie) suddenly found himself on the front lines of mutology after encountering one in his rural neighborhood in 1975. Curiously enough, the only evidence discovered at the cattle mute scene was drops of blood that led back in the direction of Perkins' home. Perkins later learned that the local sheriff had considered him, at least for a short time, to be a suspect in the case.

Intrigued by his initial cattle mute encounter, Perkins went on to establish the Animal Mutilation Probe (AMP), documenting his own case in addition to a slew of others he investigated in the ensuing years, along the way becoming an authority on the subject. In the summer of 1979, Perkins was contacted by Linda Howe, who was then working as a news reporter for the CBS affiliate station KMGH TV in Denver. Howe, at the time, had just started digging into the rash of mutes spreading like wildfire across Colorado and the Four Corners region, and so she reached out to Perkins to learn from him all he knew about the subject, and to tap into his extensive network of cattle mute contacts.

On June 12, at Linda Howe's request, Perkins loaded up his extensive case files into his trusty '64 Plymouth Valiant station wagon (known endearingly as The Mutemobile) and hauled them 200 miles to the KMGH offices where Howe immediately began making copies of everything and hashing out plans with Perkins to take her and a film crew on a road trip later that year, the end results of which appeared in Howe's documentary, *A Strange Harvest*. During their June 12 meeting, Perkins promised he'd give Howe a heads-up if any new cattle mute cases came to his attention. A couple weeks later, on June 25, Perkins was alerted to a mute discovered on the Potts Ranch in Walsenburg, Colorado. According to Perkins:

> By the time I got there, the animal had been lying in the blazing sun for several hours. Its mouth was only partially open and I wanted to see if the tongue had been removed. I tried to pry open the jaws by hand but was unsuccessful. I found a stick and used it as a crowbar. After a few tries, the jaw finally popped open. In that process, I apparently opened up a pathway for the bull to release an explosive noxious spew of heated stomach gases and gross particulate matter…directly into my face. Indeed there was no tongue, at least as far back in the throat as I could see…I took a photo of Linda and her cameraman crouching over the mute, and in it you can see the very stick I used for that misadventure….

Due to his involvement in the field of mutology, as well as Perkins' academic background, Harrison Schmitt and Gabe Valdez (who were the prime movers behind the Albuquerque conference) tapped him as the keynote speaker for the event. Perkins recalled:

> Getting in front of that group at the conference was pretty rough, and Valdez and Schmitt had picked me for reasons unknown to send me in first. Whether they were feeding me to the lions or what, I don't know…and I didn't say a whole lot; I simply provided an overview of the phenomenon. My most memorable line was: 'The only thing that makes sense about the mutilations is that they make no sense at all.' That was my first comment to

Linda Howe and cinematographer Richard Lerner investigate one of Howe's first cattle mutilations near Walsenburg, Colorado in June of 1979. The stick on the ground is the one David Perkins used to pry the cow's jaw open (Photo credit: David Perkins).

the group, and it was a very Zen comment. And for some reason people picked up on it, and it was repeated by news outlets. And what I was trying to point out was that the whole thing seemed senseless. It just made no sense. I was trying to convey the fact that this was a real conundrum, kind of like a Zen puzzle of some sort for us to figure out.

Following Perkins keynote speech, Tom Adams presented a "preliminary report regarding the appearance of unidentified helicopters at or near mutilation sites."[10] An expanded version of this report was later released under the title of *The Choppers...and the Choppers: Mystery Helicopters and Animal Mutilations* (1980) documenting over two hundred helicopter/mute cases.

Next up to the podium was Gabe Valdez, who spoke about the strange lights in the sky he'd witnessed in the Dulce area that appeared to be associated with the mutilations. During one of his patrols, Valdez observed one of these lights (a UFO by any other name) flying directly toward Mount Archuleta, near the town of Dulce. Valdez had expected to see the craft crash into the mountainside, but at the last second it vanished into thin air, as if it had somehow flown into, or through, the mountain. Following Valdez's talk, Paul Bennewitz approached Gabe and the two men became fast friends. Soon after, Bennewitz accompanied Valdez during his nighttime patrols in and around Dulce during which they chased a number of strange lights in the night.

The Albuquerque cattle mutilation conference received mixed reviews, although to those in attendance it seemed a sincere effort on Harrison Schmitt's part to bring together the principal players in the scene to discuss the impact that the phenomenon was having on the livelihoods of ranching communities throughout the American West.

Among the more vocal critics of the event was reporter Mark Acuff, who in an editorial for *The New Mexico Independent* described the conference as an "exquisite farce" featuring "the strangest collection of weirdos ever assembled in New Mexico." Such negative portrayals as these were believed to have contributed to Harrison Schmitt's failed re-election bid in 1982.

Chapter 4
Ground rules for regression

On May 6, 1980, the state police office in Cimarron, New Mexico was contacted by a hysterical twenty-six-year-old woman named Myrna Hansen who claimed that she, her six-year-old son Shawn, and an unfortunate cow had been harassed by interplanetary visitors near the town of Eagle Nest. With nary a clue as how to deal with this traumatized young lady, the local cops contacted Gabe Valdez for assistance as by this time he had acquired the reputation as the go-to guy for cut-up cows and unexplained lights in the sky.[11]

Valdez phoned his running mate, Paul Bennewitz, figuring Bennewitz could tap his APRO contacts to bring in some specialized expertise for the Myrna Hansen case. In response, APRO's Jim Lorenzen put Bennewitz in touch with Dr. Leo Sprinkle, a University of Wyoming Professor with over ten years of experience investigating UFO cases using hypnotic regression. In early May of 1980, Sprinkle traveled to Albuquerque to conduct an hypnosis regression with Myrna Hansen at Bennewitz's home.[12]

Bennewitz, by this time, had convinced himself that the ETs were transmitting a mind control beam to repress Myrna Hansen's memories. Bennewitz believed that the ETs were likewise beaming him in an attempt to disrupt his ongoing UFO probe. To thwart this extraterrestrial electronic harassment, Bennewitz arranged for Hansen's regression to take place in his 1979 Lincoln Town Car with multiple sheets of aluminum foil draped over the windows to deflect the dreaded alien beams.[13] Bennewitz connected these perceived beams to cattle mutilations:

The alien does KILL with the beam generally. Results on a human will exhibit a three to four cm purple circle. If done from the rear, on one or both shoulders. The results on cattle are the same, essentially exhibiting purple beneath the hide, with burned circles on the outside."[14]

Hansen's regression sessions featured many themes that would later litter UFO lore, including such alien abduction tropes as "missing time" and a female subject placed in a trance—and in a state of undress—undergoing medical procedures.

During Hansen's first regression, on May 8, 1980, she described a hovering ET craft that sucked a cow up from the ground with a "tractor beam":

They're landing. Oh God! Cattle are screaming! But I've got to know who it is. Shawn wants to go. The light is so bright. It's orange. I want to see them. I want to go to them. I'm out of the car...[the] screaming of the cattle; it's horrible—it's horrible. It's in pain—incredible pain!

Hansen found herself inside the alien spaceship where one of the crew brandished a long silver knife and "plunged it 6 inches into the [cow's] chest; then they worked on the genitals while the cow was still alive and struggling..."

On May 12, during her second regression, Hansen recalled being transported to an underground facility. During a medical examination, a metallic object was implanted in her brain, apparently as a means to later track her and beam her with malevolent messages. At one point, the ETs left Hansen unattended, and she attempted an escape. As she was running through an underground tunnel, Hansen came across multiple vats of liquid containing the remains of human and animal body parts. Bennewitz somehow deduced that this underground facility was located in Dulce.

During a June 3 regression, Hansen described rows of vats filled with body parts that reminded her of:

...pickled pig's feet, although not that good. Pickled! Oh God! Wondered if that was where I was going [into a vat]...I was horrified...fluid was circulating! That's why those body parts drifted up and away...Edges of the tank were sharp, like the edge of a tin can...They were big tanks. I was crying...I wish I had looked in all the tanks. But [the aliens] weren't far behind me...

If brain implants and pickled body parts weren't awful enough, the aliens—according to Bennewitz—introduced into Hansen "a vaginal disease like streptococci-bacillus..."[15] This extraterrestrial vaginal disease was described by Bennewitz in an August 1980 letter to APRO's Jim Lorenzen:

Dear Jim,
...The situation here is serious but not out of hand—she [Myrna Hansen] is getting the best of treatment by the pathologist and the doctor at no cost to her, for an apparent alien bacteria. We are trying to culture it—no luck as yet. Also it has evaded all of our known antibiotics and penicillin.

She is also being badly beaten on by the alien with their beams—24 hours a day. These beams have been measured and we are now getting a handle as to what they may be.

Film footage is piling up—over 1000 feet now—Scientific data and documentation excellent and piling up.

Jim, if you could possibly observe the following precautions in any of your present and future regressions, your data will be more accurate.

1) Use as many different expert psychologists as possible;

2) Do not regress unless, A) There is an unbiased witness acquainted with the process present taking verbatim notes if possible. B) The regression must be done in a shield enclosure. The best option I'm aware of are:

1A) An automobile in a garage—use 3 layers of heavy aluminum (barbeque type) foil to cover all windows—grounded to the chrome trim around the windows thoroughly. Masking tape can be used to hold it in place.

Precaution: do not ground the auto. If the alien senses he cannot get through, he will attempt to modulate the beam ultrasonically—about 18 to 23 KC. The intent is to vibrate the atmosphere within, sympathetically, thus reaching the victim. Closed windows and cotton in the ears will deaden this reasonably effectively.

2A) The very best option is to use an x-ray room. It is lead shielded. A two story or larger building where the room us totally shielded. Not a one story building because generally the ceiling will not be shielded. Inspect and make certain the room is shielded.

3A) Last and least best option—a hotel room in a multistory hotel with the room on an inside corridor midway or so up. Anyone taken to the room should not know nor look at the floor numbers or room numbers. This type of room is obviously not shielded—concrete will not work. This is a method of "cloaking" because of the many other minds present in the hotel, the alien is confused and will have difficultly searching out the victim.

I know I don't need to re-express how serious this is. Please instigate these procedures if at all possible. Your data will be accurate, much more detailed and without contaminative programming. The apparent prime intent of the alien is to instill a feeling supposedly of their true benevolence thru the victim, when in reality with this particular alien culture, exploring and encountering on earth, if the intent is truly malevolent in its worst sense.

I would suggest if you can do it quietly, that you relay these ground rules for regression to other UFO organizations, asking them, at least at this point not to question—just try to do it this way. We must take a very serious investigatory position on documenting in as great a detail as possible. I am basing everything I tell you on a solid, tried and working hypothesis, not an imagination, guessing or paranoia. I can assure you it is not a beautiful "religious experience" that some investigators would have us believe. There are always some "good apples" in any bad basket—hopefully sooner or later we will encounter some of those and find some allies.

Again—to lend credibility when final government access is gained—none of what I've discussed must get to the media. Leo's idea of video-taping for TV and publication will only create propaganda for the alien—it is self defeating. When the final absolutely provable facts are gleaned, we must carefully control their presentation to the proper authorities.

I will appreciate any feedback you can give me concerning the new regressions you mentioned, methods, etc., when you have the data for cost relative procedures.

P.S. One last thing—A must if the hotel room is used. Place an EKG electrode (with rubber strap) on the right inside forearm prior to application—wet the contact area with saliva or saline solution. Our most recent regression tapes indicate no alien interference using this method in a hotel room.

Use a banana plug and heavy wire to ground the room outlet hotel ground system.

Best regards,
Paul F. Bennewitz[16]

Chapter 5

The attack of the computer ETs

In December 1979, Paul Bennewitz—equipped with an eight-millimeter movie camera—began filming UFOs over the Manzano Weapons Storage Area at Kirtland Base, which at the time housed the largest cache of nuclear weapons components in the U.S. Bennewitz installed an arsenal of tracking antennae on his roof to record signals apparently emanating from these UFOs, which he claimed he could "D.F." (direction-find) at distances of up to 60 miles. Alarmed that these craft posed a national security threat, Bennewitz alerted Kirtland Base officials of his findings.

Not long after, Bennewitz received what he believed were alien transmissions that included information about a battle between ETs against U.S. armed forces at an underground base located in Dulce, New Mexico. Bennewitz claimed that Major Ernest Edwards—Commander of Kirtland's security detail—was present for this broadcast. "Major Edwards has witnessed closely all events throughout including establishment of the first communications with the Alien since Jan. 27, 1980. He has unofficially provided valuable logistic judgment as the Project progressed."[17]

In October 1980, the Air Force Office of Special Investigations (AFOSI) alerted Bennewitz of their security efforts against this perceived ET threat—or at least that's the line AFOSI allegedly fed Bennewitz. Official documents later surfaced to the contrary, indicating that the Air Force denied any involvement in UFO investigations or attempts to come up with any sort of defense strategy against this perceived alien threat. Whatever the actual truth, AFOSI—and in particular, Special Agent Richard Doty—made no attempt to dissuade Bennewitz of the notion that what he'd observed were genuine ET craft. Around this time AFOSI launched a counter-intelligence investigation into Bennewitz's activities.

As it turns out, it wasn't alien beams or underground bases that aroused the AFOSI's interest in Paul Bennewitz. AFOSI's concerns stemmed from the fact that Bennewitz had intercepted secret transmissions from a laser-based tracking system located at Kirtland.[18] According to Greg Bishop: "The satellite messages were supposedly sent by laser light. The radio bursts were most likely a way to communicate with weapons or battlefield operations."

Bishop noted that these encrypted messages sounded like sped up gibberish—until they were decoded and slowed down—which was the process Bennewitz was trying to figure out. It was these activities that specifically concerned AFOSI, and so part of their investigation was to determine how far along Bennewitz was in this decoding process, and to identify anyone else who may have been privy to his activities.

At some point, the NSA (who maintained a presence at Kirtland base) launched a separate counter-intelligence investigation and set up surveillance in an empty townhouse across the street from Bennewitz.[19] This operation included beaming electromagnetic signals at Bennewitz's antenna set-up with the intent of scrambling whatever transmissions he had been intercepting from Kirtland. According to Greg Bishop: "The NSA had become a major player in the Bennewitz drama, especially since a signal intercept from the Soviet bloc had referred to him as a possible source of information, even if he was unaware of his role...."[20]

In the Summer of 1981, former Project Blue Book scientific advisor and Air Force consultant Dr. J. Allen Hynek confided to Bill Moore (over an adult beverage or two) that he had gifted a computer to Bennewitz to "aid" him in his UFO research. However, Hynek neglected to inform Bennewitz that this computer had been provided at the behest of the U.S. Air Force, and embedded in the software was a code that generated an "alien language."[21] With the aid of the Air

Force computer, Bennewitz claimed he "Established constant direct communications with the Alien using...a form of Hex Decimal Code with Graphics and print-out."[22] According to Richard Doty:

> Bennewitz had [the computer] rigged up to antennas on his roof that included a small microwave dish...and he would look at the screen, and there would be images on the screen that certainly wasn't an alien, but he was convinced that it was...I would actually tell him, 'I don't see anything.' And he said, 'I see it, and I can hear them,' and he had these earphones that he would put on, and he said, 'I can hear them talking.' And I asked Paul: 'What language are they speaking?' He said, 'They're speaking their language'...And he wrote a hundred page document about the alien language...When he went out to Kirtland to give his presentation, to all these generals, he presented them with that information."[23]

The allegation that J. Allen Hynek was involved in the AFOSI's disinformation campaign (with his role in providing Bennewitz with the Air Force computer) will no doubt raise the hackles of current day Hynek enthusiasts. Nonetheless, there is tenuous evidence which suggests that Hynek met with Bennewitz during the relevant timeframe when the computer came into his possession. In a phone interview with San Francisco-based ufologist Jim McCampbell, Bennewitz stated that: "...at his house, he showed Hynek

Paul Bennewitz

films and out in the back yard a flying saucer. He asked Hynek about his view with regard to abductions as to how many people might have been abducted. Hynek, unhesitantly said about one out of forty [UFO witnesses had been abducted]…"[24]

In *Dulce Base: The Truth and Evidence from the Case Files of Gabe Valdez*, author Greg Valdez (Gabe's son) recalled visiting Bennewitz and receiving a demonstration of how he used this computer to communicate with the ETs:

> He would type a question into the computer in a very complex for the time period form of a computer program, much like a current e-mail. Much to everyone's surprise, he would get an answer to the questions he was asking. Sometimes he would get an immediate response, and sometimes it would take several minutes. He would even receive very crude and basic pictures or graphics on his computer of these 'aliens.' Some of these pictures resembled birds with reptile features, and some resembled reptiles with bird features. During this question and answer session, Gabe instructed Paul to ask the simple question, 'Where are you from?' Paul already knew the answer to the question because he had already asked the question and he answered it verbally when a response came back on the computer. It simply said the Zeta Reticuli Star System.

Due to these alarming computer messages and images, Bennewitz came to believe that the U.S. government had signed on to a secret treaty with treacherous ETs who had double-crossed their earthly counterparts and overtaken Dulce Base. To address this dire situation, Bennewitz composed a report titled "Project Beta" detailing his UFO investigations and outlining a strategy to combat the alien intruders. Bennewitz shipped off his Project Beta report to Senators Pete Domenici and Harrison Schmitt, hoping they would assist him in his efforts. In his report, Bennewitz described a "beam weapon" he was developing, all part of his plan to neutralize the ETs and ultimately save the human race.

After one of his trips to Dulce—where he rode shotgun with Gabe Valdez, visiting cattle mute sites and observing strange lights in the night—Bennewitz checked in with his AFOSI contacts, informing them of these strange happenings. Special Agent Doty further encouraged Bennewitz's belief that ETs were not only responsible for the peculiar goings-on at Kirtland, but that he was also on the right track with his Dulce underground alien base theory. The ultimate intent of stringing Bennewitz along (according to researchers like Greg Bishop and Christian Lambright) was to shift Bennewitz's attention away from Kirtland to a remote area like Archuleta Mesa (near Dulce) where AFOSI could ramp up their disinformation operation and more easily stage "UFO events." As Lambright writes in *X Descending*:

The primary and most obvious goal was to convince everyone that Paul was not credible when it came to anything even remotely related to UFOs. A good amount of effort went into ensuring that outcome. Equally important however, was a secondary goal of diverting attention away from Paul, if not the entire Albuquerque area. This would be done in part by intriguing documents that mysteriously began to appear, as well as other sightings and witnesses. But it also included pushing stories of an alien base near Dulce. Third, and less obvious, was an effort to obscure and dilute Paul's role and the significance of what he saw. There was a deliberate attempt to shift the perceived time frame of his sightings, creating the impression that his films and his call to Air Force Security had come much later than they actually did. It was a coordinated effort utilizing confusion and diversion— and having the right people in place to carry it out.[25]

Chapter 6
Agent Dody and Mr. Huck

"In the case of UFO 'leaks', the general researcher profile is well-known. All that needs to be done is to feed information about a previously unknown event, or sensational revelations about an old case to the target, who gleefully spreads the story around the grapevine. In recent years, many researchers have become savvy to this method of deception, and most are now more careful before making announcements. This may have caused the disinfo mill to abandon the lone UFO researcher in favor of anonymous postings on various internet sites and blogs."

- Greg Bishop, *It Defies Language*

In July of 1980, APRO's Jim Lorenzen received a two page letter with no return address, which related the following alleged incident:

Dear Sir;

On July 16, 1980, at between 10:30 – 10:45AM, Craig R. Weitzel, 644 Wind Glove Rd, Marietta, Georgia, a Civil Air Patrol Cadet from Dobbins AFB, Ga, visiting Kirtland AFB, NM, observed a dull metallic colored UFO flying from South to North near Pecos, New Mexico. Pecos has a secret training site for the 1550th Aircrew Training and Testing Wing, Kirtland AFB, NM. WEITZEL was with ten other individuals, including USAF active duty airmen, and all witnessed the sighting. WEITZEL took some pictures of the object. WEITZEL went closer to the UFO and observed the UFO land in a clearing approximately 250 yards, NNW of the training area. WEITZEL observed an individual dressed in a metallic suit depart the craft and walk a few feet away. The individual was outside the craft for just a few minutes. When the individual returned the craft took off towards the NW.

On July 17, 1980, at about 2210hrs, Weitzel was in his temporary billets on Kirtland AFB, when an individual dressed in a dark suit, came to his door. The individual was described by Weitzel as being: 6'3" tall, weight, 170 lbs, slender built, dark black hair, dark eyes, wearing sunglasses, narrow shaped face. The individual identified himself as a Mr. Huck from Sandia Laboratories, a secret Department of Energy Contractor on Kirtland AFB. Mr. Weitzel, not being from the Albuquerque area, did not know what Sandia was. After obtaining an explanation from the individual, Weitzel allowed the individual in. The individual told Weitzel that he saw something yesterday near Pecos that he shouldn't have seen. The individual demanded all the photographs. Mr. Weitzel explained that he didn't have any photographs, that all the photos were with a USAF airman and Weitzel didn't know the individual's name. The individual warned Weitzel not to mention the sighting to anyone or Weitzel would be in serious trouble. After the individual left Weitzel's room, Weitzel wondered how the individual knew of the sighting because Weitzel didn't report the sighting to anyone. Weitzel became scared after thinking of the threat the individual made. Weitzel called the Kirtland AFB Security Police and reported the incident to them. They referred the incident to the Air Force Office of Special Investigators (AFOSI), which investigates these matters according to the security police. A Mr. Dody, a special agent with OSI, spoke with Weitzel and took a report. Mr. Dody also obtained all the photographs of the UFO. Dody told Weitzel he would look into the matter. That was the last anyone heard of the incident.

I am a USAF Airman assigned to the 1550th Aircrew Train-ing and Testing Wing at Kirtland AFB, NM. I was with Weitzel during the sighting, however, I did not see the craft land. I spoke with Weitzel after this Mr. Huck visited him. Weitzel was very upset and wanted something done about it. But after Weitzel spoke with OSI, Weitzel changed his attitude. Weitzel didn't want to talk about the matter anymore. I called and spoke with Mr. Dody. He disavowed any knowledge of the photographs and stated Weitzel decided not to make a report of the sighting.

I have every reason to believe that USAF is covering up something. I spent a lot of time looking into this matter and I know there is more to it than the USAF will say. I have heard rumors, but serious rumors here at Kirtland that the USAF has a crashed UFO stored in the Manzano area, which is located in a remote area if Kirtland AFB. This area is heavily guarded by USAF Security. I have spoke with the two employees of Sandia Laboratories, who also store classified objects in Manzano, and he told me that Sandia has examined several UFO's during the last 20 years. One that crashed near Roswell NM in the late 50's was examined by Sandia scientists. That craft is still being store [sic] in Manzano.

I have reason to believe OSI is conducting a very secret investigation into UFO sightings. OSI took over when Project Blue Book was closed. I was told this by my commander, COL Bruce Purvine. Col Purvine also told me that the investigation was so secret that most employees of OSI doesn't[sic] even know it. But Col Purvine told me that Kirtland AFB, AFOSI District 17 has a special secret detachment that investigates sightings around this area. They have also investigated the cattle mutila-tions in New Mexico.

I don't expect you people can do anything about this, but I thought I'd let you know. I must remain anonymous because

I am a career airman [sic] with tIme [sic] remaining on active
duty. I know you people can't guarantee my anonymity.

Although Lorenzen viewed the Weitzel Letter as suspect, he nonetheless forwarded it to APRO investigator Bill Moore as it contained
investigatory breadcrumbs that could be followed up on.[26] Moore
agreed to look into the matter, and soon after tracked down Craig
Weitzel, who confirmed that he and some fellow cadets had indeed
witnessed a silvery object that sped away suddenly "like you never saw
anything accelerate before." However, Weitzel denied authoring the
anonymous letter, and pointed out a number of inaccuracies in it, such
as the inclusion of a silver-suited entity. Weitzel also denied having
taken any photos or of being hassled by the mysterious Mr. Huck.
Weitzel noted that he reported the sighting to Sgt. Richard Doty at
Kirtland Air Base. (Not "Dody" as stated in the letter.)

Bill Moore later came to the conclusion that the Weitzel Letter was
among the first phases of the AFOSI disinformation operation—chum
tossed into the ufological waters to see who might nibble. Apparently,
AFOSI was impressed that Moore didn't swallowed the bait, and in
fact it appeared to be a test that he passed with flying colors. As Moore
later wrote:

[In September 1980] I was approached by a well placed individual within the intelligence community who claimed to be directly
connected to a high-level government project dealing with
UFOs. This individual, who subsequently came to be known as
'the Falcon,' told me that he spoke for a small group of similar
individuals who were uncomfortable with the government's
continuing coverup of the truth and indicated that he and his
group would like to help me with my research into the subject
in the hope and expectation that I might be able to help them
find a way to change the prevailing policy and get the facts to

the public...I knew I was being recruited, but at that point I had
no idea for what.[27]

A deal was agreed to that Moore would be given access to classified UFO reports, and in return he'd keep tabs on prominent UFO
researchers, and report back on their activities. After their meeting,
Falcon put Moore in touch with Richard Doty, who going forward
would serve as the Falcon-Moore liaison. Among those Moore was
assigned to keep tabs on was Paul Bennewitz, who by this time was
already knee-deep in his belief of a mounting ET menace.

Chapter 7

The Mount Archuleta mystery

In late 1981, Richard Doty arranged an Air Force helicopter flight in which he took Bennewitz for a spin around Archuleta Mesa, pointing out a location where a secret alien base was presumably located.[28] Bennewitz, a licensed pilot, began his own reconnaissance flights out to Dulce searching for further evidence of this alien base. These flights apparently played perfectly into Doty's hands, who—in cahoots with fellow AFOSI agents—allegedly set up props around the area that included a large air vent planted into the ground to give the impression that it was connected to the suspected underground base. Later, reports of air vents loomed large in Dulce Base lore. Greg Valdez suspects that Doty's claims about setting up props was likewise disinformation, and that there actually was a secret facility located at Mount Archuleta—as opposed to Archuleta Mesa—which in reality are two different locations. This fact in itself suggests that Archuleta Mesa was thrown into the mix to lead researchers astray.[29]

During one of his Dulce recon flights, Bennewitz spotted what he believed were the remains of a delta-wing shaped aircraft that had crashed and broken into two sections. Somehow, Bennewitz arrived at the conclusion that the remains were those of an atomic powered spacecraft that the ETs had given to the U.S. Air Force, but then for some reason the ET's turned around and decided to shoot it down. Bennewitz flew over this supposed crash site on multiple occasions, taking photos and using a device called a scintillator that detected elevated radiation levels in the area. Bennewitz documented his findings in a report titled "Results of Re-analysis of Aerial Films and Atomic Ship," which included drawings and measurements that looked suspiciously like the F-18 stealth fighter that at the time was still classified.

After discovering the crash site, Bennewitz contacted Gabe Valdez (who had access to Jicarilla tribal lands), and requested that an expedition be made to Mount Archuleta to see if they could locate the site. Using a hand drawn map by Bennewitz to guide them, Gabe Valdez and Edmund Gomez (son of rancher Manual Gomez) first accessed the crash site in late 1985. At the site they discovered a large gouge in the soil, broken treetops, and charred vegetation indicative of some type of ground impact. En route there, Valdez and Gomez came across what they described as a "highway" that had recently been constructed—a "highway" in this instance meaning a well-maintained gravel road that would allow access to large trucks and heavy equipment. Bear in mind that Mount Archuleta is a remote location, which inevitably led to speculation that the military had some sort of operation going on there due to the construction of said "highway." Doty later took credit for this road construction, the intent of which was to plant a seed with Bennewitz that some major operation was underway at Mount Archuleta related to the supposed underground alien base.[30]

Concurrent with the Mount Archuleta expeditions, a series of military maneuvers were conducted in the area by Delta Forces in black helicopters, reportedly from Fort Carson, Colorado. Doty later claimed he'd arranged for these maneuvers, part of his grand plan to dupe Bennewitz into believing the alien invasion was nigh at hand. These activities—in combination with reports of cattle mutilations in the area—so thoroughly muddied the waters that if there was some secret operation going on at Mount Archuleta no one would ever be able to discern its true purpose.

Gabe Valdez trekked out to Mount Archuleta on numerous occasions. The most well-known account was documented in a report titled *Recollections and Impressions of Visit to Dulce, New Mexico - October 23, 24, 1988*. This report surfaced in the early 1990s, authored by "Jason Bishop". Many of the details therein are consistent with Greg Valdez's account in *Dulce Base: The Truth and Evidence from the Case Files of Gabe Valdez*:

In 1988, Dr. John Gille from France and his wife, Elaine, accompanied Edmund Gomez, his brother Manuel Jr., Gabe and his two sons, Geoff, my brother, and myself for an overnight expedition to Mount Archuleta. Another man, who refers to himself as Jason Bishop on certain documents, also accompanied the expedition. Jason Bishop is not the true name of this individual, and there are in fact several individuals known by that moniker including Tal Lavesque [sic]...To make sure we are on the same page, we will call this person Bill McGarity to avoid any confusion. Bill has an interesting résumé, which at the time of the expedition was not fully disclosed to Gabe...

At the time of the Mount Archuleta expedition, Thomas William "Bill" McGarity worked at Los Alamos Laboratories, reportedly involved in stealth aircraft development. McGarity's rationale for using the Jason Bishop cover name was because he didn't want his Los Alamos superiors to discover he was investigating UFOs and cattle mutes, and then end up getting fired due to these extracurricular activities. McGarity claimed he was taking this risk because he was a concerned citizen who simply wanted to get to the truth.

Greg Valdez later obtained a copy of Bill McGarity's résumé, which confirmed his employment history at Los Alamos and Nellis Air Force Base, although what wasn't known at the time of the Mount Archuleta expedition was that McGarity was also moonlighting with the CIA.[31] As Greg Valdez recalled: "Edmund [Gomez] never trusted McGarity. Edmund told me: 'There's something shady about that guy.' And Edmund was right..."[32]

According to "Jason Bishop" (aka Bill McGarity) in *Recollections and Impressions of Visit to Dulce*:

At 19:51 hrs. all seven of us spotted a very bright light coming from the northwest at a very high rate of speed. The object appeared to be boomerang shaped with a very bright light just below its center.

The light was a bright white, blue and green. As it approached, it slowed down [obviously under intelligent control], seemed to reverse direction, finally stopping. When it stopped, a shower of what appeared to be sparks were emitted from each end of the boomerang, and then it began moving forward again and disappeared from sight at a very high rate of speed. All this took place in approximately 10 to 15 seconds. We attempted to take a picture of the object but were unsuccessful.

About 2200 hours we climbed to the summit of Mt. Archuleta and watched for about an hour and a half. We could see across the canyon in the moonlight. This canyon wall is where Paul Bennewitz claimed an 'alien' base is located and that during the night their ships are seen entering and leaving cave openings in the cliff wall.

During our stay on the peak, we saw two very bright lights on the cliff walls in the exact location where Paul said the base openings were. There are no roads on this cliff. The lights would appear suddenly and then fade over a period of time until you could not see them. At this time we also heard voices that sounded like radio transmissions..."[33]

One of the more befuddling aspects of *Recollections and Impressions of Visit to Dulce* is that the individual who disseminated this report was Tal Levesque. And to make matters even more confusing, Levesque—for some of his own writings—adopted the pen name of Jason Bishop III. (Bishop in French is 'Levesque'). However, Levesque and McGarity were entirely different individuals.

Greg Valdez suspects that McGarity's interest in Mount Archuleta had less to do with what his father, Gabe Valdez, was up to, and probably had more to do with the activities of Dr. John Gille, who—it was later learned—worked with French government intelligence. During this period, Gille was making the rounds of MUFON conferences and interacting with UFO researchers presumably as part of an intelligence-gathering operation. McGarity, in turn, was monitoring Gille's activities on behalf of U.S. intelligence.[34]

At Mount Archuleta, McGarity took a number of soil and vegetation samples, which he afterwards analyzed and, from this data, concluded that an F-117 Nighthawk had crashed at the site, although it was later discovered that McGarity was quite possibly passing along erroneous information to confuse the facts as to the specific type of aircraft that had actually crashed.[35]

At a location north of Mount Archuleta, Bill McGarity and Edmund Gomez discovered a ventilation shaft in the same general area where Bennewitz had previously observed what appeared to be UFOs flying into the mountain. Afterwards, Gomez obtained aerial photos of Mount Archuleta that revealed military vehicles and an aircraft hangar in the vicinity of the supposed underground base. At some point during their Mount Archuleta odyssey, Valdez and Gomez were informed by Jicarilla Tribal Police that they'd no longer be allowed to access the site due to an ongoing Drug Enforcement Agency operation, a claim that later turned out to be false.[36]

Someone was hiding *something.*

Chapter 8

Mystery orbs and wobbulating beams

During his Mount Archuleta fly-overs, Bennewitz took a series of photos, and when they were developed he was able to pick out what appeared to be an alien spacecraft. On one occasion, Bill Moore was hanging out with Bennewitz on the deck of his condo—looking toward Manzano Mountain—when he instructed Moore to set the shutter speed of his camera to 1000 and snap some random photos. When Moore later developed these photos, several shots revealed a curious tube of light that was only visible at this 1000th of a second setting. By using this shutter setting, Bennewitz had presumably employed a method of photographing images otherwise unseen by the naked eye. Similarly, during the 1988 Mount Archuleta expedition, Gabe Valdez's group took a number of random photos that when later developed revealed an object (of the unidentified variety) which none of them had noticed at the time, as if the camera lens setting had somehow bypassed a camouflage system deployed by the craft.[37] Greg Valdez recalled:

> Around the time Bill McGarity started coming out to Dulce we found a way how to photograph the [stealth] aircraft. It was just by dumb luck. We were up at Mount Archuleta and we were taking random photos of the area, and that damn aircraft would appear in the photographs...And so we gave one of the photos to Bill McGarity, because he had a contact at Los Alamos labs, and he had the photo superimposed by some of the lab people; it came up so clear that you could see the insignia of the pilot's squadron...and so because of that, my dad felt that Mount Archuleta was a military test site. That's why he never made a

big deal about it [the secret test site], because in theory, they [the government] are protecting American citizens. Do you want to disclose that we have this fancy aircraft to Russia or China? So for my dad, it drove him crazy, because the government was still killing these cows. He thought they should just go buy them!

Another oddity Bennewitz observed were orange orbs that materialized inside his home. Bill Moore later confirmed seeing one of these softball-sized orbs, which he described as three dimensional and self-illuminating, hovering near the ceiling. According to film maker Mark Pilkington:

> Others had noticed the orbs too. On one of his many trips out to the Bennewitz home to check up on things when the family was out (i.e., break-ins) Doty and two NSA operatives had disconnected the alarm system and were just about to start snooping around when they noticed one of the balls floating underneath a central stairway in the large entry room. "It was orange and had sparkles in it," said Doty. "I asked the other guys: 'Is it one of yours?'" But the NSA men were mystified as well, and the trio tried to see if the phenomenon was projected from outside of the house somewhere. No dice. 'We never did figure out what that was,' said Doty. Perhaps the NSA was in fact responsible, but if so, they never admitted this to anyone outside their circle.[38]

More recently, Dr. Howard Elliason—while conducting research on anomalous events in the Dulce area—followed up on a report by a local rancher who had encountered an inert orb on his property. Elliason took photos of this orb, which appeared to be composed of a crystal-like material. On another occasion, the same rancher witnessed an orb levitating in the same general area where several cattle mutilations had occurred.

Greg Valdez has noted recent incidents of military engagement between Israel and Hezbollah that included reports of orbs that appeared in advance of bombing runs. Valdez theorizes that these might have been the same type of orbs examined by Dr. Elliason, and that the crystals Elliason observed inside these orbs were a form of memory chip used for data storage and navigational control. In the case of Paul Bennewitz—it could be conjectured—the orbs he observed were ostensibly used to monitor his activities.

Orbs weren't the only weird things buzzing around Bennewitz. As noted earlier, NSA agents (or some other alphabet soup spooks) had moved into a vacant building across the street from his home in an attempt to scramble Bennewitz's signals. Although Bennewitz didn't know if the strangers across the street were actually government agents, or aliens in disguise, he somehow determined they were scanning him with high tech equipment. Bennewitz said he could "sense their sweep" and that it caused a stinging sensation across his body. Over time, Bennewitz grew to suspect that this "sweep" had been performed by an ET beam. On one occasion, Bill Moore was visiting Bennewitz and also experienced this sensation, describing it as a beam that scanned his body.

To combat this perceived ET beam, Bennewitz constructed his very own spacegun. "The speed of my weapon exceeds that of their weapons and in its most sophisticated form can be readily computer controlled to allow extremely rapid tracking and lock-on regardless of speed along with electronic wobbulation of the beam."[39] Bennewitz further claimed that: "Two small prototypes have been funded and constructed by my Company. Tests conducted to date indicate they do work and work rather well considering their small size..."[40]

The beam or "scan" that Bennewitz and Moore experienced could have conceivably been a form of directed-energy weapon that was first reported in development during the late 1990s by the Air Force Research Laboratory (AFRL) at Kirtland Base. According to Christian Lambright in *X Descending*:

In 2001, the AFRL publicly revealed the existence of Active Denial Technology (ADT), which was referred to, behind closed doors, as the "pain beam," a science fiction sounding "microwave beam that heats the water in the surface layer of the skin where the pain-sensing nerves are, and can do so from a considerable distance... By all accounts, the sudden and intense pain is enough to cause virtual panic as people desperately try to get away from the beam. Research into such 'non-lethal' weapons has reportedly been going on since the mid-1980s, though it is an outgrowth of research into radar and electro-magnetic pulse technology.[41]

During the ADT's 2001 public roll-out, a contraption called the Active Denial System (ADS) was demonstrated, which consisted of a large antenna mounted atop a military transport. In 2003, Eric Adams—an associate editor with *Popular Science Magazine*—volunteered himself, guinea pig style, to test the effects of this technology. According to Christian Lambright:

> [Adams] had the system fired at him from a half mile away with the directed-energy beam controlled to hit him only in the middle of his back. In less than two seconds, he experienced a warm sensation that quickly grew to feel like an 'electric burner.' Though in this demonstration the purpose was to show that the ADS could generate only enough pain to motivate someone to leave the area, in a 2007 accident at Moody AFB, Georgia, an exposure of four seconds at 100% power injured one person seriously enough to require being flown to a local burn center. However, at lower power levels the beam can produce only a mild feeling of warmth and, as the above demonstration showed, it can be focused on a relatively small area even over a substan-tial distance...[42]

Christian Lambright notes the existence of "man-portable" ADS-like systems in development as far back as the early 1970s. A 1972 *Time Magazine* article entitled "The Death Ray" described "a portable chemically-powered laser" that could "silently burn a fatal, quarter-inch-wide hole in the body of an enemy soldier up to five miles away... Much of the Pentagon's laser weaponry research is being conducted in great secrecy at Kirtland Air Force Base, outside Albuquerque." Lambright goes on to say:

> The above *Time Magazine* article was written forty years ago, and we are left to wonder where the research may have gone since then. Perhaps it melded into the Air Force Research Laboratory's Directed Energy Directorate and a little-known research group located at Kirtland Air Force Base...Even more interesting, is word of the Portable Efficient Laser Testbed (PELT), which was described in the above *New Scientist* article...as the 'first man-portable heat compliance weapon of its kind.' Cursory information on this weapon appeared in a Department of Defense (DoD) document titled Joint Non-Lethal Weapons Exercise Reference Book published in 2003, which listed the PELT laser rifle as a classified program. Included in the document is an illustration of this decidedly futuristic-looking weapon and, if you look closely, it sports the unique logo of the ScorpWorks...
>
> What about the choice of the unusual name 'ScorpWorks'? It was one of the questions I addressed to the AFRL Public Relations Office and, as expected, they acknowledged that the name is a play on the infamous Skunkworks, the secretive advanced aircraft division of Lockheed. The reference to a scorpion is supposed to reflect the Southwest flavor of their New Mexico location. But a scorpion being selected to symbolize the types of weapons the ScorpWorks develops, directed

energy beam weapons with painful effects, also brought to mind what Paul Bennewitz complained about. It is what scorpions do. When a scorpion strikes... it stings...[43]

Chapter 9

Leaving New Mexico with a strange feeling

In December of 1981, Special Agent Richard Doty showed Bill Moore an official-looking teletype concerning a secret government project code-named "Aquarius." At a later date, Moore claimed that Doty provided him with a revised version of this teletype that included additional material on ETs that had not been present in the original teletype. Doty instructed Moore to pass this along to Paul Bennewitz, a prospect Moore was none too enthused about, as he suspected that an official government document had been doctored as a means to seed disinformation.

Instead of immediately passing along the "Aquarius" document, Moore sat on it for a while, hoping Doty would ultimately let the matter go. Doty eventually became impatient with Moore's slow roll, instructing him to either pass along the document or he would terminate their working arrangement. When Moore eventually provided the document to Bennewitz, in June 1981, he did so with the caveat that he hadn't validated its authenticity. Bennewitz, however, was immediately convinced that it provided proof of what he'd been saying all along about an imminent alien invasion of Earth.

On January 10-11, 1983, Peter Gersten of the Citizens Against UFO Secrecy (CAUS) met with Doty and Moore in Albuquerque. On January 25 of that year, Gersten conducted a teleconference in which he recounted this two-day meeting. The highlights of this teleconference, recorded by an unidentified note-taker, included the following:

- Doty informed Gersten that the government was "studying UFOs & knows they're extraterrestrial," and that there were various agencies involved, including the military, but that the NSA was the "primary mover."

- Doty revealed that there had "been 3 crashes where bodies were 'retrieved' – one was Roswell – one was in the late 1950's, one in the 1960's…[Doty] indicated retrievals [were] once stored at Kirtland, but [were] no longer there." Gersten was allowed to view some allegedly classified documents related to "Project Aquarius" that included a 1977 "Executive Briefing" given to President Jimmy Carter by a secret government group identified as Majestic 12, or MJ-12. Aquarius, according to the documents, was a secret U.S. government project related to UFOs that included information about a human-alien exchange program. Doty also said that the "aliens are coming from 50 light years away, but [the] location is classified."

- Doty mentioned that he had spoken to a woman in the "Cimarron Case" [Myrna Hansen] who had witnessed "aliens & military types together in [an] underground installation—tanks with organs in them—she was told they were making humanoids." Doty acknowledged that there was some sort of "agreement" between the aliens and the U.S. government, and that the aliens had been allowed to conduct cattle mutilations in exchange for technology and given "land for a base." Doty quoted Paul Bennewitz as saying that "…in 1979 aliens & military had some kind of 'fight over weapons' & 66 military people were killed by the aliens."

- Doty informed Gersten that there is "indeed 'programming' going on via movies, media—to help [the] population accept [the] ET presence" and that the last scene in *Close Encounters of the Third Kind* "may have been close to reality—re: pilot exchange—rumor is that Spielberg met Reagan at the White House & Reagan told Spielberg that the movie was 'more real than people think.' Spielberg supposedly has confirmed this to BM [Bill Moore]."

- Doty ended the meeting with this cryptic comment: "How do you know that I'm not here to either give you mis-information or give you information which is part of the programming, knowing you're going to go out and spread it around?"

Afterwards, Gersten noted: "When you take what [Doty] says and what PB [Paul Bennewitz] says together, you really leave New Mexico with a strange feeling."

Chapter 10
UFOs: The human factor

"Whether UFOs are or are not extraterrestrial is really only a part of the picture. In the final analysis, the process of studying this phenomenon and the people involved with it, of assessing the claims and the counter-claims, and of dealing with the question of how we, as earthlings, will react to the discovery of a race of extraterrestrial visitors and how they will react to us—all of this and more, when finally looked at in perspective, leads us to the inescapable recognition that in studying the UFO phenomenon, we are at the same time becoming more aware of ourselves as individuals and learning something about the society that we are a part of."

– Bill Moore

In early 1983, Linda Howe—hot off the success of her regional Emmy Award-winning documentary *A Strange Harvest*—had been tapped to produce an HBO special with the proposed title of *UFOs: The E.T. Factor.* On April 9, 1983, Howe met with Doty at Kirtland Air Force Base, an incident that seemed lifted straight out of a spy novel. As Howe recounted in *An Alien Harvest*:

I sat down with my back to the windows. [Doty] sat behind the desk.

"You know you upset some people in Washington with your film *A Strange Harvest*. It came too close to something we don't want the public to know about."

That began a brief discussion about my documentary. I asked him why extraterrestrials were mutilating animals. Richard Doty said that subject was classified beyond his need to know. He told me I had been monitored while I was making the film...

...[Doty] reached with his left hand to a drawer on the left side of the desk and opened it. He pulled from the drawer a brown envelope. He opened it and took out several standard letter sized sheets of white paper.

"My superiors have asked me to show this to you," he said, handing me the pages. "You can read these and you can ask me questions, but you can't take any notes."

I took the papers and I read the top page. It was entitled "Briefing Paper for the President of the United States of America" on the subject of unidentified and identified aerial craft or vehicles...

Richard Doty then stood up and said, "I want you to move from there." He motioned me toward the large chair in the middle of the room. "Eyes can see through windows."

I got up and moved to the big chair, confused. I didn't know what was happening. As I looked at the pages in my lap a second time, I wondered why he was showing them to me?

I was very uncomfortable, but I wanted to read and remember every word...[44]

The documents Howe viewed described four separate saucer crashes that occurred in Aztec, Roswell, Kingman (Arizona), and Mexico. The lone survivor of the Roswell crash was identified as "EBE" (Extraterrestrial Biological Entity). EBE was held in captivity at Los Alamos Laboratories until his death in 1952, and was described as four-feet-tall, gray-skinned and hairless, with a large head and big eyes, "like a child with the mind of a thousand men." One of the documents stated: "Two thousand years ago extraterrestrials had created a being" who had been placed on Earth to teach peace and love, and it seemed obvious that this was a reference to Jesus Christ.

After EBE died, a couple of other ETs (EBE-2 and EBE-3) visited Earth as part of an exchange program. Doty informed Linda Howe that EBE-3 was still alive and that she might get an opportunity to interview him. In addition, Doty told Howe that high-level government intelligence officers had in their possession film footage of a UFO landing at a military base, as well as other photos and classified materials she could use for her documentary. Doty said he'd contact her at a later date using the code name "Falcon." After several months of stringing Howe along, Doty informed her that he'd been removed from the case, and passed her on to other intelligence contacts that likewise strung Howe along for a period of several months, but never produced the promised UFO footage. This delay eventually caused HBO to opt out of the project, leaving Howe high and dry. To this day, Howe stands by the "amazing" material Doty presented to her as authentic evidence of ETs—although she must obviously be aware now of all the erroneous information and documents that Doty has disseminated over the years.

Howe's experience wasn't the first episode of military intel types dangling supposed flying saucer footage—or proof of little green men—before the noses of Hollywood producers. In 1975, an Air Force official contacted producers Robert Emenegger and Alan Sandler (who were then working on a documentary entitled *UFOs: Past, Present and Future*) with a promise of 16mm footage of a UFO and ETs supposedly filmed at Holloman Air Force Base in 1971. Like Linda Howe, Emenegger was similarly strung along until the 11th hour when his Air Force sources decided to pull the plug on the project.

Chapter II

The Cosmic Watergate

After spending three years trying to convince anybody who would listen that our planet had a serious ET problem, Paul Bennewitz no doubt found some measure of vindication when a collection of Air Force documents (obtained by Barry Greenwood of CAUS through an FOIA request) emerged in 1982. These documents revealed that there had indeed been some type of strange aerial activity going in the vicinity of the Manzano Weapons Storage Area during August of 1980, as documented on the front page of the April 8, 1983 edition of the *Albuquerque Tribune* with a story entitled "UFOs: U.S. reports tell of five sightings in 1980 over Kirtland; city man claims alien contact." The "city man" in this instance was Paul Bennewitz, who was featured prominently in an article authored by Susie Gran, stating that:

> Just released government reports document five sightings of unidentified flying objects during August 1980 over Kirtland Air Force Base.
>
> The mysterious encounters, as described in Air Force reports and revealed through the Freedom of Information Act, were:
>
> *On Aug. 8, "three security policemen…on duty inside the Manzano Weapons Storage Area sighted an unidentified light in the air that traveled north to south over the Coyote Canyon and eventually landed in the canyon, according to the security policemen, who then witnessed it 'take off and leave proceeding straight up at a high speed and disappear.'"
>
> *The next day, Aug. 9 a security guard at Sandia Laboratories on the base observed a bright light near the ground behind a

building in Coyote Canyon. As he drove nearer, he saw a round, disc-shaped object and tried to radio for help. But his radio would not work.

The guard, who did not want his name divulged for fear of harassment, then walked up to the object armed with a shotgun. Suddenly, it took off, going straight up at a high speed.

The guard, a former Army helicopter mechanic, stated that the UFO was not a helicopter.

*The following day, Aug 10, a New Mexico state policemen saw a flying object land in the Manzano Mountains between Belen and Albuquerque. When he reported the sighting to the Kirtland command post, he was told by the public relations office that the Air Force did not investigate sightings unless they occurred on the air base.

*Three days later, Aug. 13, radar equipment at Kirtland and the Albuquerque Airport experienced a total five-hour blackout from an "unknown cause." An Air Force report concluded that "the presence of hostile intelligence jamming cannot be ruled out," but went on to say "no evidence would suggest this."

*Nine days later, on Aug. 22, three other security guards observed the same aerial phenomenon described by the first three guards two weeks earlier.

"Again the object landed in Coyote Canyon. They did not see the object take off," the report said.

*The final Kirtland document is dated Oct. 28, 1980. In it, Air Force scientific advisor Jerry Miller concluded that a film taken by Four Hills resident Paul Bennewitz "clearly shows... some type of unidentified aerial objects" at Kirtland.

Miller is a former investigator for Project Bluebook, the Air Force's massive investigations of UFOs that ended in 1969.

Bennewitz, president of a local electronics firm, lives adjacent to the northern boundary of Manzano Base.

He said it was on Feb. 2, 1980, that he saw four "saucer or hat-shaped objects lined up behind the outside fence" of the Manzano area.

"A black spot and big blue halo appeared, establishing their force field. There was a flash under each one as they jumped off the ground in sync 300-400 feet, turned right and were gone to the south," he recalled.

He filmed the spectacle from about 2,500 yards away.

Bennewitz, according to the official Air Force report written months later, produced still photographs and 2,600 feet of 8mm motion picture film "depicting unidentified aerial objects flying over and around Manzano Weapons Storage Area and Coyote Canyon Test Area."

But investigator Miller reported only that "no conclusions could be made whether these objects pose a threat to Manzano-Coyote Canyon areas."

On Nov. 19, Bennewitz was told that the Air Force would not investigate the objects and "was not in a position to evaluate the information and photographs he has collected."

However, the sightings reportedly caught the interest of former New Mexico Sen. Harrison Schmitt, who inquired why the Air Force refused to investigate, the report said.

Within the past year or so, Bennewitz, who is convinced the UFOs are alien ships, has called Kirtland to again request an investigation, said George Pearce, Kirtland public affairs officer.

"He said he was in contact with alien beings through his computer and wanted us to investigate," Pearce said.

"I told him we don't investigate those things since Project Bluebook concluded in 1969 after 22 years of investigation. Of course, he wasn't pleased with the answer."

Bennewitz earlier this week in Albuquerque briefed a group of UFO enthusiasts on his personal three-year investigation into alien activities in New Mexico. He said he plans to put his observations into a book.

Among his conclusions are that there is an alien base inside an isolated mesa near Dulce, and that the aliens intend to enslave earth.

He said his study includes a statement taken from a New Mexico women who was taken hostage near Cimarron by aliens after she saw them mutilate a calf.

Bennewitz said he has seen the aliens on a video screen, said he described them as green and about 4 feet tall and "strong little bastards."

He told those gathered for the UFO briefing session that cattle mutilations are the aliens' source of supplies needed to build humanoids through gene splicing. They take the organs and blood from the animals while they are still alive in order to maintain a tremendous supply of DNA—the carrier of the genetic code—for this purpose, he said.

The Kirtland sightings in 1980 were described in reports sent to the Mutual UFO Network, a Texas-based UFO international study group, by the Department of the Air Force in December 1982.

MUFON's effort to gather documents has been a tough, uphill battle with countless arms of government and military agencies.

"We call it our Cosmic Watergate," Andrus [National Director of MUFON] said.

On the heels of the *Albuquerque Tribune* story, its competitor, the *Albuquerque Journal*, published an article the following day, April 9, 1983, covering most of the same ground as the *Tribune*, along with a closing quote by Bennewitz claiming that he had discovered that "the government is aware the objects are in fact extraterrestrial and is currently studying them under a project code-named 'Aquarius'."

Chapter 12

Do you believe in MAJIC?

In 1982, Bill Moore approached film producer Jaime Shandera with a pitch to develop a documentary based on his Roswell research. Although this project never got off the ground, Shandera instead became Moore's research partner, an arrangement that continued through the course of the decade.

On December 11, 1984, Shandera received a delivery at his home in Burbank, California, that had been sent anonymously with no return address, postmarked December 9 from Albuquerque (shades of the Weitzel Letter). The envelope contained a roll of 35mm film that when developed revealed photos of what became known as the MJ-12 papers. This included the Eisenhower Briefing Document or "EBD." Dated November 18, 1952, this eyes-only document had been allegedly prepared for President Elect Eisenhower to brief him on "Operation Majestic-12...a Top Secret Research and Development/ Intelligence operation responsible directly and only to the President of the United States."

After receiving the MJ-12 papers, Moore and Shandera were reluctant to release the materials until fully vetting them. By 1986, Falcon (or whoever was actually orchestrating the release of the MJ-12 papers) had become impatient with Moore and Shandera's slow roll, and to speed up the release approached British ufologist Jenny Randles to serve as a conduit for the release of the materials. The intermediary in this instance was a young man named Robert, who claimed that he had previously served in the British Army. Robert offered Randles over six hundred pages of material that had been allegedly obtained from U.S. military intelligence sources, the content of which sounded remarkably similar to the MJ-12 papers. Randles suspected something was amiss and decided to steer clear of entering into an agreement she might later regret. It was subsequently discovered that during this period Randles had been under surveillance by British and U.S. intelligence due to her UFO research.[45]

As it turns out, Randles had previously been on the business end of a hoaxed letter concerning the 1980 Rendlesham Forest incident. The hoaxed letter in question was sent in 1984 and later appeared in a book Randles co-authored called *Sky Crash*. According to Randles: "We have investigated [the letter]...and our conclusion is that it is a deliberate fake by certain parties, whose identities are strongly suspected by us...This hoax has clearly been planned to test us or, more likely, to impugn our credibility should we fall for the trick." Written on British Ministry of Defense stationery, the undated letter read:

Dear [Blacked out],

As you know, OSI has completed a report on the landing of a craft of unknown origin crewed by several entities near RAF Bentwaters on the night of December 29/30 1980. Interestingly, OSI reports that the entities were approximately 1 1/2 metres tall, wore what appeared to be nylon-coated pressure suits, but no helmets. Conditions on the night were misty, giving the appearance that the entities were hovering above ground level.

Tape recordings were made on which the entities are heard to speak in an electronically synthesized version of English, with a strong American accent. Similar transmissions intercepted irregularly by NSA since 1975. According to OSI, entities had claw-like hands with three digits and an opposable thumb. Despite original reports, OSI said the craft was not damaged but landed deliberately as part of a series of visits to SAC bases in USA and Europe. Reports that craft was repaired by US servicemen or was taken on to the base are not confirmed by OSI.

Landing is not considered a Defence issue in view of the overt peaceful nature of the contact, but investigations are to be continued on [Blacked out] authority. Precautionary plan for counter-information at a local level involving [Blacked out] and a [Blacked out] is strongly recommended.

Randles' run-in with the Rendlesham hoaxed letter no doubt influenced her decision to steer clear of the MJ-12 material, and afterwards the same anonymous source who approached Randles apparently found another British ufologist willing to bite, in this case Timothy Good, who agreed to publish the MJ-12 papers in his forthcoming book *Above Top Secret: The Worldwide U.F.O. Cover-Up*. This arrangement was made with the caveat that Bill Moore would have the first shot to publicly announce the release of the documents in mid-June 1987. Using this two-pronged approach, *Above Top Secret* would provide independent corroboration as a follow up to Moore's forthcoming announcement. These best-laid plans were derailed when Good's publisher announced a hastily arranged press conference for May 29, 1987, that would include an MJ-12 sneak peek. When Bill Moore caught wind of these developments, he decided to beat Good to the punch and officially release the MJ-12 papers on May 28 at the annual National UFO Conference (NUFOC) in Burbank, California. As Jenny Randles recalled:

> The MJ-12 documents surfaced in May 1987. Tim Good had received them at some point after our meeting with Robert, and published them—more or less at the last minute—in *Above Top Secret*. I thought that what was happening was this: someone had first approached Moore, Shandera, and Friedman with those papers. And because they'd sat on them for a couple of years and hadn't published them, they had given up on them. It was not unknown in October 1986 that I was writing *The UFO Conspiracy*—which deals with government investigations of UFOs—and that maybe they were hoping that by feeding this story to me, I'd publish it in [the book].[46]

Researchers began scouring the MJ-12 papers and soon keyed in on a number of peculiarities. For example, the typeset on the documents corresponded with a Smith-Corona model that was manufactured after 1952, the year that the Eisenhower Briefing Document was supposedly authored. Arch debunker Phil Klass noted that the dating system on the MJ-12 papers didn't correspond with the standard system he'd seen on other government documents. The MJ-12 papers used the following format: "18 November, 1952," whereas the formats Klass had seen most commonly used was "November 18, 1952" or "18 Nov. 1952." Furthermore, Klass claimed to have seen the MJ-12 dating system used on documents and correspondence produced by Bill Moore prior to 1984.

In June 1987, Klass contacted William Baker, then Assistant Director in the Office of Congressional and Public Affairs for the FBI: "I am enclosing what purport to be Top Secret/Eyes Only documents, which have not been properly declassified, now being circulated by William L. Moore, Burbank, California, 91505..."

At Klass' urging, the FBI opened an investigation to determine if the MJ-12 papers were either a hoax or classified documents that had been illegally leaked. On November 30, 1988, a meeting took place in Washington D.C. between FBI and AFOSI agents. At that time, "...[t]he Office of Special Investigations, US Air Force, advised...that the document was fabricated. Copies of that document have been distributed to various parts of the United States..."[47] What remains a mystery is how the Air Force determined that the MJ-12 papers had been faked, and by whom.

In 1998, UFO researcher Nick Redfern was contacted by a former FBI agent who had been worked on the MJ-12 papers. One area of inquiry—according to this former agent—included the theory that the MJ-12 papers had been fabricated by Soviet agents to be used as "bait" to reel in civilians working in the defense sector who were involved in UFO research.[48] Conversely, Falcon once remarked to Bill Moore that the AFOSI counterintelligence operation had been designed to flush "a few moles out of their holes"—the moles, in this case, being Soviet spies.[49]

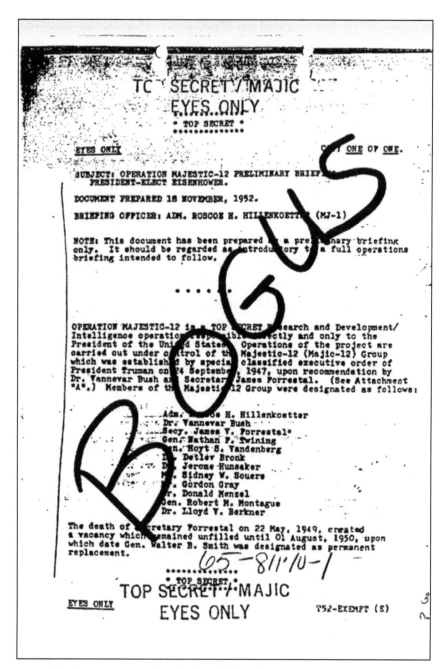

MJ-12 papers stamped marked as 'BOGUS' by government investigators.

Prior to the emergence of the MJ-12 papers, Bill Moore and Stan Friedman had speculated about the existence of just such a group as Majestic-12, and had compiled a list of its most probable candidates. Moore later shared these names with Doty in the hopes that he or Falcon might be privy to inside information that would confirm their list of MJ-12 candidates.

In *TOP SECRET/MAJIC* (1996), Stan Friedman stated that: "... the simple fact of the matter is that Moore, Shandera, and I had already picked up on all the names of the [MJ-12] list prior to receipt of the film as a result of the many days spent in archival research begun a decade ago...We had noted who was where in early July 1947, when the Roswell incident occurred."

Some of these very same MJ-12 candidates that Moore and Friedman identified (such as Roscoe Hillenkoetter, then director of the CIA, and James Forrestal, then Secretary of Defense), later surfaced in the MJ-12 papers, providing confirmation to Moore and Friedman that they'd been on the right track.

After the MJ-12 papers surfaced, Moore and Shandera received a series of cryptic clues from their spooky sources instructing them to travel to the National Archives in Washington D.C., to examine a series of recently declassified Air Force documents. In July 1985, Moore and Shandera spent several hours going through over one hundred boxes and, in the 126th box they examined, discovered a document wedged between two file folders. The document in question, dated July 14, 1954, had been dictated by Robert Cutler—Special Assistant to President Eisenhower—to Gen. Nathan Twining, stating that that "The President has decided that the MJ-12 SSP [Special Studies Project] briefing should take place during the already scheduled White House meeting of July 16 rather than following it as previously intended. More precise arrangements will be explained to you upon your arrival. Your concurrence in the above change of arrangements is assumed."

At the time, Moore claimed that the Cutler-Twining Memo "unquestionably verifies the existence of an "MJ-12" group in 1954 and definitely links both to the National Security Council and the President of the United States to it." However, there was no actual mention of UFOs in the document, and it only stated that "MJ-12" was a "Special Studies Project" without identifying what it actually pertained to.

After the Cutler-Twining Memo surfaced, Jo Ann Williamson, chief archivist of the military reference branch at National Archives, dictated a three-page memo stating that:

> ...the military reference branch had conducted a search in the records of the Secretary of Defense, the Joint Chiefs of Staff, Headquarters to US Air Force, and in other related files. No information has been found on this subject [MJ-12]...Inquiries to the US Air Force, the Joint Chiefs of Staff, and the National Security Council failed to produce further information...The acting Director of the Freedom of Information of the National Security Council informed us that 'Top Secret Restricted Information' is a marking that did not come into use at the National Security Council until the Nixon Administration. The Eisenhower Presidential Library also confirms that this particular marking was not used during the Eisenhower Administration...

An equally quizzical Phil Klass pointed out that all of the other declassified documents filed in the National Archives boxes (identified as Group 341) had been stamped with a register number—all of the documents, that is, except the Cutler-Twining Memo. This led Klass to speculate that the document had been surreptitiously planted by Moore and/or Shandera. Stan Friedman likewise suspected that the document had been planted, although he fingered Falcon, or one of his feathery underlings, as the culprits in the caper.

Chapter 13

UFO cover-up lie

Although Linda Howe's proposed UFO documentary ultimately ran aground, what Richard Doty and his AFOSI cohorts probably intended all along was rolled out in a nationally televised special that aired on October 14, 1988, called *UFO Cover-up Live!* hosted by Mike Farrell of *Mash* fame.

In *UFO Cover-up Live!*, Bill Moore and Jaime Shandera coordinated the "appearances" of two government intelligence officers code-named Falcon and Condor, who were shown in the shadows with their voices electronically scrambled. The person appearing as Falcon was eventually revealed to be our old pal Richard Doty, who later claimed he wasn't the *real* Falcon, and had simply performed the role as a surrogate on *UFO Cover-up Live!* to protect Falcon's identity. Condor was later revealed to be former Air Force officer Robert Collins. According to Phil Klass:

> Robert Collins was then a Captain in the Air Force assigned to the Air Technical Intelligence Center in Dayton. In his later years he transferred down to Kirtland; what is now called the Phillips Lab. It was called then the Air Force Weapons Lab. He retired shortly before the TV special [*UFO Cover-up Live!*].[50]

UFO Cover-up Live! was broken into several segments, each roughly ten minutes in length, featuring a variety of UFO witnesses, researchers, scientists, whistle-blowers, as well as people-in-the-street interviews filmed in the U.S. and the Soviet Union. One segment featured film producer Robert Emenegger who, in 1975, had been dangled the proverbial carrot at the end of the stick—or saucer at the end of a string—only to have it snatched back at the last minute. Appearing with Emenegger was the very same former Air Force official, Paul Shartle, who had first told him about the film with the UFO and ET footage. Emenegger recalled that "in 1973 when I was vice president of Grey Advertising I took time out and went to Norton Air Force Base to explore subjects for television specials related to the defense department. While discussing several of the subjects, UFOs came up and Paul here told us about a film about the landing of alien craft at Holloman Air Force Base." Shartle described the film as:

> ...footage of three disc shaped crafts. One of the craft landed...it appeared to be in trouble because it oscillated all the way down to the ground. However, it did land on three pods. A sliding door opened, a ramp was extended and out came three aliens...they were human sized, they had odd gray complexions and a pronounced nose. They wore tight-fitting jump suits and head dresses that appeared to be communication devices and in their hands they held a translator, I was told. The Holloman base commander and other Air Force officers went out to meet them.

Emenegger added:

> This film footage sounded very, very special and we wanted to use it as the ending of our television special...although the Pentagon had been very cooperative all the way, at the last minute the film was confiscated and we lost the whole finale of our show, but what I saw and heard was enough to convince me that the phenomenon of UFOs is real.

Perhaps the most compelling *UFO Cover-up Live!* segment was introduced by Mike Farrell: "From the piney woods of east Texas on December 23rd 1980 comes a bizarre close encounter of the second kind experienced by our next guests, Betty Cash and Vickie Landrum," a couple of middle-aged ladies who shared the harrowing tale of driving home from bingo one night with Landrum's seven-year old grandson, Colby, when they witnessed:

"... a bright light in the sky above the pine trees. A tremendous amount of heat was coming from this diamond shaped thing. Fire was coming out of the bottom of it. When it moved it made a swishin' sound, and there was a beeping the entire time; a deafening beeping that I still hear in my mind at night...I just stood there terrified for about ten minutes. The object lit up the surrounding pine woods like it was daylight and I was burning, my skin was burning...The craft hovered over us about 20 minutes. Fire was coming out of the bottom like a blowtorch. It lifted up and then flew away over the trees. That's when we saw the helicopters come out..."

Farrell: "I understand that you in fact later identified them as CH-47 Chinook military helicopters?"

Landrum: "Yes, it seemed like they were trying to escort the craft somewhere. Looked like they were about to collide. The roar sounded like a tornado. When we got home I washed Colby off and put him to bed. When the water touched his skin he cried out like he'd been burned, as if he had been in the sun too long."

Cash: "And I was too sick to work the next day. My eyes swelled closed and welts appeared on my face and head and I thought I was going to die. Vickie came and took me to the emergency room of the hospital. They treated me like a burn patient. Over the next few days I kept losing big patches of skin on my face and about half my hair fell out. They kept me in the hospital over a month with no improvement."

Following Cash and Landrum's testimony, video footage of Falcon (portrayed by Doty in the shadows) provided this stunning revelation:

> The Cash-Landrum incident—the craft that was observed— was an alien craft, piloted by military aircraft pilots. Although they were trained and were somewhat familiar with the craft, they found that the aircraft did not respond to certain control. They radioed that they thought that the craft was going to crash. Standard procedures for the military in a situation where the aircraft was going to crash, the military would send up search and rescue helicopters. The helicopters were following the craft. The craft experienced severe problems. It was thought that the craft was going to crash. However this craft did not crash.

Following the incident, Betty Cash was diagnosed with cancer, which she suspected was a result of radiation exposure. The two women took legal action, and—with the aid of Peter Gersten of CAUS—sued the federal government to the tune of $20 million. On August 21, 1986, the Cash-Landrum lawsuit was dismissed by a U.S. District Court Judge on grounds that the defense team failed to provide sufficient evidence that the government owned any type of aircraft resembling the technology the women described.

Whether the Cash-Landrum incident actually constituted a test drive of a real deal alien spaceship—or more likely the testing of some secret all-too-human craft—it might lend credence to the theory that the two women (and child) were unintentionally irradiated as a result of a covert government operation. It should be noted that during this period secret atomic-powered craft were in development.

Doty's role as Falcon on *UFO Cover-up Live!* seemed designed to present a version of events (a UFO test drive gone awry) designed to conceal secret state-of-the-art U.S. government technology—or at least get it muddied up in a fanciful UFO yarn that most media would dismiss or, at best, belittle.

Curiously enough, the Cash-Landrum sighting occurred one day after the Rendlesham Forest UFO incident, which many researchers now suspect was some sort of government Psy Op.

Chapter 14

Flying saucers are real! Period!

Bill Moore appeared in two segments of *UFO Cover-up Live!*, the first of which he shared the stage with Stan Friedman, who claimed that their research had uncovered incontrovertible proof that a UFO crash had occurred near Roswell, New Mexico in 1947, with dead alien bodies recovered from the wreckage. To close the segment, Friedman boldly proclaimed: "Flying saucers are real. Period!" The other segment in which Moore appeared featured his running mate Jaime Shandera, who related the story about how the MJ-12 papers had miraculously landed on his doorstep one day, ostensibly adding more fuel to the fire that Roswell was a real deal saucer crash, and that the government had been suppressing this knowledge for over four decades.

In retrospect, *UFO Cover-up Live!* comes across like an infomercial for the Roswell crash religion. Mike Farrell asked obviously scripted questions, which elicited canned answers ostensibly connecting Roswell to MJ-12. In other words, since Roswell was mentioned in the MJ-12 documents, this provided evidence supporting the Roswell crash itself. Moore later claimed that...

> ...there were a lot of things on that show that were very hastily thrown together...[it] was supposed to be a spontaneous show and, in the end, they insisted that it had to be scripted, and we had to read what we were told, and it really was a very disappointing experience...if I had that to do over again, I would not have gotten involved...Some of the stuff on the show was real, and some was disinformation."[51]

During *UFO Cover-up Live!*, an executive news producer for the CBS affiliate in Los Angeles named Peter Leon stated that in 1983—in the presence of Bill Moore and Jaime Shandera—he verified Falcon's credentials as those of a "government intelligence official." One might assume that Leon was referring to Richard Doty's credentials, who was indeed a bona fide intelligence agent. The unspoken caveat, however, was that Doty's stock in trade was disinformation.

In one segment of *UFO Cover-up Live!*, Mike Farrell interviewed Falcon and Condor in what was made to appear as a real time discussion; in reality, Farrell was talking to video clips of the two feathery spooks with questions that had obviously been scripted to present a pre-determined narrative.

Falcon: "[The Red Book], or it's called The Bible within the MJ-12 Community, contains historically everything that occurred from the Truman Era up through the three aliens being guests of the United States Government, technological data gathered from the aliens, medical history gathered from dead aliens that were found in the desert, and information obtained from the extraterrestrials regarding their social structure and their information pertaining to the Universe."

Farrell: "Was there an additional source of information?"

Falcon: "Presently, as of the year 1988, there is one extraterrestrial being. He's a guest of the United States Government and he's remained hidden from public view. The Yellow Book is a book that was exclusively written by the second alien. The book relates to the alien's planet, solar system, suns, the culture and societal make up on the planet, the social structure of the aliens and the alien's life among Earthlings. What was most intriguing to me in my experience with the aliens is...an octagon shaped crystal which when held in the alien's hand and viewed by the second person displays pictures. These pictures could be of the alien's home planet or pictures of Earth many thousands of years ago."

Farrell: "Where did the EBEs come from?"

Falcon: "He was in the Zeta Reticuli star group."

Farrell: "Now Condor, tell us about a deal our government made with the aliens."

Condor: "There has been an agreement signed between our U.S. Government and the extraterrestrials and essentially the agreement says that we won't disclose your existence if you do not interfere in our society, and we allow you to operate from a designated base here in the United States. It's in the state of Nevada in an area called Area 51 or Dreamland."

Falcon: "The extraterrestrials have complete control of this base...My understanding is that three different aliens of the same species have resided within the United States from 1948 or '49 until present day. The first alien was captured in the New Mexican desert after its craft crashed. The alien which was named EBE by the Government was kept in captivity for three years. We learned a great deal of information about the alien's race, culture and spacecrafts. The second alien was part of an exchange program. I don't recall what year that alien visited. The third alien was also part of an exchange program and has been a guest of the United States Government since 1982."

Falcon described the ET's physical attributes in terms of "The Grey" motif soon after to populate alien abduction accounts. Falcon also claimed that one of the ET saucer crash survivors was crazy about strawberry ice cream, and a huge fan of Tibetan music.

Chapter 15

Strange breezes in the Gulf

An audience was assembled in Gulf Breeze, Florida to participate in *UFO Cover Up Live!*. As the studio announcer explained: "The story of Gulf Breeze will play a major role in our program tonight. We're down here in Florida where we've assembled a whole town-hall full of people who say they've seen a UFO that has haunted this community since last November."

Around this time, Gulf Breeze experienced a flurry of UFO sightings that first came to public attention courtesy of a fellow named Ed Walters (real name Ed Hanson). According to Walters' account, he'd been the victim of a failed abduction when ETs attempted to suck him up into their ship via a blue beam that momentarily paralyzed him, but before being sucked all the way up, Walters snapped out of it and was able to extricate himself. Walters—who happened to have a Polaroid camera handy—snapped a series of photos of ET ships with luminous tops that indeed appeared quite impressive at first blush.

Before you knew it, Walters' photos were all the rage, as many prominent ufologists enthusiastically jumped aboard the Gulf Breeze spaceship for a ride. During Walters' ascendance into UFO celebrity status some inconvenient facts emerged, which included the discovery of miniature flying saucers in his attic (constructed with plates and scrap paper) that had apparently been used to create his series of stunning saucer photos.

Among Walter's most fervent supporters (before these inconvenient facts of plate and scrap paper saucers emerged) was UFO researcher, and former Navy physicist, Dr. Bruce Maccabee, who conducted an extensive analysis (supposedly) of Walters' photos and confirmed that they were, in his estimation, authentic. Maccabee even appeared on *UFO Cover-up Live!* declaring: "Ed could not have faked the pictures!"[52]

A bizarre episode connected to the Gulf Breeze sightings concerned a group of U.S. Army intelligence specialists stationed in Augsburg, West Germany, who went AWOL on July 9, 1990, high-tailing it to Gulf Breeze where they planned to meet up with a landed saucer and save the world from the anti-Christ. This group subsequently became known as Gulf Breeze Six (GB6).

According to the de facto leader of the group, Vance Davis, Ouija board sessions played a role in motivating him and his cohorts to go AWOL. Between December 1989 and July 1990, the GB6 received a series of dire predictions from an otherworldly entity named Safire that included information about the imminent return of the anti-Christ, who, it appears, was in cahoots with evil aliens. Before deserting their posts, each member of the GB6 drafted a letter (dictated by their spirit guides), addressed to President Bush, alerting him of the forthcoming return of the anti-Christ.

Apparently this wasn't Vance Davis' first encounter with otherworldly entities. In the 1980s, he enrolled in a Silva Mind Control course and learned self-hypnosis through "active imagination." During one of his self-induced trances, Davis encountered a green-skinned woman named Kia, who—over the course of one very memorable evening—corrected his flat-footedness while clueing him into the mysteries of the universe. Kia informed Davis that:

> ...she came from a planet forty-five light years away from Earth, that had been destroyed by another race. Her race, the Kiasseions, were telepaths that were enroute to Earth to assist the Alliance in protecting the human race. They were scheduled to arrive by late 1992. The Kiasseion civilization had been reduced to five spacecraft carrying about three thousand people per ship. Her husband had been killed, and she had taken his

place as Commander of this small armada, with her two grown sons in charge of two of the remaining ships.[53]

Upon landing on U.S. soil in July 1990, the GB6 split up into separate groups and made their way to Gulf Breeze to rendezvous with the landed saucer. The wheels came off this grand plan to meet the saucer people and thwart the anti-Christ when—on Saturday, July 14—a member of the group, Michael Hueckstaedt, was pulled over by police due to a broken tail-light and a computer check identified that Hueckstaedt was wanted for desertion. In short order, the rest of the GB6 were rounded up at the home of a psychic named Anna Foster in Gulf Breeze.

These events coincided with the 1990 MUFON Symposium held in Pensacola, Florida, just a few miles from Gulf Breeze. Although it was reported that none of the GB6 attended the symposium, apparently their psychic friend, Anna Foster, was said to have been present. Among the speakers were Ed Walters, detailing his dubious Gulf Breeze encounters. According to UFO researcher Jack Brewer: "One MUFON account stated the Gulf Breeze Six identified Ed Walters as the anti-Christ and intended to kill him."[54]

Chapter 16

Spooks of a feather

According to Robert "Condor" Collins, a secret group unofficially dubbed the Aviary was hatched in 1986, and it appears one of the driving forces behind the Aviary's conception was retired Air Force officer Ernie Kellerstrauss.[55]

According to Collins, he had been shooting the bull one day in the mid 1980s with co-workers at Wright-Patterson AFB when the topic of UFOs came up, and one of Collins' colleagues name-dropped Kellerstrauss as someone in the UFO-know. Afterwards, Collins sought out Kellerstrauss at around the same time—in the spring of 1986—that he became acquainted with Bill Moore, who had showed him copies of the MJ-12 papers.

These interactions led to a meeting hosted by Kellerstrauss at his home in Beavercreek, Ohio, in 1986 that included Collins, Doty, Moore, Shandera and U.S. Army colonel John Alexander. This gathering of "intelligence agency insiders" would form the core of what later became known as the Aviary. As Robert Collins recalled:

> Even amongst fellow spooks there was a cat and mouse game going on during the meeting. Rick [Doty] and Ernie [Kellerstrauss] ostensibly had not met before, and they were doing a little challenging back and forth as to who knew what. One would start to describe a certain classified room in the Pentagon or something, and then say, 'Oh yeah, and then when you go through this door...um what was it again on the other side of that wall?' If the other spook could pick up the conversation from there and describe it, and everybody was in sync, then everything continued along. At the same time, they began

talking about the E.T. who was an 'ambassador' or liaison to the U.S. Among the things discussed was that the extraterrestrial ambassador was a female, Extraterrestrial Biological Entity...[56]

In 1985—a year before the Aviary first began flapping its wings—Bruce Maccabee met with Ernie Kellerstrauss and conducted a series of interviews called *Hawk Tales* (eventually published in 2005). *Hawk Tales* disclosed information that would resurface in *UFO Cover Up Live!*, including stories of a crashed saucer at Roswell, captive ETs and the existence of a "Yellow Book" and a "Red Book." The Red Book—according to Robert Collins—was a compilation of ongoing government research on UFOs and ETs dating back to 1947. The Yellow Book, however, was a horse of another color: an octagon-shaped crystal that, when held by the ETs, would project holographic images, such as the story of how ETs seeded Jesus on our planet. Rick Doty claimed that "he had seen that crystal, and in fact had handled it, but couldn't make it work. It seemed to work only when an E.T. handled it."

In *Hawk Tales*, Kellerstrauss (referred to pseudonymously as "Hawk"), identified the insider source for much of his information as Dale Graff, a physicist with the Air Force's Foreign Technology Division at Wright-Patterson. In the mid-1970s, Graff organized an informal remote viewing group at Wright-Patt, and some suspect that these remote viewers provided the "insider" information that would evolve into the MJ-12/Project Aquarius revelations.

At the time of *Hawk Tales*, Bruce Maccabee was unaware that similar info was being fed (via Doty) to Moore, Shandera, Howe, et al. To this end—it could be conjectured—that Doty and Kellerstrauss coordinated to seed the same narrative to different researchers, essentially creating a feedback loop, as these researchers interacted and shared information with one another, receiving what appeared to be independent confirmations from multiple sources within the military intelligence community.

A legend has grown around the Aviary that they were a latter day version of MJ-12, and some have even cast them as sinister spooks that were trying to poison the well of UFO research. A more benign take on the Aviary suggests it was simply an ad hoc group of current and former intelligence personnel and researchers with an avid interest in UFOs, some of whom apparently had inside knowledge, or pieces of the puzzle, and engaged in a meeting of the minds aimed at ultimately discovering the truth about UFOs, or at least inching themselves closer in that direction. Below is a list of reported Aviary members derived from multiple sources:

- Richard Doty = Sparrow
- Robert Collins = Condor
- Ernie Kellerstrauss = Hawk
- Dale Graff = Harrier
- John Alexander = Penguin
- Jaime Shandera = Woodpecker
- C.B. Scott Jones = Chickadee
- Dr. Christopher "Kit" Green = Blue Jay
- Dr. Hal Puthoff = Owl
- Dr. Ron Pandolfi = Pelican

Perhaps the most obscure Aviary member was Jack Vorona (code name Raven). According to ufologist Dr. Richard Boylan:

Vorona [was] apparently the most covert of all the Birds. He is believed to have been a liaison between Capitol Hill and Los Alamos. Was once involved in Project Sleeping Beauty, an attempt to disable enemy troops using electromagnetic radiation. Vorona has recently 'vanished,' and his present whereabouts are unknown.

Although Bill Moore never directly identified himself as an Aviary member, his arch-nemesis-critic Robert Hastings described Moore as a "carrier pigeon" used to deliver documents to the UFO research community as part of the AFOSI counter-intelligence operation.

Other names have been put forth as possible Aviary members, such as Jacques Vallee, rumored to be "Parrot," and Dr. Bruce Macca-bee, "Seagull." Over time, Aviary speculation became a fanatical hobby for ufologists and conspiracy buffs alike, and the biggest mystery of all was the secret identity of Falcon, that enigmatic bird at the top of the Aviary pecking order.

Chapter 17

The alphabet soup working group

It's conceivable that the Aviary was a cover story for an actual group identified by *New York Times* reporter Howard Blum as "The UFO Working Group" in his book *Out There: The Government's Secret Quest for Extraterrestrials* (1990).

Officially formed in 1987 under the direction of "Colonel Harold E. Phillips," the UFO Working Group was an ad hoc collection of intelligence officers from various alphabet soup agencies assembled to investigate UFOs and the possibility of ET contact.

The UFO Working Group identified their secret project as "Aquarius," which was the same code-name attributed to the spurious briefing documents Richard Doty had disseminated in the early 1980s. One might presume that if enough layers of disinformation are attached to a story—even though some of that information is legit—the true stories will then get wrapped around the false ones and at the end of the day no one really knows what's actually going on. In other words, if the *real* Project Aquarius was leaked, there would be a cover story already in place to discredit any factual reporting that might eventually surface.

After the publication of Blum's *Out There,* rumors circulated that the true identity of Col. Harold E. Phillips was none other than Col. John Alexander. In recent years, Alexander has gone on record confirming he was indeed in charge of the UFO Working Group —although who knows what to believe in this hall of mirrors—and perhaps that's the whole point; to keep researchers stumbling down blind alleys. In recent years, Alexander has stated that the UFO Working Group was involved with what was known as the Advanced Theoretical Physics Project (ATP).

Alexander retired from military service in 1988, at around the same time the UFO Working Group was calling it a wrap. He then slid into a sweet government contractor gig developing non-lethal weaponry at Los Alamos National Laboratories, a facility which some suggest played a pivotal role in whatever went down in Dulce related to UFOs and cattle mutilations.

Another member of the UFO Working Group was Dr. Ron Pandolfi, a former "Scientific Advisor on the Advisory Board to the Directorate of Intelligence, CIA," also rumored to be Aviary member, "Pelican." According to researcher Armen Victorian, in 1991 Pandolfi began using an intermediary named Dan T. Smith to backchannel classified information into the UFO research community, including revelations about the existence of a captive ET housed at Los Alamos.

In the early '90s, researcher Vince Johnson recounted a series of phone calls with Dan T. Smith, who was supposedly known to the Aviary as "Chicken Little." According to Smith's sources, there were "grave concerns" at this time "by high government officials about impending metaphysical catastrophe—The Eschaton, or the end of the world." In his 1993 article entitled "The Aviary, the Aquarium, and Eschatology", Johnson writes:

According to Smith, UFOs are primarily a psychological/ metaphysical phenomenon which are both preparing us and pressuring us to develop our own psi abilities. Not that UFOs are a single type of entity, Smith asserts that there are 'powers and principalities' at work—presumably supernatural entities like angels and demons.

Furthermore, he said that a radical program of parapsychological research and development is currently underway near Los Alamos, New Mexico. This group's development of psychokinesis, and psychotronics (a term used to denote psychic warfare techniques) represents a danger of eschatological proportions. 'These techniques have been available, but controlled, throughout history. Now, other entities are forcing the issue,' said Smith.

To corroborate Smith's claims, Johnson was able to get a phone call through to Ron Pandolfi at CIA headquarters. While Dr. Pandolfi confirmed he was indeed in contact with Smith, he denied ever sharing classified information, and also dismissed all the hullabaloo concerning the Aviary. Pandolfi informed Johnson that:

> ...the Aviary is nothing more than the product of the somewhat-deranged mind of...retired Air Force Captain Robert Collins...Pelican [Pandolfi] said that Collins was discharged from the Air Force after breaching the security perimeter at the Manzano nuclear weapons storage facility at Kirtland AFB... When taken into custody by base security, Collins told them he was there 'to meet the President.'

Johnson came away from his conversation with Pandolfi unsure what to believe, noting that:

> Of course, nobody is shocked any more by government denials that turn out to be less than truthful, but as I said before, Pelican was very convincing. He reiterated Dan Smith's proviso that I keep his name confidential—not to keep him from being deluged by UFO kooks, but rather, so he wouldn't receive unwanted attention from foreign agents—a condition that I'll honor, even though Pelican's real name is already well known to researchers following this story.

In Jon Ronson's *The Men Who Stare at Goats*, psychic Uri Geller is quoted as saying he had been recruited into President Bush's "War on Terror." According to Geller: "The man who reactivated me is called Ron." From all accounts, Geller was referring to the mysterious Dr. Pandolfi.

Chapter 18
Dancing with Mr. D

hroughout 1981, Robert "Bob" Pratt surreptitiously recorded phone conversations with Bill Moore at a time when the two were collaborating on a book project titled *MAJIK-12*, based on the purported UFO encounters of Richard Doty (identified by Moore at the time as "Ronald L. Davis").[57]

Initially proposed as non-fiction, Pratt later insisted that the book be presented as a fictional account, mainly because they had little, if any, actual evidence to corroborate Doty's claims. Moore grudgingly agreed, and the duo authored a 250-page draft manuscript with the revised title of *The Aquarius Project*. Although the book was never published, the first proposed title suggested that Moore was aware of something called MAJIK-12 at least three years before the appearance of the MJ-12 papers.

The Aquarius Project told the story of "Mr. D" (aka Doty), a disgruntled Vietnam vet who returns to the States and is reassigned as an Air Force intelligence officer. Also appearing in this draft manuscript was a certain "Dr. Berkowitz," a character based on Paul Bennewitz. As Pratt recalled:

Our 'hero' was an AFOSI agent who scoffed at UFO reports, etc., but comes to believe because he has to investigate the 'infamous Ellsworth AFB incident' and later has his own UFO encounter. Because he realizes UFOs are real—knowledge most AFOSI agents don't have—he is assigned to keep tabs on people and things in the UFO world from his new posting at Kirtland. To give him a thorough understanding of the phenomenon, the Air Force sends him to Bolling Field in Washington, DC, where he is given access to a number of secret UFO files, and it is there that he first learns of Project Aquarius...

Somewhere in doing all of his dirty deeds, the hero's conscience takes over and he finds himself rebelling against official policies ('the people have a right to know ...'). He winds up a dead hero, his body shipped off to planets unknown on a UFO operated by aliens in cahoots with the government.

Doty was stationed at Ellsworth Air Base at the time of this alleged UFO encounter. According to a supposed top secret document leaked to the *National Enquirer*, this incident occurred in November 1977, when a spacecraft landed carrying three ETs (dressed in green glowing metallic suits) who melted an M-16 rifle from the hands of one of the sentries, and then deactivated a nuclear missile at the base.

Bob Pratt investigated the Ellsworth Incident for the *National Enquirer* and determined it was a hoax based on a number of findings, one of which was the absence in the official Air Force records of the names of personnel listed in the Ellsworth document. In other words, the names were made up. Given this discrepancy, it should come as no surprise that Richard Doty later informed Bruce Maccabee that the Ellsworth document had indeed been fabricated, although Doty denied having any direct involvement in the fabrication thereof.

Chapter 19

The man who bumped into walls

In 1972, a group of young, cutting edge scientists—headed up by future Aviary alumnus Dr. Hal Puthoff—obtained funding from the CIA to the tune of $50,000 to conduct a psychic research project code-named Stargate. The CIA liaison for Stargate was another future Aviary member, Dr. Kit Green. Headquartered at the Stanford Research Institute in Menlo Park, California, Project Stargate tested a number of psychics, among them the spoon-bending sensation, Uri Geller.

Like many involved in the paranormal field, Geller had some odd associations with UFOs and ETs reportedly dating back to his childhood. During the same period as Project Stargate was active, Geller had been closely associated involved with another CIA-linked scientist, Dr. Andrija Puharich, who made a practice of placing Geller into hypnotic trance states as a method to further enhance his psychic abilities. During one such hypnosis session, Geller recalled an encounter from his youth with a "silvery mass of light" that made time stand still. The light identified itself with a name straight out of a James Bond movie: Spectra. Geller described Spectra as his "programmer."

Puharich came to believe that Geller was "specifically created to serve as an intermediary between a 'divine' intelligence and man," and that his mission was to alert the world about an imminent mass landing of spaceships carrying a race of ETs called the Hoovas. In addition to channeling Spectra, Puharich and Geller claimed to have witnessed a wide range of paranormal activity, including mysterious messages that appeared on blank audio tapes, not to mention several UFO sightings, and the teleportation of objects.

Secretly funded government remote viewing projects appear to have played a role in the genesis of the Project Aquarius and MJ-12 mythos. If true, this puts a whole new spin on the stories promoted by Doty and the Aviary, including the possibility that forged documents were distributed to advance these narratives, and perhaps as a method to falsely corroborate remote-viewed intelligence gathered on UFOs and ETs. As previously noted, Dale Graff—one of the early military remote viewers—was allegedly a source for a large part of the MJ-12 information.

In 1989, a remote viewing firm called PSI-TECH was launched by former military remote viewers Captain David Morehouse and Major Ed Dames (who after their discharges continued using their former military ranks as a means to legitimize the endeavor). Included on the PSI-TECH board of directors were such spook luminaries as Major General Albert Stubblebine and Col. John Alexander.

The former commanding general of the U.S. Army Intelligence and Security Command (INSCOM), Stubblebine earned the nickname "Spoonbender" from military cohorts due to his keen interest in psychic phenomenon and how it could potentially be utilized on the battlefield. According to Jon Ronson in *The Men Who Stare At Goats*, Stubblebine was constantly walking into walls with the intent that he would eventually walk through one using the powers of his mind. But, alas, he just kept bumping his nose against the wall, and never made it through to the other side.

Stubblebine's entrée into psychic research came courtesy of Col. John Alexander, who served under Stubblebine. In the mid 1970s, Stubblebine attended a "PK party" at Alexander's apartment in Alexandria, Virginia. This party included a psychic medium named Anne Gehman, who under Alexander's direction attempted a number of psychokinetic feats, one of which was intended to bend forks. Gehman—who had never attempted fork bending before—had the fork prongs immediately melt and bend over in her hands just like a Dali painting. It was this alleged incident that set forth Stubblebine on his path of psychic discovery.

Stubblebine was equally intrigued by ET contact and was married to psychiatrist Dr. Rima Laibow, who was considered one of the foremost alien abduction therapists at the time. Laibow—a former close associate of Budd Hopkins and said to be an alien abductee herself—appeared on *UFO Cover Up Live!*, which featured footage of Laibow placing a fellow abductee under hypnotic regression.

At the International Symposium on UFO Research in Denver, Colorado in May of 1992, Stubblebine gave a presentation called "Remote Viewing as a Research Tool." On the subject of remote viewing UFOs, Stubblebine stated:

> As far as UFOs are concerned, they can be accessed, they can be tracked, we have looked at the propulsion system for them, that's not a hard job, you can track them back to where they come from, whether they come from a place here on this planet or whether they come from a place on another planet, they are trackable and you can take a look inside as well as outside. So again, it is a tool that is available to be used for the UFO research and...that's the reason that I am standing on this platform in spite of my misgivings and feeling a little bit nervous like a tree in a Lassie movie.

In the early 1990s, Aviary member C.B. Scott Jones (another former longtime spook with a variety of alphabet soups) attended a series of conferences in Europe and the Soviet Union accompanied by Stubblebine, Laibow and a young ufologist named Victoria Lacas (who later married Col. John Alexander). At the time, Stubblebine, Laibow and Jones had formed "a prodigious UFO/Psi network," partnering with Russian scientist Dr. Igor Smirnov. These activities, one might surmise, were fronts for a sophisticated intelligence operation using the cover of UFOs and the paranormal to penetrate the Iron Curtain.[58]

From 1985 to 1991, Jones served as a Special Assistant to the Senate Foreign Relations Committee chaired by Senator Claiborne Pell, one of the senior-most politicians on Capitol Hill, and was reportedly on a first name basis with then Secretary of Defense, Dick Cheney. Along with reputed Aviary member Jack Vorona, Jones has been linked to classified electronic mind control research. To this end, Vorona purportedly headed up a project code-named Sleeping Beauty dealing with research into microwaves and how they affect the human mind.

Jones was also linked to Dr. Michael Persinger, a clinical neurophysicist and professor of neuroscience, whose research focused on the effects of electromagnetic fields on biological organisms and human behavior. In collaboration with Stanley Koren, Persinger invented the so-called "God Helmet," which was literally what it sounded like: a contraption you could place on your head that would induce an ecstatic God state experience through a process of stimulating the test subject's temporal lobe with a low-level magnetic field. According to researcher Walter Bowart:

> In the Summer of 1989, Dr. Michael Persinger of Lautentian University of Ontario, Canada announced he'd invented a helmet that could induce UFO abduction experiences. The helmet is reported to be able to send specific frequencies into the hippocampus area of the back brain. During such stimulace, volunteers report UFO abduction experiences, out of body experiences, and a wide range of altered states of consciousness."[59]

Under the umbrella of New Age "science", Jones was involved in ESP research with John Alexander, which included an attempt to establish telepathic communications with dolphins to see if they could locate the remains of flying saucers that had crashed in the ocean. Who knows if that ever happened, but whatever Jones and Alexander were actually up to, one can only imagine the military and espionage uses of trained dolphin spies swimming international waters on suicide missions for Uncle Sam.

Chapter 20

The G-men give Lee Graham a pep talk

In 1979, Dr. Kit Green—who ran the CIA's so-called "weird desk"—extended an invitation to Bruce Maccabee to meet for periodic UFO briefings at spook central in Langley. In 1984, Green retired from the CIA and passed on his "weird desk" duties to Dr. Ron Pandolfi, who continued conducting periodic UFO briefing sessions with Maccabee. During one such briefing, Pandolfi informed him that the CIA had "firm evidence" that the KGB had devised plans during the '70s to establish contacts with American ufologists as a ploy to penetrate US defense systems and gather intelligence.[60] In this regard, a number of prominent UFO researchers have been employed as civilian defense contractors, many of whom maintained security clearances. For example, one of the founding members of MUFON was John Schuessler, a senior executive with McDonnell Douglas who had been involved in the NASA space shuttle program. Other civilian contractors active in UFO research included such high profile players as MJ-12 researcher, Robert Wood, who also worked for McDonnell Douglas; Robert Bigelow of Bigelow Aerospace; Jim McCampbell, who worked in scientific development for Bechtel Corporation; and John Andrews, a Lockheed engineer who worked on Skunk Works projects, including the stealth fighter program.

Not only did Maccabee interface with stateside spooks on the subject of UFOs—he was also approached about the topic by Russian nationals:

> After I spoke at a UFO conference near Washington, D.C. in February 1993, I was contacted by an assistant military attaché who was stationed at the Russian Embassy. He wanted to know

how to obtain U.S. government files on UFOs. You can imagine my surprise and amusement when, about six months later, while I was at work I got a call from the 'dreaded' FBI. It became obvious to me that the agent didn't know much about the UFO phenomenon and was amused to learn about the FBI files on the subject. But he was especially interested in my interactions with the military attaché.[61]

Many researchers first became aware of something called MJ-12 in late 1985 courtesy of an article by Barry Greenwood referencing UFO researcher Lee Graham, an employee at Aerojet Electrosystems in Azuza, California. One of the things that initially sparked Graham's interest in the subject came from reading Moore and Berlitz's *Incident at Roswell*, and a specific passage alleging that Sen. Barry Goldwater had been denied access to a facility at Wright-Patterson called the "Blue Room." It was in the Blue Room, it has been claimed, that the Air Force stored dead alien bodies. Graham sent a letter to Goldwater in an attempt to confirm this Blue Room anecdote, and Goldwater responded to Graham confirming that this "Blue Room" incident had indeed occurred.

Graham and a fellow Aerojet co-worker, Ron Regehr—who shared an interest in UFOs—built parts for the secret stealth fighter, although neither knew exactly what the aircraft looked like. On their days off, Graham and Regehr would go out "Stealth hunting" at Tonopah and other remote California airfields, hoping to catch a glimpse of these elusive craft.[62] It was during this period that Graham filed a series of FOIA requests related to the stealth fighter program in an attempt to uncover what these craft actually looked like, and as a means to differentiate them from UFO observations.

In April 1987, Graham "was the first person to have been provided with copies [of the MJ-12 documents] without restriction as to how they could be used." Moore later stated—in the September 30,

1989 issue of *Focus*—that he had approached Graham at the direction of the AFOSI:

> After considering several likely 'candidates' and discussing them with Rick [Doty] and others (including 'Falcon' himself), we settled upon Lee Graham. Our reasoning was that Lee could be depended upon to carry the banner on this thing without making a cloak and dagger affair out of it. Lee, for his part and without really being told what was expected of him, grasped the nature of his role almost at once and seemed to feel very content with it. All he needed to do was to write letters and ask questions—all I needed to do was keep in contact with him and monitor the feedback...

At one of their meetings, Graham asked Moore how he'd acquired the MJ-12 papers, and Moore reportedly flashed a badge identifying himself as a government agent. (Moore later claimed that Graham misidentified the badge as a government ID, and that he had actually flashed his MUFON membership card.) Due to this badge flashing boondoggle, and the possibility he may have received classified information, Graham forwarded copies of the documents to Aerojet's chief of security, who, in turn, contacted the Defense Investigative Service (DIS), a government agency responsible for handling security matters related to the aviation industry. Eventually, the MJ-12 papers and other documents Graham provided to DIS were returned to him marked "unclassified." This material also included the Aquarius documents, which listed within them a number of supposedly classified projects, one of which was Snowbird, a secret operation to fly recovered alien craft.

Not long after, Graham was paid a visit by FBI Special Agent William Hurley, accompanied by another fellow in civilian clothes who refused to identify himself, but appeared to be some sort of high-ranking government mucky-muck. The main theme of their one-hour interview concerned the MJ-12 and Aquarius documents.

After discussing the matter at some length, the two G-Men delivered something akin to a "pep talk" praising Graham for his work in bringing the materials to light

After they were done discussing MJ-12 related matters, the amiable government agents decided for some reason to confirm that the code name for the F-117 Stealth fighter program was Senior Trend, which was information Graham had been pursuing through a series of FOIA requests. Graham was given a form to sign certifying that this information was on a "need to know" basis.

Afterwards, Graham used his contacts in ufology to try to ascertain the identity of the mysterious government man in civilian clothes with whom he had met. The answer was shortly after disclosed to him by the Aviary's own C.B. Scott Jones, who informed Graham that the mystery man in "civvies" was Major General Michael Kerby who, at the time, was in charge of the Air Force's stealth fighter program.

Chapter 21

The Crestone Manifesto

Although Paul Bennewitz lit the initial Dulce Base fuse, it took the better part of a decade for the story to go viral when John Lear burst on to the scene with his hair on fire. Lear—who seemingly added some measure of credibility as a Dulce Base promoter—was an airline captain and former CIA contract pilot, as well as the son of William Lear, inventor of not only the Learjet, but also the eight-track tape player.

On the June 11, 1994 edition of Don Ecker's *UFOs Tonight* radio program, Bill Moore stated that the bulk of John Lear's Dulce Base information came courtesy of Paul Bennewitz, including the term "Greys" that first appeared in Bennewitz's "Project Beta" report, describing the aliens who had entered into a secret treaty with the U.S. government. According to Moore:

> Many people out there have heard these little aliens referred to as 'Greys'—that term was invented in the Bennewitz counterintelligence affair. They made it up. They dumped that in Bennewitz's lap and he proceeded to repeat it to all kinds of people in the UFO community and today it's standard word of mouth. And it's crap!

In early November 1987, a mini-conference, comprised entirely of UFO researchers, was organized by Tom Adams and held in Crestone, Colorado. Among those attending were John Lear, Linda Howe, Christian Lambright, David Perkins, Gary Massey, Lockheed engineer John Andrews, and Jim Speiser, founder of the ParaNet Bulletin Board System (BBS).

It was at this Crestone "meeting of the minds" —according to Bill Moore—that the Dulce Base story was fleshed-out using Paul Bennewitz as the primary source of information, or at least that was the scenario that Moore laid out in his interview with Don Ecker.[63] What Moore was most likely referring to as the "Dulce Base story" later evolved into "The UFO Cover-Up", a controversial seven-page document that Lear posted to ParaNet in December 1987.

During the Crestone conference, Lear suggested that the group put their heads together and come up with a joint statement addressing the current state of ufology. Initially everyone was receptive to this idea, and on the second day they gathered in a meeting room to come to a consensus as to what this group statement would say. As the discussion progressed, everyone seemed in agreement that some form of unidentified aerial phenomenon was involved with the cattle mutilations, but John Lear wanted to take it several steps further and definitively declare that Earth was under attack from an alien race. As David Perkins recalled:

I was horrified about where Lear wanted to take our statement, but I was trying to be polite, and I said, 'I can't quite get behind that one, John. I'm not signing my name to that.' And from there this whole idea of putting out a statement quickly fell apart. Lear got miffed; he thought he could come away from our conference with this Crestone Manifesto, and it didn't happen—so he was kind of pouty the rest of the day, as I recall—and then later that evening he and Linda Howe suddenly decided to take off and go on a road trip together, leaving the conference early. And I said to her: 'What? You can't leave now, we still have another day.' And she said, 'Well, we have to go right away to Roswell to see Clifford Stone. It's very important. He has some information for us.' And that really seemed out of character for Linda, and raised a few eyebrows, because she never left anything early. She'd stay to the bitter end if there was some sort of gathering happening. And we thought it must be really damned important whatever Clifford Stone had to tell her.[64]

On their way to Roswell, Lear and Howe had a stop-over in Albuquerque where they "had dinner with Col. (Ernie) Edwards who kept track of Dr. Paul Bennewitz for the Air Force and met with Condor (Robert Collins)...who showed us some transcripts regarding EBE3, one of the living aliens sequestered from the Roswell crash. One of the messages said, 'EBE3 wants to see the ocean. We had better comply or he'll disappear again.'"[65]

Howe and Lear's next stop was Roswell where they met up with another spooky ex-military type, the aforementioned Sgt. Clifford Stone, who claimed that as a child growing up in Southern Ohio he had encountered extraterrestrials, and that these encounters had come to the attention of the U.S. government, who monitored Stone throughout his youth and into adulthood.

During the Vietnam era, Stone enlisted in the Army and in short order (or so Stone claimed) he was whisked away to a top secret movie-screening room at Fort Belvoir and shown a film of a UFO retrieval, then afterwards placed on a special military team assigned to crash-retrievals, during the course of which Stone identified no less than fifty-seven different alien races.

In the summer of 1986, Stone had been in correspondence with Paul Bennewitz, receiving what could best be described as two rather lengthy and rambling letters in which Bennewitz went into exhaustive detail about the different alien races at Dulce, perhaps comparing notes about the different aliens that Stone himself had allegedly encountered during his crash-retrieval assignments. It was Stone's involvement with Bennewitz that appears to have been at least one of the factors that motivated Howe and Lear to skip out early from Crestone to rendezvous in Roswell with Stone. All of these peculiar peregrinations seemed have the singular focus in mind of finding out more of what Bennewitz knew about the ETs and the alleged Dulce underground base.

Not long after his road trip with Howe, Lear returned to Albuquerque to meet with Bennewitz. According to Christian Lambright:

> Sometime in 1987, or possibly 1988, John Lear went to meet Paul [Bennewitz] at Paul's home. I found out later that John spent several days there, though to the best of my knowledge it was the first time they had met in person. A few days after John's departure, I got a call from Paul. He was extremely angry about something involving John and, from the strong words he used, it was very clear that he did not care to see John again.

Following his interactions with Lear, Bennewitz changed his phone number and withdrew from the front lines of ufology. Lambright suspects that the cause behind Bennewitz's self-imposed ufological exile had something to do with his meeting with Lear, not to mention that by this time Bennewitz was teetering on the edge of a psychological meltdown.[66]

Chapter 22

Welcome to the Universe

In Paul Bennewitz's first letter to Clifford Stone, dated March 15, 1986, he categorized the different alien races at the Dulce underground base as the Low, the High and the Very High. Bennewitz refers to the Low, or the "aliens in the North," as a bunch of ill-tempered, limping little bastards ruled by fear, who are:

> ...extremely jealous [in] nature...[and] resent the human totally. Their anger is fantastic, extending to outright out of control rage. So there are, despite being totally Pragmatic—some emotions. Unfortunately the wrong kind.
>
> There is a Council in the North called The Nine—all of these seem to be cut from the same pattern. All appear to be highly vindictive and ego-oriented.
>
> It is quite strange—they feel that they are in a position to judge each—there is no jury. And in particular they appear so ego oriented that they try to impress themselves upon one who wants nothing to do with them. If they are ignored then they resort to threats—to tell the truth I have never seen such total social ignorance. They for some reason exhibit a 'hate' syndrome that just won't quit...So you can rate The North and their so-called God 'TA' as Low."

The next set of aliens Bennewitz describes, the High, are from:

> ...the culture of IO or JO. They don't limp for one thing. They do exhibit kindness, empathy, and extreme intelligence in transmissions through my computer...they—as I told you in

our telecon today (3/18/86)—have the EOKU and the Gray with them...

Bennewitz's reference to "the Gray" appears to be the "grey alien" that has since became ingrained in UFO lore and the model for the iconic alien face that appeared on the cover of Whitley Strieber's *Communion* (1987). The "Gray—according to Bennewitz—was basically a group of lower-caste worker drones within the ET societal hierarchy. The EOKU, it appears, were those who piloted the spaceships of the High, although in other parts of the letter Bennewitz says that the Gray also piloted the spaceships. Bennewitz writes that the High:

> ...gave indication that bodies of their group are here in Albuquerque in Cryogenic Containers. Location tentatively is the FAA Complex north of Albuquerque. It is a fenced and highly secured area—periodically what appears to be O2 (liquid) vapor exhausts there. They indicated by the computer that 8 of the EOKU were shot—and 11 crashed. There are more in storage than that so I don't know who the rest are... I know the bodies had been moved from Md. [Maryland] and are presently under Navy jurisdiction. Yesterday the computer indicated a total of 40.
>
> I was shown a color photograph by Rick Doty two years or more ago of a purported alien life-form being held prisoner. Supposedly it was taken to Los Alamos. He was alive—a light green color—big eyes standing directly in front of the camera. He may have been from IO's group.
>
> So far I know very little about "The High" except for what I have experienced. They are Homo-Sapien and I would guess are some of the same type who zapped Travis Walton. If the numbers are correct from my computer, they number over five thousand. Indications also that they are operating from a Star Ship in a far orbit...

Next on Bennewitz's ET hit parade was the Very High, who he said:

> ... are just that. Very High. Apparently few in number, their entire structure of knowledge, social-interaction credo and way of life is so far advanced that it is nearly impossible for us to relate. They are God-like and near 'GODS' as aligned with knowledge and power, yet they apparently lord it over no one.
>
> They are at such an advanced state that if you confronted one with a weapon—and though he might be totally able of taking YOU out—he would stand and allow you to shoot him. Again, please know that much of this information is based upon personal input of which I have never spoken to anyone about and in fact—you are the first.
>
> The Very High obviously are the ultimate. I would guess that these Very High aliens are quite old, one thousand years is not unrealistic...
>
> Now let's expand further—eons ago in the universe 16 billion years old by our estimate, probably billions beyond that, the Very High reached status. That status being so far advanced that they understood all. To the extent of understanding how to create life and human or near human form....
>
> One approach would be to say that in their travels in Star Ships they did seek out 'New Worlds.' 'Incubators' created by the Great Creator—the law of the Universe. They created those in the North to be pragmatic deliberately. Pragmatic, but perhaps quite physically perfect. And due to their incubator environment they were made vegetarian and because of a less temperate climate they were given high metabolisms. Then they took the next step and created Humans. The Humans were given emotions and were given full span control and because of the atmosphere and a very ideal climate, Earthwide, gave us lungs and by our standards, climate temperatures and a different method of elimination.

The North, because they were the first, were at some point in time given the 'enlightenment' to create Ships of Light and so they advanced further than we and more rapidly. Then the North, now stating via the computer, they control the cosmos and because of their pragmatic nature became aggressive and war-like.

The High and Very High thus seeing this did declare war, following them throughout the Universe. This war as indicated by the High has been ongoing for three hundred years....

What Bennewitz was referring to, in the above passage, was an ongoing war between these different alien factions, and that the Low were the bad guys in the battle, the very same alien scum Bennewitz had been tangling with since 1979. In a follow-up letter dated March 19, 1986, Bennewitz alerted Stone to some troubling developments:

To show you the ill logic used by those weak ones with their false God 'TA' in the North, they again showed their ignorance during the night. It would appear they are near frantic to stop me from talking to IO; 'JO' via the computer.

This morning I have a dark red streak down the left side of my face about two and three-fourths long and a quarter inch wide. Based upon past experience, I would guess it was done by a spherical in the bedroom during the night. This is typical of their totally distorted logic. They think they can operate upon the basis of fear—though with me—they have a problem—I do not experience fear—never have. All they achieve is that I totally ignore them and continue until I find a way to meet this IO. So for all the trouble they showed me, by their actions, only one thing—and that is their fear. It would appear that they are deathly afraid of IO and the other—fearful that I will achieve direct contact, which, in time, I will.

You will find, if you have not already, that constant inter-action will result in learning how to be aware of, and in turn use, Alien logic. Our own superior logic along with this other logic, though distorted, allows you to read the real intent behind anything they try to do. In that, there is advantage.

IO or JO whichever, she uses both, has indicated a number of times she is 'by me', indicating a protective attitude (on the computer).

So one could say—reading the Alien in the North—with the obvious streak on my face, that they are saying—See? She can't protect you—

To me that is quite childish and in fact all of their logic tends to be childish and weak. In point of fact, though so very obvious, from the very onset seven years ago, they have never recognized one fact...

Elsewhere in the letters, Bennewitz reminds Stone that Jesus was not a Jew and that we are all "Star Progeny" created under "The Law of the Universe" giving us "The Force". Bennewitz mentions the "four of us who came together...A Morman, a Lutheran, a Catholic and an atheist," although he does not identify by name these other three individuals who were "contacted at a very early age." In essence, Bennewitz seemed to be suggesting that he was chosen at a young age by the Very High to be one of their Earthly emissaries, which sounds similar to Clifford Stone's claims that he had likewise been chosen early on in life to carry out a mission of advancing the ETs' agenda.

Bennewitz's final words of wisdom to Stone: "The soul may be the final key—Welcome to the Universe."

Chapter 23

Subterranean alien base blues

During the Crestone conference, Tom Adams approached John Lear with a letter he'd received from a lady in Las Vegas going by the name of "Ann West" who claimed to have in her possession explosive information concerning the Dulce underground base. As Lear recalled, "Tom told me he didn't have time to respond to this letter and since I lived in Las Vegas would I check it out. I agreed and he gave me the letter."[67] In the letter, Ann West claimed that she knew two men who were "extremely private" and "asked that their names not be given. One man is an ex-CIA type person," who informed her that he had:

> …been inside the facility in Dulce. He managed to get a 'job' in the underground plant. I have seen his pictures that he took there. He is currently in hideing [sic], and in fear for his life. He has made copies of those pictures. He has told me that four other people know the locations of those pictures and documents… The pictures show large tanks or vats that hold liquid. In that liquid is something that looks like deformed bodies. Other shots show tiled walls that go on forever, there is a lot of guages [sic] or meters and screens. Needless to say those pictures were fascinating to me, and I would prefer to tell the 'world' about them, but…the man's life depends on the five people who have the copies…[68]

In recent years, "Ann West" has been revealed to be Cherry Hinkle, a Henderson, Nevada housewife with her own odd history of purported ET encounters. According to Tal Levesque, he lived a couple of blocks from Tom Castello in Santa Fe, New Mexico, when their mutual friend Cherry visited them both there (separately) in April of 1979. Tal claimed that, at one time or another, he and Castello were employed by the same security firm in Santa Fe.

During Hinkle's '79 visit, she recalled that Castello seemed on edge, and had some sort of earth-shattering story he wanted to share with her, but due to his security clearance couldn't talk about whatever was eating at him. The day she departed, Castello pressed a piece of paper into Hinkle's hand and cryptically said, "don't let anyone see this."

[Hinkle] slipped it into her pocket. That night, alone at a motel in Durango, she opened the paper. There were three things on its yellow page: a sketch of an alien; an inverted triangle; and the name Dulce. She stared at the mysterious drawing and tried to figure out what it all meant. The alien in the drawing had a large head, big black eyes, no nose and no hair. The triangle was shaded black. After looking at it, she flushed the paper down the toilet. That night she had nightmares about aliens.

The next morning, over coffee, she was looking at a map for a route back to Las Vegas when she noticed the name of a small town near the New Mexico state line called 'Dulce.' Were there aliens in Dulce? What was Tom trying to tell her?

Early in December of that year, Tom paid Ann a surprise visit. He told her that he had walked out on his job some months ago after a major dispute broke out between security workers and a military group. Tom said that the security force used 'flash guns,' but the military group was armed with machine guns. He said it was like a war with screaming and panic in all the tunnels. A lot of people died in the conflict. He wondered what story the government would use to coverup the deaths. In February, 1980, the media reported a prison riot near Los Alamos and that many prisoners died. Was this the coverup?

Thomas was ready to go into hiding. But, when he went to pick up his wife and young son, he found a van and government agents waiting. He had been betrayed by K. LOMAS [a fellow worker] who was instrumental in the kidnapping of his wife and child. The agents wanted what Thomas had taken from the facility for which he would get his wife and son back. It became apparent to him that his wife and son would be used in biological experiments and were not going to be returned unharmed. That was a little over ten years ago [1979].[69]

After the Crestone conference, John Lear made contact with Hinkle, who...

...spent a couple of days telling me all about Costello [sic], how he had escaped, how he had given her one of the 5 boxes [of Dulce Base materials], how he had shown her the photos and how she made pencil drawings of them and where she hid her box...

At one of our meetings she said that she had been contacted by a strange man dressed all in black, with a strange briefcase and had wires coming out of his sleeve. He told her that she should caution me that I was risking federal charges of 'sedition' if I continued my UFO research.

At another meeting she brought 4 pencils drawings, 2 diagrams and 1 page of technical information. Since the pencil drawings were so faint she asked me if I would copy them with a black felt tip pen. She also asked me to type up the technical information which was hand written. I spent a couple of days carefully making the drawings, typed up the information and then she asked me to send copies of everything to my friends. These became the infamous 'Dulce Papers.' Since my name was nowhere on the drawings or information I was never able to prove that I was the one who made the drawings. The only thing that could identify me was the fact that in 1965 when IBM came out with their proportional spacing 'Executive' typewriter, I bought one of the first ones and kept it in good shape. That proportional spacing would prove that I had typed the information because it was very unlikely that anybody else had that particular type of IBM 'Executive' electric typewriter 23 years after its introduction. I still have it...[70]

The Dulce Papers describe:

...what the aliens are after and how the blood (taken from cows) is used. Aliens seem to absorb atoms to 'eat'. Aliens put hands in blood, sort of like a sponge, for nourishment. It's not just food they want, the DNA in cattles and humans is being altered. The 'Type One' creature is a lab animal. 'They' know to change the atoms to create a temporary 'almost human being'. It is made with animal tissue and depends on a computer to simulate memory, a memory the computer has withdrawn from another human being. The 'almost human being' is slightly slow and clumsy. Real humans are used for training, to experiment and to breed with these 'almost humans'. Some humans are kidnapped and used completely (even atoms). Some humans are brainwashed and used to distort the truth. Certain male humans have a high sperm count and are kept alive. Their sperm is used to alter the DNA and create a non-gender being called 'Type Two'. The sperm is grown some way and altered again, put in large wombs, many destroyed – certain are altered again and put in separate wombs. They resemble 'ugly humans' when growing but look normal when fully grown which takes only a few months from fetus size. They have a short life span, less than a year. Some female humans are used for breeding. Countless women have had a sudden miscarriage after about 3 months pregnancy. Some never knew they were pregnant. Others remember contact some way. The fetus is used to mix the DNA in types one and two. The atomic makeup in that fetus is half human, half 'almost human' and would not survive in the mother's womb. It is taken at 3 months and grown elsewhere.

One of the more curious examples of Dulce Base "evidence" was a photo purportedly taken by Tom Castello of the genetic experiment vats on Level 6, a copy of which Tal Levesque disseminated during the early 1990s. If you do a web search for "Dulce Base labs" you will find a somewhat blurry black and white photo with the name "TAL" in a retro-futuristic looking science fiction font in the lower right-hand corner. The image itself resembles an upscale meth lab. According to Bill Hamilton in *Cosmic Top Secret*:

Level 6 [of Dulce Base] is privately called 'Nightmare Hall.' It holds the genetic labs, where experiments are done on fish, seals, birds, and mice that are vastly altered from their original form. There are multi-armed and multi-legged humans and several cages (and vats) of humanoid bat-like creatures as tall as 7-feet...

It was when [Castello] encountered humans in cages on Level 7 of the Dulce facility that things finally reached a climax for him. Row after row of thousands of humans, human-mixture remains, and embryos of humanoids were kept in cold storage. He says, 'I frequently encountered humans in cages, usually dazed or drugged but sometimes they cried or begged for help. We were told they were hopelessly insane, and involved in high-risk drug tests to cure insanity. We were told to never speak to them at all. At the beginning we believed that story. Finally in 1978 a small group of workers discovered the truth. That began the Dulce wars.'[71]

Among the half dozen researchers that purportedly received these Dulce Base materials, Cherry Hinkle was unique in the respect that Castello passed on to her (supposedly) the original documents. This Holy Grail of Dulce, according to Hinkle, is now hidden in a sealed oxygen-free box buried on a remote Arizona mountaintop—known as "Death Trap Mountain"—the contents of which include twenty-seven 8x10 photos and videotape footage of alien greys, computer banks, cages, burbling vats and various shots of the notorious Nightmare Hall. Not to mention Tom Castello's actual flash gun—which can levitate, vaporize and cause a temporary state of death!

According to Hinkle, there's a good reason why the location was dubbed Death Trap Mountain, as it takes an all-day hike, over rough terrain inaccessible to vehicles, to reach the summit where the box is buried. Hinkle claims that she hiked in with Castello and helped him bury the box there. In recent Facebook posts, Hinkle revealed that several attempts have been made over the years to retrieve this box, but that she and her cohorts either began their trek too late in the day to make it to the spot during daylight hours, or that the location where the box is supposedly buried now looks different. John Lear recalled:

> One of the boxes was hidden in the mountains near Dolan Springs, which is southeast of here on your way to Kingman... And I think 1993 or '94 was when Castello missed his connections. In other words, he missed the contact at the first 4 months and the second at 8 months. So it was decided to go and get the box...I didn't go myself, but I believe Bill Hamilton did. I think he was one of them. And I think Tal [Levesque] was another one, but I'm not sure, I don't remember. It's been, you know, almost twenty years ago. But I do remember that it was a serious effort, that they made at least six expeditions in to find this box and it was never found...[72]

Chapter 24

Bill Moore's MUFON meltdown

The 1989 MUFON Symposium, held on July 1st at the Aladdin Hotel in Las Vegas, became ground zero for a battle then brewing on the frontlines of ufology. At the time, John Lear had taken over the reins as State Section Director for Nevada MUFON, and part of his duties included organizing this event.

That year's symposium was titled "The UFO Cover Up: A Government Conspiracy," the very same name of a controversial paper Lear had posted to ParaNet in December 1987. Also known as the "Lear Statement," this seven-page tract laid out in brain-gobbling detail the entire saga of how the MJ-12 group had made a diabolical deal with malevolent ETs to bring humankind to its knees. According to Lear:

> The 'deal' was that in exchange for 'technology' that they would provide to us if we agreed to 'ignore' the abductions that were going on and suppress information on the cattle mutilations... The various parts of the body are taken to various underground laboratories, one of which is known to be near the small New Mexico town of Dulce...Witnesses have reported huge vats filled with an amber liquid with parts of human bodies being stirred inside...

Walt Andrus, National Director of MUFON, had lined up a number of 'mainstream' UFO researchers to speak at the '89 symposium, many of whom, ironically enough, had become ensnared in the Bennewitz affair, and who were central (either wittingly or unwittingly) in promoting the MJ-12 and Dulce Base stories. These speakers included Stan Friedman with an "Update on Majestic-12"; Linda Howe with "An Alien Harvest" about the creation of human-alien hybrids; Timothy Good presenting MJ-12 material from his book *Above Top Secret*; and last, but not least, Bill Moore, who was given the prime-time slot on Saturday night.

Just prior to the event, when Lear caught wind of the scheduled speakers, he proposed a list of additional presenters—some of the more, shall we say 'extreme', views then emerging in the field—views that mirrored, in many ways, the sort of mania Lear himself was promoting about underground bases and dastardly deals with ETs. These speakers included himself, Bill English and Bill Cooper.

Initially, Andrus vetoed Lear's list of speakers, whom he considered "unscientific." In response, Lear threw a hissy fit: "I blew up. Andrus was taking my own conference away from me. I told him if he wasn't going to let us talk, I'd hire another hall down the Strip. The people would follow us there and our speakers would outdraw his. He must have known I was right because we wound up speaking at the Aladdin after all."[73]

There was much anticipation, and an equal measure of uneasiness, about what Bill Moore might reveal during his MUFON presentation. In the run-up to the event, rumors ran wild that he had turned coat and was now a well-paid government agent spreading UFO disinfo, allegations fueled by an article by Robert Hastings published in the June 1989 *MUFON UFO Journal*.

Moore arrived in Las Vegas shrouded in a cloak of mystery, checking into a different hotel than where the event was being staged, so no one knew his actual whereabouts. To add to the mystery, Moore refused to submit his paper for publication in the symposium proceedings, so whatever he was planning to say was likewise shrouded in mystery. To address all the rumors swirling around him, Moore delivered a historic and equally incendiary speech called "The Status of the UFO Situation in 1989" that in short order set ufology on fire. Moore began his presentation with these immortal words:

Ladies and gentlemen, friends and adversaries, associates and colleagues—in short, fellow ufologists: I had really wanted to come here tonight and 'kick ass', but fortunately for all of us, wiser heads have prevailed and we're going to keep this presentation as professional as possible...

Moore quickly laid to rest rumors that he'd fabricated the MJ-12 documents, or had profited from being a paid government agent, stressing that he was as poor as a "church house mouse." Moore openly admitted his role as an AFOSI informant, who at the government's behest had monitored ufology, reporting back to his handlers on the activities of UFO researchers and organizations. At first, this arrangement was simply an exchange of information, but over time, according to Moore, the spectre of disinformation reared its troublesome head:

When I first ran into the disinformation operation being run on Bennewitz, it seemed to me I was in a rather unique position. There I was with my foot in the door of a secret counterintelligence game that gave every appearance of being somehow directly connected to a high-level government UFO project. And, judging by the positions of the people I knew to be directly involved with it, definitely had something to do with national security! There was no way I was going to allow the opportunity to pass me by without learning at least something about what was going on. I would play the disinformation game, get my hands dirty just often enough to lead those directing the process into believing that I was doing exactly what they wanted me to do, and all the while continue to burrow my way into the matrix so as to learn as much as possible about who was directing it and why...

Moore went on to detail Bennewitz's mental deterioration:

I watched Paul become systematically more paranoid and more emotionally unstable as he tried to assimilate what was happening to him. He had guns and knives all over his house, had installed extra locks on his doors, and he worried that "they"— meaning the aliens—were coming through his walls at night and injecting him with hideous chemicals which would knock him out for long periods of time. He told me he had no idea what "they" were doing with him while he was knocked out. He began to suffer increasing bouts of insomnia. Others took over the day-to-day operation of his business as he went through this. One day I watched him eat not a bite of his lunch while he chain-smoked 28 cigarettes in 45 minutes. I knew at that time that he was not far from a nervous collapse. His health had deteriorated, he had lost considerable weight, his hands shook as if from palsy, and he looked terrible. I tried to counsel him to drop the entire UFO thing before his health was completely destroyed. He said he knew things were getting bad and he was trying to cope with it. Not long afterward I heard he had been hospitalized and was under psychiatric care.

I do know from first-hand experience that there was a tremendous amount of government disinformation involved, and that a large proportion of what we are hearing today about malevolent aliens, underground bases and secret treaties with the U.S. government has its roots firmly planted in the Bennewitz affair...

Moore next laid out how the Bennewitz affair was intimately connected to the Dulce base stories that John Lear was responsible for promoting, although he didn't name Lear directly:

Recently, one of the most prominent figures in the current disinformation wave which has been sweeping the UFO and New Age communities was quoted as having stated that he has found Paul

Bennewitz's information to be '100% true'. This person spent a couple days talking to Paul back in the summer of 1987, and has spent considerable time since spreading elaborate and increasingly sensationalistic stories based, he claims, on information gathered from a variety of unnamed sources. Strip away the fluff, and what you have left is essentially the Bennewitz story all over again...

The current crop of disinformation is really nothing new; it's just that a different crop of people are spreading it this time around. I expect that those responsible, not the rumor mongers themselves, but the ones that are feeding them, thought it would work just as well this time as it did last. The one thing I'm sure they didn't count on is that I would tell my story and thus blow their cover. And speaking of blowing covers...

At this point, hecklers in the audience interrupted: "What about the Constitution? What gives you the right to drive someone crazy?"[74]

After several stops and starts—as the heckling grew progressively unruly—Moore nonetheless soldiered on:

And speaking of blowing covers, I think it's high time I tell you what I know about another situation that has found its way into the current crop of UFO disinformation. I offer this not to embarrass the person involved, but rather to shed light on the incident...In early 1983, I became aware that Doty was involved with a team of several others...in playing an elaborate disinformation game against a prominent cattle mutilation researcher who, at the time, had close connections with a major television film company interested in doing a UFO documentary...

The prominent cattle mutilation researcher to whom Moore was referring was Linda Howe. He continued:

I was able to put enough pieces of it together to conclude that the government seemed hell bent on severing the ties between the researcher and the film company. My understanding was that because the researcher was known to have close ties to Bennewitz and exhibited a strong interest in his work, certain elements within the intelligence community were concerned that the story of his having intercepted low frequency electromagnetic emissions from the Kirtland-Sandia area would end up as part of the script of a feature film...

When the film maker appeared on the scene and it looked as if Paul's story might become part of the script, the counterintelligence people simply extended their disinformation activities accordingly. Part of this game involved a meeting between the cattle mutilation researcher in question, agent Richard Doty, and others at the AFOSI office at Kirtland AFB, wherein the researcher subsequently claimed to have been allowed to view certain purportedly sensitive documents about the government's real involvement in UFOs that included information about an alleged UFO crash/retrieval at Aztec...

I can also tell you that it was a very effective deception because the researcher involved continued to believe this information and actively continues to try to convince others of its truth even now—more than six years after the fact. Unfortunately, there was no UFO crash at Aztec. Nor was there much truth to any of the other material supplied to this particular researcher. The much-touted alien harvest was really a dismal crop failure...To the best of my knowledge it was all disinformation...I've held my silence on this for more than six years. Now you know the truth...

Disinformation is a strange and bizarre game. Those who play it are completely aware that an operation's success is dependent upon dropping information upon a target, or 'mark,' in such a way that the person will accept it as truth and will repeat, and even defend it to others as if it were true…Once this has been accomplished, the work of the counterintelligence specialist is complete. They can simply withdraw in the confidence that the dirty work of spreading their poisonous seeds will be done by others. Those of you who want proof of how well the process works need only look around you. Every time one of you repeats an unverified or unsubstantiated bit of information, without qualifying it as such, you are contributing to that process; and every time you do it, somebody in a need-to-know position sits back and has a horse laugh at your expense.

At this point, Moore launched into a question and answer session, but instead of actually fielding questions from the audience, he posed a series of questions to himself. This seemed like a deliberate slap in the face to many in attendance, who again began venting their spleens. In response, Moore stood sternly gazing out into the crowd, as the emcee, Hal Starr, took to the stage, attempting to restore order. "Frankly," said Starr, "I'm a little ashamed of some people in this audience, regardless of what you believe, or not. This is not a debate. It is a paper trying to be presented. Now, please show a little courtesy." As Greg Bishop remembered:

It was the best speech I had seen anywhere. Not just a UFO conference, but anywhere, for the audience reaction. The crowd erupted at several points….People got mad and ran out of there. Bill English said I'm going to get a fire hose and ran out…I remember Vickie Cooper [*UFO Magazine* editor] start-ed crying…a lot of the yelling was coming from the back where Lear, Bill Cooper and Bill English were standing…After Moore finished his speech, he ran out of the room![75]

Afterwards, Moore was branded a ufological leper and eventually eased his way out of the field. Say what you will, but had it not been for his controversial speech, we may have never learned the true dimensions of the Bennewitz affair, and how ufology had been compromised and co-opted.

Chapter 25

Bill English and the human mutilators from another planet

On the second day of the MUFON symposium, Bill English— the guy who had a notion to take a fire hose to Bill Moore and blast him off the stage—presented himself to the audience as a beleaguered patriot besieged by the forces of tyranny, driven underground for many years due to his dangerous ET knowledge. But now he was back and ready to kick ass!

English claimed he had been a member of a Special Forces unit in Vietnam dispatched to a B-52 crash in the jungles of Laos. Before the B-52 went down, it sent out a May Day alert that it was under attack by a "large light." When English's team arrived on scene they discovered the B-52 completely intact with no evidence that there'd been a crash. The B-52 crew, however, didn't fare as well; every single one of them was dead, victims of ghastly mutilations, although each was still in their seat and harness. Despite the condition of the bodies, little if any blood was discovered in the aircraft, as if they had been completely drained of blood, similar to many cattle mutilation cases. After photographing the scene and retrieving a list of items, English's team set off a series of charges that caused the bombs on board to explode, incinerating the bodies inside. Shaken by this incident, English was shipped back to the states and processed through a psychiatric institution, then afterwards reassigned to RAF Chicksands in Bedford, England, to serve as an intelligence analyst.

In July 1977, English found a sealed diplomatic pouch in his inbox containing a copy of a six-hundred-plus-page document called the "Grudge Project Bluebook Report #13" that included photographs of ETs, dead and alive, as well as classified information about their spacecraft and technologies. It took English four days to review the report and prepare an analysis, which he then deposited in his outbox and, in short order—as he told the rapt audience at the MUFON Symposium—his "life went to hell in a handcart." Just a few days after preparing his analysis, English's commanding officer informed him that his performance had been deemed "unsatisfactory" and he was terminated from service. English was then deported from England as an "undesirable alien" and separated from his wife and children, who were told that he had deserted them. Afterwards, English claimed that over a twelve-year period there were a total of fifteen attempts on his life, presumably by the Men-in-Black or some other clandestine bad actors who were trying to keep a lid on the startling truth about UFOs and ETs.

In May of 1982, one of the many supposed attempts on English's life apparently occurred—at least according to English—when he was contacted by his former Commanding Officer from RAF Chicksands, who apparently had also been relieved of duty not long after the Grudge Project Bluebook Report #13 fiasco. English's former C.O.—who he referred to as The Colonel—had retired to New Mexico and apparently acquired information regarding the site of a UFO crash. English and The Colonel, accompanied by a third unidentified individual, drove a four-wheel drive van to the suspected site in the New Mexico desert. After arriving, English "walked some distance from the van while examining the area and the other two men were near the van working with equipment. Suddenly, a noise and flash attracted [English's] attention, and he watched as a 'rocket' tore through the night sky, exploded on or near the van, apparently killing the other two..."[76]

The next stop on English's tragic course brought him to Tucson, Arizona, where he worked in the APRO offices of Jim and Coral Lorenzen. This is where he first met Bill Moore, who was then serving as an APRO field investigator. At the behest of the Lorenzens, English sent Moore a copy of the infamous Weitzel letter, which led to Moore's investigation of the case. English—as part of his APRO duties—was the first investigator to interview the Cash-Landrum witnesses, and a summary of his report on the incident appeared in *The World Weekly News*.[77]

Later on there were rumors that English had been "banished" from APRO after an "unsuccessful attempt to wrest control…from its long-time organizer/leaders…An incumbent official who survived the organizational coup attempt has characterized [English] as 'unstable' and that the Grudge Report story 'springs from an internal need for attention rather than from external fact.'"[78]

After delivering a spiel to the MUFON Symposium audience about how the UFO research community needed to stop fighting amongst itself and come together in unity, English then fired off a full-throated harangue of Bill Moore, who literally overnight had become ufology's favorite whipping boy. English claimed that he first met Moore in Tucson in 1979, at which time he related his Grudge-Blue Book story that he claimed Moore afterwards "later twisted around" and used to create his own material on Roswell, MJ-12 and Project Aquarius.

English authored a now-impossible-to-find-book called *The Grudge/Blue Book Incident*, and claimed that Moore had attempted to sabotage this work by going around telling everyone that English had written it under the influence of LSD. In his MUFON speech, English rambled on, visibly agitated:

Then Moore came out with that caca UFO show of his [*UFO Cover up Live!*] that was intended to do nothing more than discredit the science of ufology, and that's exactly what it did. It was poorly produced, poorly written, and made UFO investigators look like utter absolute idiots…to add insult to injury, Mr. Moore had his two buzzards [Falcon and Condor] pronounce the stuff he said I'd lied about for 13 years. Word for word they parroted everything I had told him in 1979! When after viewing this travesty, I got on the telephone…I tracked down Moore in Washington, D.C., and

I spoke with Mr. Shandera. I told Mr. Shandera that I wanted a piece of Mr. Moore's ass so bad I was ready to crawl through the phone and bite him on the ear. I told Mr. Shandera that show was bullshit! For a man that had said for 12 years that Bill English is a liar and a drug addict and a paranoid schizophrenic, and every kind of perverse son of a bitch you could imagine, produced a television show that parroted everything I had been saying for 12 years! My question now is, after producing that piece of shit, why would you stand in front of an audience of qualified intelligent people and tell them that it was a disinformation ploy? Another lie! Quite frankly, if Moore was not in this for the money, then what the hell was he in it for? He has not done any good for UFO investigations that I can determine. Except hurt it. I would like to take this opportunity right now to apologize to those of you who support Mr. Moore, but the facts are facts!

Chapter 26

A chain of apparently related documents

While Bill Moore had seemingly flown the ufological coop following his 1989 MUFON Symposium presentation, behind the scenes he and Jaime Shandera continued their research into the MJ-12 papers. In 1990, the duo released *The MJ-12 Documents: An Analytical Report*, which examined what they referred to as "a chain of apparently related documents and events dating at least as far back as late 1977."

Moore and Shandera determined that this chain of documents were part of an intelligence operation initiated in mid-1977 with the infamous Ellsworth document that was created in response to "several stories that appeared in the *National Enquirer* which led Air Force security people to believe that someone at Ellsworth was leaking small amounts of material to the tabloid about sensitive Air Force projects, none of which seems to have had anything to do with UFOs." In response to the leaks, AFOSI launched:

...a CIA-sponsored training program which had to do with the formulation and use of disinformation as a counter-intelligence tool. They would create a document as an example of how such things were done, and then send a copy of it to the *Enquirer* along with an anonymous cover letter indicating legitimacy. If, as suspected, sources at Ellsworth had indeed been in contact with the *Enquirer*, then it seemed reasonable to assume that those individuals would be among the first the *Enquirer* would try to make contact with in an effort to obtain more information about the 'ED' and its contents. All that was needed was to monitor the activities of the *Enquirer*'s people and of those individuals at Ellsworth suspected of being in contact with them. Those with whom the *Enquirer* made contact would immediately be questioned about the matter. And, since the target was, after all, the *National Enquirer*, what better topic around which to build a phony document than UFOs? It was the one topic the *Enquirer* could be counted upon to take an immediate interest in...

Such programs are often a double-edged sword in that while they offer training to a relatively large number of people, those sponsoring them often make a point of identifying specific individuals among those involved either directly or peripherally (i.e. as trainees, or perhaps organizers and assistants), who might prove useful in future situations. It seems to have been through such a process that Richard Doty's name came to the attention of a shadowy figure in Washington who would later find ways to make considerable use of him. That man was 'the Falcon'..."

Bob Pratt—while working the UFO beat at the *National Enquirer*—concluded that the Ellsworth document was a hoax, although at the time this finding wasn't shared with the larger world of ufology. The Ellsworth document was later dusted off and presented to Linda Howe when Doty did his number on her at Kirtland Air Force Base in April of 1983.

Shandera and Moore identified the Weitzel letter as the next link in this chain, and that it was used by AFOSI to recruit Moore into their counterintelligence operation. According to Moore's '89 MUFON speech:

The letter, which is loosely based upon an actual UFO case, was written anonymously to APRO in July, 1980 by Richard Doty and is directly related to the Bennewitz affair. Essentially it was 'bait'. AFOSI knew that Bennewitz had close ties with APRO at the time, and they were interested in recruiting someone within the APRO organization who would be in a position to provide them with feedback on Bennewitz's activities and communications. Since I was the APRO Board member in charge of Special Investigations in 1980, the Weitzel letter was passed to me for action shortly after it had been received. It was not long thereafter that I came to know Richard Doty and began providing him with information about the Bennewitz case.[79]

The next link in the disinformation daisy chain was the Aquarius Document (or "AD") that first surfaced in February 1981. According to Moore, in the June 30, 1989 issue of *Focus* magazine:

('AD') is an actually example of some of the disinformation produced in connection with the Bennewitz case. The document is a retyped version of a real AFOSI message with a few spurious additions. It was apparently created by AFOSI, or at least I always assumed it was, and it was handed to me in February 1981 with the intention that I would pass it to Bennewitz. My understanding, although I never knew for sure, was that Bennewitz was expected to wave it to the press and others as proof of what he was saying about an alien invasion, at which point the document would be denounced as a counterfeit and Bennewitz would be further discredited. Unfortunately (or perhaps fortunately, depending upon one's point of view) it didn't turn out that way.

The next piece of this odd puzzle, or link in the chain, was revealed in March 1983 when Bill Moore was sent on a cloak and dagger trip to New York City where he was met in a motel room by a courier bearing a mysterious manila envelope. The courier informed Moore that he had exactly nineteen minutes to view the documents. Moore asked if he could photograph the items and read the contents into his tape recorder. The courier replied, "Both are permitted. You have seventeen minutes remaining."

When Moore's seventeen minutes were up, the courier collected the documents, returned them to the manila envelope, and departed. These documents were thereafter identified as the "Carter Briefing Documents" and contained information about a number of secret government projects that included Project Aquarius, Project Pounce, Project Sigma, and Project Snowbird. The Project Aquarius identified in the documents referred to a different Project Aquarius than the Aquarius documents passed on to Bennewitz. The other projects related to research on green fireballs (Pounce), laser programs (Sigma), and the testing of stealth aircraft (Snowbird).

The next and final links in the chain was the mother lode of them all, the MJ-12 documents, to be followed shortly after by the Cutler-Twining Memo. After the release of *The MJ-12 Documents: An Analytical Report,* both Moore and Shandera receded ever deeper into the ufological shadows, creating a vacuum soon to be filled by a new wave of MJ-12 riders.

Chapter 27

Rogue Agent Doty?

In 1984—around the time the MJ-12 documents surfaced—Richard Doty was transferred to Lindsey Air Force Base in Wiesbaden, West Germany. In July 1986, he was reportedly stripped of his AFOSI agent status due to "unauthorized" activities. Doty later claimed his decertification was unrelated to the Bennewitz affair, although the timing seemed suspect. According to Phil Klass:

[Doty] began submitting reports claiming he was in contact with high-level Soviet KGB agents and East German KGB agents and wrote the kinds of stories that he had earlier written about UFOs. Except that he had a much less credulous boss in in West Germany. They began to suspect those were simply tall tales and investigated. He took a lie detector test, I'm told, which he flunked. Not that polygraph is always 100% accurate. And so he was then, the politest word is to say "eased out" of Air Force Office of Special Investigations and ended up his last two years in service running the mess hall out at Kirtland...I don't mean to put down the importance of feeding the troops, but if you've got a very, very high intelligence officer, if he is serving top intelligence people in the government, you don't let him spend the last two years running the mess hall. There are other people that can do that...

All you need to do is look at his record...that this is clearly a guy that moves in the very top intelligence circles. What do I mean. Well, he was a guard at the gate at such and such an Air Base and then he moved to another Air Base and he was a gate guard there. And you know guards at gates of military bases are really top intelligence people. Then he took a course, I think in police investigation and so on and became, in effect, a military policeman, investigating such things as minor theft and so on. If you were ever to look at his record he never moved in high circles...

In contrast, Greg Valdez suspected that the disciplinary action taken against Doty was due to the leaking of classified information to Bill Moore, Paul Bennewitz, Gabe Valdez and others in the UFO research community. It was during this period that bugging devices were discovered at the homes of both Gabe Valdez and rancher Manuel Gomez. Recently, I asked Greg Valdez how they'd determined their phones had been tapped.

GV: "Because we found the bugs! (Laughs) They were analog bugs...before they started using digital. My mom found it. It's a funny story. My dad came back from Manuel Gomez's house, the rancher who had been having all the cattle mutilations. We were at the dinner table, and my dad said, 'You know, Manuel found something weird by his phone.' And so my dad pulled it out, he had it in a little envelope, and my mom said, "I found one of those the other day, too! It was there by the dishwasher.' This was when Howard Burgess was alive, and so we took the things down to Burgess [who worked at Sandia labs], and he said, 'This is a listening device.' He activated them—he turned them on. I was a kid, and he said, 'Kid, go into the other room.' He put the bug in there, and they could hear it—they were recording everything we said!"

AG: "What do you think the intent was? Was it an attempt to intimidate or freak you guys out so you'd quit going out to Mount Archuleta?"

GV: "No, this surveillance had to do with Ernest Edwards and Richard Doty, who provided a lot of classified information to Paul Bennewitz.... They weren't interested in what my dad or

Manuel were up to. They were tracking what Doty was leaking out, and what Ernest Edwards was leaking out—which made its way to my dad and some of these other outside sources—about what was going on in Dulce. And that's why they ended up transferring both of them [Edwards and Doty] out of Kirtland, basically kicking them out of there."

AG: "So they [AFOSI] were spying on Doty, too?"

GV: "Well, they were covering their tracks. They were trying to access how much information had gotten out. Did my dad know about it? Did Manual Gomez know about it? They also tapped the tribal police. They found listening devices at the tribal police department."

AG: "So, obviously, it wasn't Doty behind the wiretaps?"

GV: "No, not in that instance. And that's where it gets confusing because you had a lot of agencies involved—it wasn't just the Air Force. You had the NSA, CIA—all these other three letter groups were involved. They were trying to track where their leak was coming from. They knew they had a leak, and who that leaker was, but they were trying to do damage control

Richard C. Doty
(Photo credit: Mirage Men/Perception Management Productions)

to see just exactly what had gotten out, and at the same time to monitor their progress with Bennewitz. Do they [the UFO research community] believe in this, or are they on to us? It was Spycraft 101."[80]

During the period that the Bennewitz affair was reaching critical mass, Doty and his superior officer—Col. Ernest Edwards—had come under increased scrutiny. This was due in part to Gabe Valdez pulling some political strings through his friendship with champion race car driver, Bobby Unser. According to Greg Valdez:

> Bobby Unser was a political contributor to Senator Pete Domenici—they were good friends. Domenici was very influential with the [Sandia] labs, so my dad had Bobby contact Domenici to put pressure on the Air Force to get to the bottom of what was going on with these secret test projects out in the Dulce area. For example, the Geiger counters we used at Mount Archuleta to test for radiation—the funding for those came from Pete Domenici's office...I didn't put it in my book, but this was fairly important, because this pressure coming from an outside political force—in this case, Senator Pete Domenici's office—is how things started unraveling for Doty. He had made such a mess of things that the Air Force could no longer cover it up—Doty was bringing too much heat down on Kirtland Base—so it was damage control when they shipped him to Germany."

As noted, Doty returned to Kirtland as a "food service specialist" until his discharge on November 1, 1988. Following his military retirement, Doty started a second career as a state trooper in Grants, New Mexico, the same job Gabe Valdez held in Dulce, which could lead to speculation that Doty used his law enforcement position as a cover for ongoing counterintelligence work.

Although it's commonly accepted that Doty played the role of Falcon in *UFO Cover Up Live!*, he has continued to deny that fact. In a letter to the June 1, 2001 edition of *Saucer Smear*, Doty wrote, "On October 14th, 1988, I was a cadet in the New Mexico State Police Academy, Santa Fe, N.M. Unless Scotty beamed me up from Santa Fe to Los Angeles, I did not appear on that show. Robert Collins appeared live on that show..."

Doty's denial of portraying Falcon is the usual game he plays wiggling around the margins of truth. Although *UFO Cover Up Live!* was broadcast on October 14, 1988—at the same time Doty was going through trooper cadet training—the actual video footage of Falcon in *UFO Cover Up Live!* had been shot years earlier as part of a documentary Moore and Shandera were working on that was never completed.

In September 1987—a year before *UFO Cover-up Live!* aired— *Saucer Smear* editor Jim Moseley got a sneak peek of some of this footage when he visited Moore and Shandera in Burbank. According to Moseley:

I arrived in California firmly committed not to be hypercritical, but I just couldn't help being highly unimpressed by all aspects of what I was shown. To begin with, there were the cheap theatrics of an alleged intelligence agent in shadow, with his back to the camera and his voice disguised electronically. If his disclosures were matters of vital importance to the government, it wouldn't have been hard to figure out who Falcon was, though as far as I can recall, he never has been publicly identified despite a lot of informed and semi-informed guessing behind the scenes.

The content of the videos was, if anything, worse. Falcon raved at length about Jesus Christ being a spaceman; Earth being under alien surveillance for twenty-five thousand years; a shipwrecked saucer pilot kept alive by the U.S. government in a secret location, where he enjoyed strawberry ice cream and

Tibetan music; and on and on and on. I remember going easy on Moore when I wrote this up in *Smear*, but Bill was sorely disappointed, as he'd hoped I would take a much more positive attitude toward what he had let me in on. He as much told me that he hoped I would help convince The Field about the validity of his tapes (an interesting insight into Moore's judgment). He also tried to pump up my enthusiasm by telling me that there were more tapes that were so secret he could not show it even to me, whom he trusted implicitly (see my above observation about his judgment).

One theory about Doty is that he was a "rogue agent" who of his own volition spearheaded the Bennewitz affair—or at least took the AFOSI's disinformation campaign way farther than his superiors ever intended. The "rogue agent" label itself may have been yet another layer of disinfo that the government used to distance itself from culpability.

Chapter 28

My breakfast with Tal

> "There are many reasons you would self-edit
> yourself if you discovered the Truth."
>
> - Tal Levesque, 6-24-2012

y initial contact with the mysterious Tal Levesque came courtesy of an unsolicited email I received in 2007 inquiring if I had knowledge of paranormal activity occurring in or near the mountain town of Mariposa, California, not far from where I live. The anonymous emailer went on to say: "Right now I'm working on a program about the Dulce, N.M. Underground Base, for the History Channel's *UFO Hunters*."

As there was no name assigned to this email (just the "questal" handle), I was a tad dubious as to the sender's claimed association with *UFO Hunters*, 'cause let's face it, I get all kinds of sketchy email from dubious sources alleging involvement in everything from multidimensional time-travel scenarios to mind-control victims seeking help to combat shape-shifting New World Order reptilians.

Afterwards, I contacted *UFO Magazine* editor Nancy Birnes (wife of head *UFO Hunter*, Bill Birnes) and asked if she knew the identity of the shadowy persona behind this anonymous email. Nancy, in turn, referred me to her hubby Bill, who confirmed that the unidentified email correspondent indeed "knew a lot of things" and had been used as a source for a *UFO Hunters* episode focusing on underground bases.

I was intrigued by the information provided by Bill and Nancy Birnes, which initiated a correspondence with the mysterious email sender, whom I soon discovered was the one and only Tal Levesque of Dulce base legend. And so it was that in early 2009 I was invited to break bread with Tal and his longtime colleague John Rhodes (aka The CryptoHunter), another avowed reptilian believer and frequent guest on such shows as *UFO Hunters, MonsterQuest* and *Coast to Coast AM*.

Our conclave commenced at a Mariposa greasy spoon, where after ordering from the breakfast menu—as a model choo-choo train chugged overhead along the wood paneled walls of the rustic dining room like a scene straight out of *Twin Peaks*—our conversation soon gravitated from mundane cordialities to a wide ranging discussion of all forms of high strangeness and, in particular, entrances to the inner Earth.

Before delving too deeply into those rascally reptilians and associated inner-Earth mysteries, let me provide a brief description of Tal, who—if encountered during a chance meeting on main street Mariposa—would leave the casual observer with the impression of an unassuming fellow in a long sleeve flannel shirt and jeans, eyes partially concealed behind tinted glasses, his head topped with an innocuous ball cap. It's the eyes, which I've never actually seen in full light— hiding behind those aforementioned spooky shades—that radiate with intensity and an equal measure of mystery.

In his early sixties at the time of our meeting—and graying with a thin wisp of moustache—Tal is a living library of arcane information, and if you're fortunate enough to land on his email list, you'll soon be inundated with a vast array of content dedicated to alternative health cures, Hollow Earth conspiracies and assorted New Age bric-a-brac.

Exchanging emails prior to our meeting, I asked Tal how I'd recognize him, and he joked that I should look for the "narc." And, indeed, there is a bit of that narc vibe to Tal, who worked many years as a security guard at government and private facilities across the southwest before settling, a few years back, in Mariposa.

Mariposa—for the unfamiliar—was the first stop on the old California gold rush trail where those grizzled prospectors back in the day dug deep into the earth, searching for treasure. Nowadays, it's among the most economically challenged counties in the Golden State, known as much for its rich history as for its growing population of meth labs and sketchy rural residents in need of immediate dental care. But like those gold prospectors of yore, Tal—as he explained—first ventured to Mariposa searching for another type of treasure, on a mission for none other than Dan Aykroyd. This Aykroyd-Levesque alliance stretched back to the mid-1990s when Tal worked as technical advisor for a Canadian television series that Aykroyd hosted called *Psi Factor: Chronicles of the Paranormal*. However, you wouldn't have seen Tal's name in the credits because he prefers to remain a "man behind the scenes." According to Tal, this arrangement had to do with a certain agreement:

> Myself and others have been taken to facilities and shown experiments being done to others and told *that* could happen to us. We were held until we agreed to certain directives and then released back to our normal lives. Some still try and push the boundaries of disseminating suppressed information, but not without *oversight*.

Like Tal, Aykroyd has apparently experienced similar "oversight." In *Dan Aykroyd Unplugged on UFOs*, a 2002 incident was recounted that occurred in New York City during the period Aykroyd was in pre-production for a new UFO-themed show called *Out There* for the Sci Fi Channel.

Aykroyd had just gotten off the phone with Britney Spears when he noticed a black limousine parked across the street carrying two Men-In-Black, one of whom stepped out and stared menacingly in his direction. When Aykroyd turned away—for what was just a matter of seconds—the MIBs and their mysterious black limo disappeared, and he later speculated that some sort of cloaking device had been employed to render the MIBs and their vehicle invisible. Two hours after this incident, Aykroyd was informed that *Out There* had been canceled without explanation!

Sometime in the early 2000s (as related between bites of eggs and slurps of coffee), Tal was recruited by Aykroyd for a reconnaissance mission to seek out a locale in Northern California where Team Aykroyd could set up a base of operations and venue for a future House of Blues franchise. Tal's ultimate mission was to locate a "safe haven" that would survive the coming Earth Changes predicted by psychics like Lori Toye, who in 1983 channeled a map of what the United States would look like after the prophesied deluge. As fate would have it, this map doesn't bode well for most of California, indicating that the only segment of the Golden State to remain unscathed will be portions of the Sierra Nevada range, soon to be a large island which incorporates Mariposa.

Not only would Mariposa provide a "safe haven" and future home to the House of Blues, but Team Aykroyd envisioned it becoming the Sedona of California; a future New Age mecca of the Golden (Island) State. According to Tal, another intriguing geographical feature of the area is an underground network of limestone caverns that stretch all the way from Mariposa to the San Francisco Bay Area. Theoretically, Team Aykroyd would fly into a small rural airport located near town and from there access this limestone tunnel network via a shuttle system that would then covertly transport Dan and his crew to a secret compound connected to their proposed House of Blues.

Ultimately, these grandiose plans never bore fruit, and before I got around to asking why this prospective gold hadn't panned out, Tal or Rhodes launched into some other mind-bending tangent, hurling information at rapid-fire speed that in retrospect I have no idea how much was fact, fiction, delusion or deliberate disinformation. This is often the case when engaged in conversation with Tal: it can be a dizzying experience that leaves the mind reeling and at the end of the day you're left with more questions than answers. In the aftermath of Tal's mission to Mariposa, he decided to plant roots there and was joined at some point by his long-time colleague Rhodes, these two rather normal-looking fellows blending in somewhat inconspicuously into the small mountain-town vibe.

According to Tal, underground bases like Dulce are part of a vast inner-Earth tunnel system that stretches across these United States, as documented in a map that Tal made back in 1979, which he brought to our meeting and unfurled on the table between our cups of coffee that we slid aside to make room for this weathered artifact. "I've discovered the locations of several more tunnels and underground bases since putting this map together, including evidence of an underground base here in Mariposa!" Tal punctuated his comment by banging his closed fist on the table, causing our plates and silverware to shake and rattle. "Oops, sorry about that," he added. "I get a bit carried away sometimes."

According to Tal, many of these secret facilities are overrun by creatures that—in many cases—have been misidentified as ETs. Tal insists that these underground dwellers are actually from *inner space*; beings that have been here on this planet for a very, very long time.

Tal and Rhodes spend much of their time these days riding around the Mariposa County countryside on quad-runners with side-arms at ready, exploring old mines and searching for inner-Earth entrances. Apparently, Mariposa is the perfect locale for just such adventures, hosting scores of abandoned old mines, from the rolling oak woodlands to the timber line.

Around the time of our breakfast meeting of the minds, Tal and Rhodes were trying to drum up interest for a reality show they were pitching called *Mysterious Mariposa*, which would include many of their inner-Earth investigations. When I asked Tal what evidence he had to support these claims of underground bases and reptilians, he suggested that if you take the time to learn who among the locals are working at these secret underground facilities, and who their family members are—and then reach out to these workers and their families and cultivate a relationship—they are more willing to reveal what's really going on down under the ground. As for Tal, he never indicated whether he was currently employed at this supposed underground facility in (or near?) Mariposa, but he did acknowledge that he was still involved with security work of some kind.

According to Tal, such secret underground facilities will be used at a time of societal collapse when that dreaded acronym COG (Continuity of Government) goes into effect, and right out of *Dr. Strangelove* our world leaders will take refuge underground with a large collection of nubile women who'll help provide "sexual fertility" to propagate the species.

COG is a government within the government—an occult, or hidden, governmental body—the shadow government that will assume command at some future date when all hell breaks loose from a natural disaster or some other cataclysmic event, like a limited nuclear exchange or, heaven forbid, a full-blown ET invasion. According to Tal, COG went into effect—at least for a limited duration—in the aftermath of the 9/11 Twin Towers-Pentagon attacks.

A matronly waitress removed our plates, then returned with a warmer for my fifth and final cup of coffee—which I probably needed like a hole in the head at this point as by now my brain was audibly buzzing due to the dizzying amount of information that Levesque and Rhodes continued unloading in rapid fire succession, which included Tal's October 1979 encounter with a utility belt-wearing reptilian from the inner-Earth.

Tal Levesque: "I woke up in the middle of the night and at the foot of my bed was this 7-foot-tall reptoid who was looking at these research maps I had on my wall."

Adam Gorightly: "What kind of maps?"

TL: "Maps I'd made that showed UFO activity in New Mexico and Colorado and were full of colored push-pins and markers to indicate these sites—not only locations of high UFO activity, but also animal mutilations, caverns, ancient ruins and suspected alien underground bases…Anyway, I saw this reptilian looking at these maps. It suddenly turned to look at me and I grabbed a heavy ashtray from the bed-stand and threw it at him. He kind of had a bioluminescent glow, but he was also translucent, and I could see the dresser on the other side of this reptilian—like I could see through him—and when I threw this ashtray, it went right through the reptilian and didn't faze him one bit! He appeared to have no ill intent for me, which was a good thing, because it probably wasn't the greatest idea to throw something at him, but I was startled and it was a natural reaction. Like here, take this you creature. Whatever the case, it quickly became clear he was curious about my research. Like he was on some sort of covert op to check my maps out.

"Then the reptilian formed a complex thought bubble within its mind and projected a visible glowing photon orb from its residual third eye bump on its forehead. The reptilian was standing about three feet from me. I saw the sphere growing and moving slowly towards my forehead. When it was about a foot away, it was about the size of a baseball and I could see within it a colorful geometric ever-changing kind of 3D holographic matrix that was transferred into my mind with the words: 'ALL IS LIGHT!'

"As it passed into my head, I went into a total sensory overload and temporarily lost my vision, but not consciousness. I was in a black void, yet the thought sphere was impressing data on my neural network. It was like a kind of time-released data dump. Later I had abilities—both spatial ones and knowledge—I could access at will. Having been within arm's length of this reptilian, I observed various details. He wore no clothes. But, he did have a utility belt with several unusual things on it."

AG: "You mean like a Batman-type utility belt?"

TL: "Well, in a sense. One device on what I'm calling this utility belt had a small orange light on it. When the reptoid touched it, it allowed him to simply disappear."

AG: "What exactly do these reptilians look like? I mean are they like those Sleestaks on *Land of the Lost*—you remember that show?—or maybe like that big lizard guy Captain Kirk traded fisticuffs with on *Star Trek?*"

TL: "Well, if we want to compare the reptilian I saw to a TV show, the head of the creature was similar to the reptoid-humanoids on *Babylon 5*. This guy had scales and the eyes were slit serpent-like and very strange—flame-like and flickery. He had three fingers and an opposing thumb, with claw-like talons on his fingers and feet, and a small tail flapping on his back. Flap, flap. His scales were large, like a breast plate on his chest. The scales were smaller where the body was flexible, like around his elbow. The scales were snake-like. I guess that is why some call them the Serpent Race. The scales were mostly green to very dark green— on each scale there was a variation of color. He glowed with an electrical blue-greenish color, like some kind of aura."

AG: "Did the reptilian speak to you in words? I mean, I know he levitated that 3D ball thing into your head, but did he speak actual vocalized words?"

TL: "No. He communicated telepathically and had very quick thoughts. Ideas driven by images and geometric impressions similar to a kaleidoscopic acid trip. It was not a linear form of communication like words. More of a symbol or image language. These reptilians react to your thoughts and can overwhelm a person with data. It can take you a long time to assimilate a reptilian transmission and integrate it. After a while I *saw* the language—these thought-form constructs the reptoid used to pass data. And man, these beings are straight out data freaks! Because of this encounter, I felt compelled to quit my security job in Santa Fe and move to Albuquerque to test at the Technical Vocational Institute as a Laser Electro-Optics Technician. My score was so high they took me immediately, instead of having to wait for years like the other applicants. I would NOT have been able to pass if the REPTOIDS hadn't put compressed data into my head!"

Our meeting of the minds came across at times like a massive data dump with a fair amount of pseudoscientific buzz words thrown in for dramatic flair, like when John Rhodes started going on about how certain humans (with highly developed chakras!) would come into alignment with the kundalini snake spirit on December 21, 2012, when the Mayan Calendar went kablooey and paradigms would suddenly shift and then those among us who had their pineal glands lit up by this December 2012 kundalini snake spirit rising would ascend to a higher plane of consciousness. Or something like that.

Quite honestly, I couldn't really keep up (nor did I even try). Yet I also sensed it was all just so much New Age psychobabble and that Tal and Rhodes may have been testing me to see how readily I would lap up any of this stuff. Just the same, I put on my best poker face and let it all roll over me, which seems the best method to employ when trying to get to the bottom of mysteries on the scale of Dulce, which is filled with as many red herrings and mis-directions as trying to navigate a carnival midway on a thousand mics of Orange Sunshine.

At one point—while deeply engrossed in conversation—a camera flashed nearby, on the edges of our peripheral view. I glanced over my shoulder to see who had taken the photo, but no one was there.

"That was interesting," I noted, to which both Messrs. Rhodes and Levesque nodded their heads in knowing unison. Afterwards, I suspected we may have been under surveillance, and someone snapped our photo—without trying to hide the camera flash—just to let us know we were being watched. Or perhaps Rhodes and Tal somehow staged the camera flash to keep me on edge or lead me to suspect that our meeting was of some grave significance. Or perhaps it was some spook that was monitoring Tal and Rhodes' movements, which is exactly what Tal has intimated on many occasions: that he's receiving constant *oversight*.

At some point during our breakfast meeting of the minds, Tal asked me if I knew his real name, and I responded that, to the best of my knowledge, it was Thomas Allen Levesque. In response, Tal said nothing, which I felt was just his way of further confusing the issue.

So here I am sitting with two other somewhat shadowy, though amiable fellows, and none of us really knows the other's real name, which doesn't much matter, that's the game we sometimes play in a world of spooks and kooks. Afterwards, Rhodes intimated via email his suspicion that I was a CIA operative, which I can neither confirm nor deny! This is the type of paranoia that permeates the fields of ufology and conspiracy research, where you form relationships, and share information, then after a while begin to suspect that those you were trading info with were misleading you and are possibly agents of a hostile foreign power.

When Tal excused himself to go use the head, I mentioned to John Rhodes that many of Tal's inner-Earth revelations reminded me of Richard Shaver's tales of the Deros, to which Rhodes responded that Tal had actually known Shaver during the 1970s, and that Tal and his ex-wife, Mary Martin, visited him at his home in Arkansas on a couple of occasions. It was during this period—the early '70s to mid '80s—that Tal and Mary published *The Hollow Earth Hassle*, a magazine devoted to all things inner-Earth.

When Tal returned, I asked him about his association with Richard Shaver, and how—over the years—many people have viewed Shaver as a head case.

TL: "My face to face contacts with Shaver impressed me. When Richard thought entities were around he would pound a shaft, three times on the floor. Well, that is something that was done in Celtic tradition also. So calling him unstable might be what some people would say. We called him a friend and gracious host."

AG: "So what were the Deros? Are they the same as the Reptilians?"

TL: "Shaver considered the Dero and Tero both to be physical beings. Other people didn't like that and wanted them to be astral Djinn-type demons. The Dero are mirrors that reflect your anti-life ways of being. The Tero are you as pro-life creator. Both are part of the illusion, the Matrix as some are calling it now. The conflict *is* in our minds...

"These beings are based within the planet, from another vibrational level inside this planet. So it all depends on perspective and point of view on how you want them to fit in with various philosophies. On the one hand, I believe they can go from physical to discorporate and that some are more ghost-like. Yet another type are able to become physical, then return to the dark plasma realms. In fact, you could enter a cavern opening on the surface as a physical human and the deeper you go, you will lose physical mass around your astral-etheric matrix body then cross over into another dimensional realm. If you returned to the surface quickly you would be glowing and be able to hover above the surface of the ground. In a short time, physical matter would start to accumulate around your matrix plasma form. You would stop glowing and return to being the person who first entered the cavern portal. Certain monks do this all the time in Tibet. Also, a Southwest Indian tribe has a cavern at a location I can't disclose where their shamans do the same thing. So everything is true. But on the surface of the planet we live in a world of conflicting points of view. It has to be one thing or another...so we have to defend our choice. I say fuck that...wake up...everything *is* possible!"

After settling our bills, we stood outside for a bit on the front steps of the greasy spoon, rubbing our satisfied tummies and gnawing on toothpicks, before bidding farewell. As a parting gift, Tal produced one of those laser light pointers; the kind that make a little red dot you can flash around that drives cats crazy and provides humans endless hours of amusement. Upon receipt of this generous Tal-provided gift, which in subsequent years I've spent endless hours indeed driving my cats crazy with, I jokingly inquired if this was a special laser pointer that would open up portals, or at least realign my chakras, to which Tal offered no direct response, aside from a slight wry smile.

Tal later emailed me with information that confirmed (more or less!) that laser pointers can indeed open inner earth portals! Everything *is* possible...

Chapter 29

Behold a pail of horseshit

At the 1989 MUFON Symposium, Bill Cooper took the audience for a wild ride with a talk entitled "The Secret Government and UFOs", in which he claimed to have become privy to top secret UFO intelligence in the early '70s while serving as a briefing officer with the Pacific fleet. At that time, Cooper allegedly viewed a series of briefing documents similar to the MJ-12 papers that included a couple dozen alien photos and information concerning sixteen saucer crashes that occurred between 1947 and 1952, not to mention the recovery of sixty-five alien bodies. If that wasn't enough, Cooper claimed that malevolent ETs had engineered JFK's assassination!

Cooper's conspiratorial cosmology included the secretive Majestic-12 group, which consisted of a twelve member body that—according to Cooper's sources—were the senior members of a larger Illuminati-like thirty-two-member group called the Jason Society that had been commissioned by President Eisenhower to "find the truth of the alien question."

During his meteoric ascent into UFO superstardom, Cooper was interviewed by the syndicated television program *PM Magazine*. While chatting up the host of the show prior to taping, Cooper mentioned the "The Krill Papers," an infamous ufological document that concerned a secret human-ET exchange program. As part of this secret program, an ET had been left behind on Earth who was identified as "Krll" or "O.H. Krill." Cooper claimed that the initials "O.H." meant "original hostage." According to Cooper, "The Krill Papers" were among a number of top secret briefing papers he smuggled out in his lunchbox in 1973 while serving as a Naval briefing officer. John Lear, who was a by-stander for the *PM Magazine* interview, recalled:

I was standing offstage a bit when I heard Bill talking to the host about the Krill Papers. Bill was telling the host that the Krill Papers were real. He said he'd seen them when he was in Naval Intelligence. I pulled him aside and asked him what the hell he thought he was doing? I told him there was no way he could have read the Krill Papers in 1973 because I'd just written them along with John Grace only a few months before.[81]

Cooper—as to be expected—took exception with Lear setting him straight, then turned the tables on Lear telling him that he was the one who was actually lying, which was Cooper's usual comeback when presented with facts that didn't square with his version of reality. In his book *Behold A Pale Horse,* Cooper claimed that damn near anyone who ever disagreed with his conspiratorial worldview was part of a sinister disinformation campaign, whom included in its ranks such ufological stalwarts as Bob Lazar, Budd Hopkins, Stan Friedman, Bill Moore, Jaime Shandera, George Knapp, Linda Howe and Bruce Maccabee. Cooper also took aim at the editors of *UFO Magazine,* Vicky Cooper and Don Ecker (who published a two-part Cooper exposé), referring to them disparagingly as "Don Pecker" and "Sticky Pooper."

In the early '90s, Cooper launched a shortwave radio show called *The Hour of the Time,* which quickly took the Great American Heartland by storm, providing fodder for those hungry for the latest scoop about New World Order conspiracies. *The Hour of the Time* was a primitive precursor to Alex Jones' *Infowars,* who obviously owes a lot of his bombastic bull-in-a-china-shop style to Bill Cooper. Cooper, not unlike Jones, was known to take a nip or two of hooch (and sometimes more) before going off on long-winded rants, occasionally berating the show's callers after he'd had a few too many pops.

During our breakfast meeting of the minds, Tal informed me that when Bill Cooper first appeared on the scene, he was among a group of insiders feeding "Wild Bill" his spiel, which Cooper then regurgitated to greater glory, performing the role of mouthpiece for this collective of insider whistle-blowers – who one can assume were some of the same names that continually crop up in this twisted tale: Tal, Lear, John Grace, Bill Hamilton, etc. Members of this insider group met a number of times, boozing it up with Cooper during his legendary appearances on *The Billy Goodman Happening*. Tal told me he also assisted Cooper with research for *Behold a Pale Horse*, as well as producing Cooper's first video interview.

Cooper's sketchiest claim to fame was a videotape he peddled at speaking gigs called *The Truth Betrayed: Dallas Revisited*, which presented "evidence" that JFK had been killed by the driver of the presidential limousine, a secret service agent named William Greer with an "electrically operated, gas-powered assassination pistol built by the CIA" containing a shellfish toxin dart.

The Truth Betrayed had been produced by a researcher named Lars Hansson, who later noted in his essay "Lear and Loathing in Las Vegas" that the videotape was intended "to serve only as a preliminary research tool to spur potential investors to underwrite a thorough professional investigation into the theory that the driver of the presidential limousine, William Greer, actually turned around and fired the fatal shot at JFK...It was never intended at any time to be considered a final statement on the issue, much less to be shown publicly and/or distributed as such."

Hansson approached John Lear (assuming he had deep pockets) and shared a copy of *Dallas Revisited* in the prospect of getting him to invest in his research. Little did Hansson know, but by this time Lear had fallen out of favor with his father, Bill Lear, losing access to those deep family pockets. After getting his mitts on *Dallas Revisited*, Lear began showing the film (without permission) at his lectures, including the 1989 MUFON Symposium, and passed along a copy to Bill Cooper, who not only afterwards trotted it out like his own baby, but also started selling copies of it at his speaking gigs.

When Hansson caught wind of these escapades, a shit-storm soon erupted between himself, Cooper and Lear. According to Hansson:

> Cooper's supporters told me a couple of months after my visit to his home that Cooper had a copy of the tape and was showing it publicly. At that time, in late October 1989, I confronted him over the phone about his dishonesty regarding his use and sale of the videotape, and have since done so publicly in print, on television, and on the radio. When he chickened out of appearing on the TV program *Inside Report*, which was taped in April and aired in May 1990, after learning that I would also be appearing to counter him, the producers deliberately left out half of my statement. I had made it clear on their videotape that at the time I threw the rough video together I believed that there was sufficient supporting evidence to warrant a complete investigation; however, after seeing a much clearer version of the Zapruder film, discussing the issue with a number of other respected researchers, and combing through the evidence at hand more closely, I had decided by November 1988 the theory was no longer tenable.

Cooper later broke ranks with ET true believers, claiming he'd been duped about UFOs and alien abductions, which he'd come to realize were actually a government disinfo op designed to conceal the New World Order agenda. According to biographer Mark Jacobson:

> Cooper said he'd begun to suspect flying saucers were not from outer space in late 1989, when a scientist of his acquaintance came to his hotel room late one night, carrying what the man called 'a mysterious briefcase.' Cooper described how when the scientist opened the briefcase, a miniature flying saucer rose out of it 'under its own power, hovered briefly, and then vanished from sight.' The scientist told Cooper this was a man-made

device, the product of Nazi anti-gravity technology brought to the USA by Third Reich physicists like Wernher von Braun during the post–World War Two 'Operation Paperclip.' It had not yet been ascertained what made the objects suddenly invisible or whether they disappeared into 'the future or the past,' but this was among the projects under study at Area 51. There were absolutely no aliens involved."[82]

In the early '90s, Cooper aligned himself with a militia group called the Second Continental Army of the Republic and told the IRS to fold it five times and stick it where the sun don't shine: that taxation was unconstitutional and if "They" wanted to try to come and take away his guns, then bring it on, Big Brother. During *Hour of the Time* broadcasts, Cooper claimed that he had been targeted by "The Illuminati Socialist President of the United States of America, William Jefferson Clinton."[83]

In 1998, Cooper was charged with tax evasion and bank fraud, and an arrest warrant was issued. The feds—well aware that Cooper was always locked and loaded—took a measured approach, realizing that any type of confrontation might escalate into violence. By the fall of 2000, the feds still had been unable to serve their warrant, and Cooper was listed as a federal fugitive by the U.S. Marshals Service.

In the meantime, Cooper had a number of confrontations with the locals in his hometown of Eager, Arizona. The straw that broke the camel's back occurred in July 2001, when a firearm-wielding Cooper chased off a local man from a parcel of land near his home. This incident triggered (no pun intended) a response from the Apache County Sheriff's office that led to Cooper's ultimate undoing when, during a raid of his home, he went out in a blaze of bullets, shot dead at age 58, on November 6, 2001.

Chapter 30

The Las Vegas nexus

In 1989, Tal Levesque (using his Jason Bishop III pen name) circulated a document called *The Dulce Base* to a collective of researchers that included John Lear, Bill Cooper, Val Valerian (aka John Grace), Bill Hamilton, and Bruce Alan De Walton. This nexus of researchers, in turn, incorporated Tal's information into their own pamphlets, books and lectures, giving the appearance that the Dulce Base story was coming from multiple sources, when in reality much of it originated with Tal, and then was afterwards embroidered upon by this nexus of researchers.

Bruce Alan De Walton first came to the attention of UFO seekers around 1990 with a flurry of BBS posts that eventually resulted in a series of books published under his nom-de-plume of "Branton." According to Branton, the United States is "the last obstacle standing in the way of the joint Reptilian-Bavarian Illuminati's new world order, which is based after the Reptilian collective mind-control/annihilation-of-consciousness system as opposed to the Christian idea of individual liberty and free thought." *The Dulce Wars*—published by Branton in the early 1990s—was the most widely distributed among the Tal Levesque inspired spin-offs, and throughout *The Dulce Wars* Jason Bishop III (aka Tal) is heavily cited.

John Grace was a former Air Force officer who had been stationed at Nellis Air Force Base in proximity to the fabled Area 51 (or so he claimed). In 1988, Grace founded the Nevada Aerial Research Group in Las Vegas, which later relocated to Yelm, Washington, and renamed the Leading Edge Research Group. Under his Val Valerian pseudonym, Grace published a series of books entitled *Matrix* that was a sort of everything-in-the-conspiratorial-kitchen-sink affair, including, of course, the Dulce Base mythos.

Grace claimed that he had been inspired to start his Leading Edge Research Group by his interactions with a courageous gal named Stacy Borland, who—along with a group of fellow Reynolds Electric Corp. employees—had purportedly blown the whistle on the fact that several of their co-workers were being held captive by reptilian ETs in an underground base below the Mercury test site, sixty-five miles northwest of Las Vegas in the town of Mercury, Nevada. (This test site is officially known as "Jack Ass Flats," so make of that what you will.) Shortly after Ms. Borland went public with these claims, she and her brother were allegedly murdered in a "gang-land"-style slaying in Las Vegas.

During an episode of *The Billy Goodman Happening*, one of the Mercury site workers phoned in, identifying himself simply as "C":

Billy Goodman: Hi! You're on the Billy Goodman Happening on KVEG! Sir, what can I do for you tonight?

C: O.K. Are you ready? Hang on to your seat! Here goes! We are going 3,000 feet underground! O.K. We get to that point, 3,000 feet. We come out into a stainless-steel atmosphere... and we come upon people that are ah...construction people... working people, and so forth that are supposed to be in that area. Then we come upon another people who push us into another little room. They tell us, "Do not come out of that area, until you're told to." These guys are 6 minute marines, all right? They tell us, "If you do, you are going to get hurt!" OK? So we are construction workers!

BG: Where are you working? Where is what you are describing to us?

C: On a certain test site!

BG: A certain test site! Which one? You can't reveal which one?

C: We're kinda mixed up! We don't know what the hell is going on. We're making ah... good bucks... and everything has come down on us... and they are hurting us! OK? So we are contractors! We are workers! OK? So there's a person that I called and explained what is happening to me and they told me to call you and tell you! So, that is what I am doing right now! Calling you!

BG: You presented it in a very odd way! First of all I didn't know if you were going to be serious or what! Are you saying to me that you are a construction worker and you had to go 3,000 feet underground? First of all what would you be doing underground? Let me ask you that!

C: We are running lights and power.

BG: And who assigned you this job?

C: It's through Reynold's Electronics. I have to say that because I get my paycheck from someone else!

BG: They tell you to put these lights underground?

C: Yeah, but there's more to it than that! I'm sort of afraid of expressing. Am I talking to you or what?

BG: Yes, you are talking directly to me!

C: OK. You know some of the things that are happening, shouldn't be. It should be made public! The public should know what the hell is going on! And it scares the hell out of me. What is not being brought out you know? For example, can I give you an example? Here's an example! A few weeks back we were inside a certain cavern going through stainless-steel halls, going north, and as we move along we are hanging lights. In the rooms are...they're like operating rooms. All of a sudden, off the elevator, our U.S. Marines come out, crash us down off our scaffold, pushing us down, and then into a room. This is taking a hell of a lot out of me to tell you this right now! The bosses come into the room and we're getting debriefed and all this kind of stuff and all of a sudden they are carrying fixed bayonets. Now I fought in Vietnam and I thought these guys were my buddies! Oh, no way!

Forget it! These guys are from outer space! These people brought these little characters on gurneys, OK? They had big heads and little bodies and they went into this little room. Then, behind them, these doctors in white coats and stuff! And we were really at, ah... we didn't know what the hell was going on! We were shocked to hell! I was scared, man!

BG: Well, sure you didn't know what was going on and didn't expect it! I guess them handling you upset you first of all. Being man to man, you thought why should you treat me this way! And that's to be expected. As far as knowing where you are I have no idea.

C: I know where I was! I worked there every day! I keep a log and if someone asks me I know what's going on! I'm telling you man they're not telling us the truth. There is something damn wrong within our government. I only got a glimpse of this scientist on television, but I know he's not telling much of what he knows. I'm just a worker. A hammer and nail man. This guy's got more brains than I do, and would know more about it than I do. There's something INSIDE they aren't telling us!

BG: OK. I understand that! Now what do you want us to do about it?

C: Expose it!

BG: I think you've done that yourself, just now! Now you haven't told us your location and I think that's important so we have some idea where this is. I hope you understand at this moment...

C: I work at Mercury, Nevada and I'm the best electrician there. This is between you and me now. I don't want anybody else to know about this!

BG: But you're on the air, sir!

C: You mean somebody knows about this besides you and me?

BG: But you are talking over the radio, sir! Everybody, all over the West Coast that is listening has just heard you! So you've gotten your word out. Now let's see if anybody else knows about it. Maybe just maybe, we'll get some calls from some of the people that work with you.

C: Wait a minute! You mean somebody else knows about this besides you and me?

BG: Now, this is a talk show, you called a talk show. I am over the radio — that's where you called!

C: Oh, my god!

BG: Why, what's wrong with that? You called a talk show!

C: I thought I was just talking to you!

BG: Now you said someone told you to call me. Was it someone you work with?

C: Yes.

BG: Nobody knows who you are. You haven't said your name or anything! Now, let's see if anyone will back up your story!

C: But I didn't know other people would hear this. Now I'm scared for my life! There's tremendous stuff out there that's being hidden. It's being corrupted inside. It's being stashed away.

BG: Well that's what we do here. We are trying to bring the information out, and it's people like yourself who are making that happen. They bring us information all the time! Are you trying to bring the information out yourself because you don't like what's going on?

C: I fear for my life because I've seen what happened. I fear for my life because the government is lying to me.

BG: OK. Why do you fear for your life? Have you been threatened?

C: Before you even go down in the pit they threaten you! That is you tell anything of what you saw, you are dead!

BG: But you're not saying more than what you saw. Is there anything else you want to say before we say thank you for calling?

C: Yes, one other thing. Whenever it gets down to the nitty gritty, it will be clear to the people, that what they are seeing on the news, is true! We've got six little bodies underground, man!

BG: Please keep in touch, OK? [Phone line goes dead.][84]

Chapter 31

Bob Lazer, superster

In the mid 1980s—prior to his ascent into the ufological strato-sphere—John Lear provided background information to Las Vegas TV station KLAS that was used for an exposé of the F-19 Stealth Fighter program, then in development at a certain secret military installation soon to become known as Area 51. In 1987, Lear paid a return visit to KLAS distributing copies of the MJ-12 papers. News reporter George Knapp was intrigued enough by this MJ-12 info that he invited Lear on to his public affairs talk show, *On the Record*, an episode that captured the imagination of the viewing public.

In the intro to the program—as fake Billy Meier flying saucer photos flashed across the TV screen—Knapp began the show with these words:

> Flying saucers, extraterrestrials, monsters from outer space. The government has been telling us for years that they're not real. They're weather balloons, or swamp gas, or reflections from the sun, or the ravings of lunatics. But serious UFO researchers say a breakthrough may be very close. Some of the government scientists who worked on the top secret project Blue Book are ready to talk. What's more, a series of revealing government documents have trickled out of the federal files, documents that paint a much different picture of the UFO phenomenon. One of the most dedicated UFO researchers is right here in Las Vegas. His name is John Lear and he is my guest today.

The "revealing series of government documents" referred to were the MJ-12 Papers, which, as mentioned above, Lear had recently passed along to Knapp. During his *On The Record* interview, Lear claimed:

I have found out that the government has retrieved between 10 to 15 actual flying saucers, three of which are in perfect condition, one which they tried to fly. They have between 30 to 50 alien bodies in cryogenic storage. We even have the name of the person whose job it is to show these bodies to the heads of state and the people who are authorized to see them. They represent at least five different civilizations.

In the aftermath of Lear's *On the Record* appearance, numerous UFO sightings started being reported in the Groom Lake area, part of Area 51. These revelations prompted George Knapp to produce a series of news segments on Area 51. One episode—broadcast in May 1989—featured a nuclear physicist with his face obscured going by the name of "Dennis" who claimed to have worked at the facility. It was eventually revealed that Dennis' actual name was Robert "Bob" Lazar, who Knapp had met through John Lear, which once again illustrates the recurring theme of how Lear (like Tal Levesque) seemed forever at the center of these emerging Dulce Base/Area 51 revelations.

According to ufological legend, Lazar was approached in December 1987 about a job working for Naval Intelligence, and afterwards was called in on an irregular basis for a secret project. Lazar reported to a pickup point where a bus with blacked-out windows would then drive him and a number of other workers to a facility in the desert called S-4 that was involved in reverse-engineering ET propulsion systems. Lazar allegedly worked on a total of nine different saucers, which he called "an assortment pack," that included the "sport model," the "top hat," and the always popular "Jello-O mold," that were fueled by "Element 115." Lazar noted that security officers wandered in and out of the facility wearing badges that said "Majestic."[85]

As a way to prove his story, Lazar snuck a vial of Element 115 out of S-4, but apparently dastardly government agents foiled his plan by later breaking into his house and stealing the stuff back. However,

Lazar had another ace up his sleeve when it came to corroborating his stories, as he'd become privy to the specific time and place where the back-engineered craft were being tested. In March of '89, Lazar drove John Lear and his buddy Gene Huff out to this viewing spot, an area called Freedom Ridge, where they witnessed a crazy UFO circus show light up the sky and blow their minds.

Lazar and Lear made frequent forays to witness these dazzling saucer spectacles—that is until one night when they were chased out by a Wackenhut security squad, who notified them they'd entered an unauthorized area, and to vacate the premises or they'd be subject to arrest. Afterwards, Lazar claimed that his Area 51 supervisor informed him he had broken security protocol by taking his pals to view these secret test flights, and Lazar was immediately terminated from his job at S-4.

One of the more intriguing angles of Lazar's story was his admission that certain things he observed at S-4 seemed staged for his benefit. This theater-like atmosphere was highlighted by one particular incident when a co-worker walked Lazar down a long corridor and directed his attention to a glass window on the other side of which Lazar observed the back of the head of something or someone that appeared unearthly. Lazar later acknowledged that what he saw could have been a doll or a dummy. During an interview with Jacques Vallee, Lazar admitted that his memories might have been "tampered with" and he stated that there was an infirmary at S-4 overseen by a lady doctor who conducted a battery of tests on the workers there, including Lazar, hypnotizing him on a number of occasions.[86]

Due to these revelations, it didn't take long for word to spread about the weird goings-on at this place called Area 51, and soon saucer seekers far and wide were showing up there on weekends to witness strange craft light up the night and perform maneuvers that seemingly defied the law of physics.

Not long after coming forward, Lazar claimed that he began receiving threats from government goons, then afterwards clammed up, pulling himself out of the media spotlight. This was around the same time that Lazar got caught up in a police sting to which he ultimately pleaded guilty to felony pandering, a charge related to a computer database he had set up for a Las Vegas brothel. Lazar's defenders claimed that the charges were a government setup designed to silence him.

Chapter 32

The further adventures of
Dr. Strangelove

Bob Lazar purportedly worked for a short stint at Los Alamos Laboratories, and while there had been recommended for his job at S-4 by none other than Dr. Edward Teller. Regarded by some as the inspiration for Stanley Kubrick's *Dr. Strangelove*, Teller was a Los Alamos Labs fixture for many years, starting with his involvement in the Manhattan Project during World War II and then on into the 1980s when he was involved in a top secret project code-named "Excalibur" designed "to explode low-yield nuclear devices in hollowed-out underground cavities at the Nevada atomic test site. The huge release of energy in the X-ray spectrum was then directed along specially designed and excavated tunnels, which channeled the pulse to a device that produced an 'X-ray laser' beam. X-ray lasers were being developed as a possible 'directed energy' weapon under the Strategic Defense Initiative..."[87]

John Lear put his own spin on Project Excalibur, referring to it as a secret project conducted in response to an "alien war" of which the MJ-12 group had decided that "there was no use exciting the public with the 'horrible truth' and the best plan was to continue the development of a weapon that could be used against the EBEs [Extraterrestrial Biological Entities] under the guise of 'SDI'...As these words are being written, Dr. Edward Teller, the 'father' of the H-bomb is personally in the test tunnels of the Nevada Test Site, driving his workers and associates in the words of one, 'like a man possessed'. And well he should, for Dr. Teller is a member of MJ-12 with Dr. Kissinger, Admiral Bobby Inman...to name a few current members of MJ-12..."

Not to be outdone, Bill Cooper put forth a similar spin, claiming that Project Excalibur was "established to develop a weapon which would destroy the alien underground base and any future underground bases which aliens might construct. It is to be a missile capable of penetrating 1000 meters of tufa/hard packed soil such as that found in New Mexico with no operational damage. Missile apogee not to exceed 30,000 feet…Device will carry 1 megaton nuclear warhead. This project is ongoing at WX division, Los Alamos National Laboratory, New Mexico, and is still in development."

Although much of what Cooper and Lear disseminated re: Project Excalibur was either intentional disinformation or misinformation, the core of the story was based on factual information. As noted, there indeed was an actual Project Excalibur that used nuclear detonations to create underground cavities, and what better way to obfuscate a real story than to overlay a false narrative?

Project Excalibur was active during the same time frame that Richard Doty was allegedly leaking information about secret projects, which included details concerning ETs and UFOs. While much of the underlying information Doty disseminated about secret projects was apparently factual, the UFO/ET elements in the stories were window dressing intended to obscure the true nature of the events. One example of this—according to Greg Valdez—was the Weitzel Letter, previously explored in Chapter 6.

As it turns out, certain details in the Weitzel Letter contained factual elements, such as the sighting of a craft that appeared to be of an advanced technology; however, the extraterrestrial trappings were inserted simply for the sake of theatrics. Another detail in the Weitzel Letter stated that the incident occurred in Pecos, New Mexico, when, in reality, it actually occurred in Dulce. The Weitzel Letter further stated that, following the sighting, the CAP cadets were questioned at Kirtland base by a security officer named "Dody."[88]

Bill Moore later concluded that the Weitzel Letter was an early phase of the AFOSI's counterintelligence operation, which, as it evolved, eventually wormed its way ever so deeply into Paul Bennewitz's brain. Injecting the ET toxin into Bennewitz's information flow was a means to discredit him, and to push false ET memes to conceal the true nature of what he had observed. To this end, the Weitzel Letter was AFOSI's attempt to pollute the ufological waters concerning the sighting of a secret craft that occurred in Dulce. One rationale for such a convoluted caper might have been to see exactly who in ufology was astute enough to extract the false parts of the story from the factual elements and thus determine what was actually being observed by the witnesses to these events.

Those UFO researchers astute enough to ferret out the essential facts in the Weitzel Letter would most likely be the same ones who would conceivably untangle the false threads being sewn into similar stories— like Cash-Landrum—thus enabling them to eventually identify the craft in question as being terrestrial in origin. By singling out these researchers, AFOSI could then target them directly and track who they were interacting with, such as someone like Bill Moore, who by this time had established contacts with scientists and "UFO researchers" in the Soviet Union suspected of being KGB agents or cut-outs.

As previously noted, Moore's investigation of the Weitzel Letter is what presumably brought him to the attention of the AFOSI. Ultimately, Moore determined that the Weitzel Letter was a hoax, which in essence meant that he had "passed the test." Soon after, Falcon contacted Moore, telling him that he was one of the few researchers in all of ufology who really knew what was going on. While this assessment was probably accurate to some degree, it also seemed designed to play on Moore's personal vanity as a means to indoctrinate him into the AFOSI's counter-intelligence operation.

Chapter 33

The Area 51 cottage industry

Listeners of *The Billy Goodman Happening*—who tuned in nightly to listen to such scene-makers as John Lear, Bob Lazar and Bill Cooper—soon discovered you could access Area 51 by taking Highway 375 (later to be officially renamed "The Extraterrestrial Highway") to mile marker 29 ½. From there you'd turn left onto a dirt road leading to a black mailbox that intersected with the main road leading into the facility, and eventually make your way to the fabled flying saucer viewing spot on Freedom Ridge.

The Rachel Bar & Restaurant (soon after renamed the "Little A-Le-Inn"—located in Rachel, Nevada, 25 miles north of Area 51) became the key meeting spot for the UFO faithful to huddle before heading out to get their flying saucer fix. One of these seekers was Norio Hayakawa, who formed a loose-knit outfit called the Civilian Intelligence Network to expose the emerging truth of whatever was actually happening at Area 51. In July 1991, Hayakawa's group organized the first "Need To Know Seminar" at the Little A-Le-Inn, and in attendance were the usual suspects: Lear, Lazar and Cooper—not to mention an up-and-coming New Age entrepreneur named Sean David Morton, who started his own paid bus tours to Area 51 for $99 a pop—and before you could say "Zeta Reticuli" a cottage industry had sprung up around this secret military base that suddenly wasn't all that secret anymore.

These Area 51 sky-watching parties proved to be short-lived, as the feds (using Wackenhut security goons in SUVs) swooped in and closed off access to the fabled black mailbox entry point, which in turn ignited protests by Area 51 enthusiasts who claimed that the government was denying them their God-given right to pursue the UFO enigma. Norio Hayakawa and his Civilian Intelligence Network were at the forefront

The fabled black mailbox at Area 51 circa early 1990s.
(Photo credit: Greg Bishop)

of these protests, which in time eventually fizzled out, as did access to the prime Area 51 viewing spots that had been effectively closed down by the aforementioned Wackenhut goon squad.

Like Kerouac's "fabulous yellow roman candles exploding like spiders across the stars," *The Billy Goodman Happening* was likewise a short-lived spectacle. Debuting in mid-1989, Goodman's show—which was originally called *The Thing*—initially aired on Las Vegas station KVEG (840 on your AM dial!) from 10:00 P.M. to 1:00 A.M., Monday thru Friday, and in short order became a regional hit. While broadcasting at a modest 25,000 watts, KVEG's signal at night nonetheless reached into ten western states and soon the word spread and a core of die-hard listeners tuned in night-in-night-out to hear the latest and greatest yarns about alien greys and the saucers they allegedly spun in on.

As Goodman continued on his mission to reveal the mysteries of Area 51 and other "government secrets," he started receiving harassing phone calls—which were more than your average I-don't-have-a-life-type phone call pranks—seemingly designed to drive him off the air. Because of this, the powers-that-be at KVEG started getting a bit fidgety—what with all the apparently sensitive material Billy's whistle-blower guests were sharing—and management decided to move his time slot to 12:00 A.M. – 3:00 A.M., then eventually to the more obscure hours of 3:00 A.M. – 5:00 A.M. when hardly anyone was listening, none of which made the least bit of sense because the show was a big hit and the only way to explain these sudden changes was that KVEG management was getting pressure to shut Goodman up. There were also rumors of bomb threats and other mischief going on at the time that only added to the hysteria. Before long, Goodman was off the air entirely, all of this happening within the span of a few months. He later resurfaced in Providence, Rhode Island, although his new show there never came close to approximating the high level of craziness that filled the airwaves during his short-lived KVEG tenure.

Around the same time *The Billy Goodman Happening* was going great guns, another Las Vegas radio personality, Art Bell, was evidently taking notes to be used at a later date. In 1988, Bell and fellow radio personality Alan Corbeth launched the nationally syndicated *Coast to Coast America* with Corbeth broadcasting the first two hours from the east coast, then Bell doing the second half from the Grand Plaza Hotel in Las Vegas. Although *Coast to Coast America* was short-lived, this model of a syndicated program stretching out across the great American heartland would later provide the architecture for Bell's subsequent endeavors in radio land.

In 1993, Robert Bigelow, an aerospace entrepreneur with an abiding interest in UFOs and paranormal phenomenon, bank-rolled a radio show called "Area 2000" on station KDWN in Las Vegas, enlisting in this effort Art Bell, George Knapp and Linda Howe.[89] The following year, Bell decided to go solo, launching *Coast to Coast AM* from his bunker in Pahrump, Nevada, featuring many of the same names that first put *The Billy Goodman Happening* on the map, such as John Lear, who Art credited as the key person that introduced him to the UFO subject. To add a supposed air of legitimacy to *Coast to Coast AM*, Linda Howe was featured regularly as the show's "science advisor." Other guests included none other than Tal Levesque's protégé John Rhodes, who regaled *Coast to Coast AM* listeners with tales of underground bases and the evil reptilians that inhabit them.

Among others Tal groomed to be one of his intermediaries, or spokespersons, was a statuesque blonde jazz singer named Pamela Stonebrooke. According to John Rhodes, he was slated to appear on *Coast to Coast AM* on February 5, 1998, and prior to the interview, Rhodes was on the phone with Art Bell when he mentioned a woman he knew (Stonebrooke) who had been abducted and enjoyed steamy reptilian sex that was literally "out of this world." As soon as Art heard this bit about Stonebrooke and reptilians doing the old intergalactic bump and grind, he about fell out of his chair and persuaded Rhodes to give up his spot that night so he could bring on Stonebrooke to share her saucy stories.

In my conversations with Tal, he indicated that Stonebrooke had gone off script during this *Coast to Coast AM* interview—or had revealed too much too soon, or something like that. Due to this perceived transgression, Stonebrooke ultimately fell out of favor with "the world according to Tal", and soon after left the ufological field for good.

Chapter 34

Mr. Mike from COM-I2

In the run-up to the "Need To Know Seminar" held at Little A-Le-Inn in July 1991, a mysterious group called COM-12 circulated a purported classified Air Force document later referred to as the "Bluefire Memoranda,"[90] that stated:

A SHUTDOWN HAS BEEN HEREBY ORDERED FOR ALL SOUTH BASE OPERATIONS AND SPECIAL SECTOR PROGRAMS. SPECIAL CONDITIONS PROCEDURES FOR SEQUENCE "BLUE FIRE" ARE NOW IN EFFECT. ALL ENLISTED PERSONNEL AND CIVILIAN PERSONNEL ARE TO BE BRIEFED ON A "BLUE FIRE" SCENARIO, ON A "NEED TO KNOW" BASIS ONLY. ALL SPECIAL SERVICE DIVISIONS, SPECIAL SCIENCES DIVISIONS AND EXECUTIVE SECURITY TEAMS WILL BE UNDER LOCKDOWN CONDITIONS OR ON RESTRICTED ROAM L.R.R.P. PROCEDURES.

ON 31 JULY 1991 AT 2000 HRS. A CIVILIAN ORGANIZED EVENT IS TO BE HELD IN THE TOWN OF RACHEL, NEVADA. THE INDIVIDUALS WHO HAVE ORGANIZED THE EVENT ARE FAMILIAR TO SECURITY TEAM PERSONNEL THAT HAVE HAD PRIOR CONTACT WITH PRIMARIES AND / OR THEIR SUPPORTERS. PRIMARY SUBJECTS ARE IDENTIFIED AS FOLLOWS:

    1.   NORIO HAYAKAWA / FOUNDER OF CIVILIAN INTELLIGENCE NETWORK
             [Address blacked out]
             GARDENA, CA.

2. GARY CLARK / AKA; SCHULTZ / FOUNDER OF
SECRET SAUCER BASE EXPEDITIONS
[Address blacked out]
SANTA MONICA, CA.

BOTH OF THE SUBJECTS OPERATE THEIR ORGAN-
IZATIONS FROM A POST OFFICE BOX IN THE CITY OF
GARDENA CALIFORNIA. (PLEASE SEE PRIOR SPECIAL
ADVISORY NOTIFICATIONS.)

BOTH SUBJECTS AND THEIR SUPPORT PERSON-
NEL WILL BE IN ADVISORY PERIMETER WITHIN A
48 HR. TIME PERIOD OF THIS NOTICE. ALL AREA
PERSONNEL ARE TO REMAIN ON ADVISORY ALERT
UNTIL 5 AUGUST 0500 HRS. AND PROCEED WITH
CAUTION IF APPROACHED BY ANYONE BELIEVED
TO BE AFFIALIATED WITH THESE GROUPS. THESE
SUBJECTS MAY ALSO BE ACCOMPANIED BY INDIVID-
UALS FROM THE NIPPON TELEVISION NETWORK OF
THE TOYKO BROADCASTING SERVICE OF JAPAN, IN
ADDITION TO VARIOUS PRINT MEDIA PERSONNEL
FROM VARIOUS ASSIGNMENTS BOTH NATIONAL
AND INTERNATIONAL. ALL BASE COMMANDERS
AND SECURITY TEAM PERSONNEL ARE TO INSTRUCT
SUBORDINATES CONCERNED TO REPORT ANY
HARRASSMENT EITHER TO THEMSELVES OR ANY
OTHER BASE PERSONNEL THAT THEY MAY BECOME
AWARE OF. FAILURE TO DO SO IN A TIMELY MANNER
WILL RESULT IN IMMEDIATE DISCIPLINARY PROCE-
DURES WITH NO EXCEPTIONS.

THIS EVENT IS TO BE HELD AT "THE LITTLE
ALE-INN" FORMERLY KNOWN AS, "RACHELS BAR
AND GRILL". MR. AND MRS. TRAVIS HAVE GRANTED

PERMISSION TO THESE INDIVIDUALS FOR THE USE OF THE FACILITIES ON THE EVENING OF 31 JULY 1991.

ALL BASE SPECIAL OPERATIONS IN SECTORS CONCERNED ARE TO BE RESCHEDULED TO AN ASSIGNMENT DATE AFTER 0500 HRS. ON 5 AUGUST.

SPECIAL SECURITY SERVICES ARE HEREBY INSTRUCTED TO COMMENCE WITH PROPER PROCUREMENT AND ENFORCEMENT OF SPECIAL SECURITY ADVISORY SECTIONS AND PRACTICES DURING THIS TIME PERIOD. IT IS EXPECTED THAT MEMBERS OF THESE GROUPS AS WELL AS OTHER FRINGE ELEMENTS WILL REMAIN IN AND AROUND THE GENERAL AREAS OF CONCERN FOR AS MANY AS A FEW DAYS PRIOR TO, AND FOLLOWING, THIS SCHEDULED EVENT.

ALL PERSONNELL BOTH MILITARY AND CIVIL-IAN WHO ARE BELIEVED TO BE COMMUNICATING OR CORRESPODNING IN ANY WAY OR BY ANY METHOD WILL BE CONSIDERED TO BE IN VIOLA-TION OF THIS SPECIAL SECURITY ADVISORY AND THEREBY CHARGED WITH WILLFUL DESREGARD OF A SPECIAL SECURITY ADVISORY AND BE SUBJECT TO IMMEDIATE ARREST AND PROSECUTION FOR VIOLATION OF THE NATIONAL SECURITY ACTS.

NOTE: THIS DOCUMENT CONTAINS INFOR-MATION AFFECTING THE NATIONAL SECURITY OF THE UNITED STATES WITHIN DESCRIPTION OF THE ESPIONAGE ACT 30 U.S.C., 31 AND 32 AS AMENDED. ITS TRANSMISSION OR THE REVELA-TION OF ITS CONTENTS IN ANY MANNER TO AN UNAUTHORIZED PERSON IS STRICTLY PROHIBIT-ED BY LAW. IT MAY NOT BE REPRODUCED IN WHOLE

OR IN PART BY OTHER THAN UNITED STATES AIR
FORCE SPECIAL SECURITY SERVICES EXCEPT BY
PERMISSION OF THE DIRECTOR OF SPECIAL INTEL-
LIGENCE T-2 USAF/NRO.

END.

The individual circulating the Bluefire Memoranda was named
Michael Younger, an imposing figure fond of donning a black trench
coat, who—when introducing himself—was known to flash a badge
of some sort indicating he was a secret agent (of some sort). Younger claimed he was a former Navy Seal now serving as liaison for
COM-12, a special operations group connected to the Office of Naval
Intelligence. COM-12, according to Younger, was allegedly at odds
with another special intelligence unit comprised of CIA and AFOSI
agents known as Aquarius. Aquarius—a fascist wing of the government—was, in turn, associated with MJ-12. According to Younger,
COM-12 was attempting to stage a "rear guard action to sustain and
preserve constitutional government."

The following year, Norio Hayakawa's Civilian Intelligence
Network hosted the "Need To Know Seminar Part 2" in Arcadia,
California. Among the speakers was none other than Michael Younger,
who Hayakawa introduced simply as "Mr. Mike." In his introductory
remarks, Hayakawa informed the audience that COM-12 had actually
helped organize the event. Other speakers included Ted Gunderson,
Jordan Maxwell, and Robert O. Dean, providing a hodge podge of
different conspiracy theories stirred up into one wild stew that basically coalesced around the overarching theory that there were all types
of coverups going on related to UFOs and secret government projects.
During the Need To Know Seminar Part 2, Michael Younger hinted
that both NSA and Wackenhut agents had infiltrated the event, as
the spectre of paranoia oozed palpably through the crowd in hushed
whispers and sidelong glances.

Much of the COM-12 material apparently emerged from the suspect death of investigative journalist Danny Casolaro that occurred on August 10, 1991, in Martinsburg, West Virginia. Casolaro's research linked the goings-on at Cabazon Indian Reservation (located in Coachella, California) with a larger clandestine project known as 'Yellow Lodge' that operated on Cabazon land and other Indian reservations, and in specific an outpost known as 'D6' located on the Jicarilla reservation, near Dulce.

The term "Octopus" was a catch-all for what Casolaro had purportedly uncovered that connected damn near everything in the 1980s conspiratorial kitchen sink: the October Surprise, Iran-Contra drug and gun running, and in particular the so-called Inslaw Affair/Promis software scandal. At the center of this many-tentacled monster was a fellow named Michael Riconosciuto (aka "Danger Man"), a scientific whiz-kid of sorts who in the early 1980s had worked for Wackenhut on a secret version of the Promis software. At the time, Wackenhut had set up a secret compound at the Cabazon Indian reservation in Indio, California where—in cahoots with Danger Man—they were developing a wide range of biological and chemical warfare weapons to be used by CIA-funded mercenaries in the jungles of Nicaragua and other South American garden spots.

Casolaro's research linked the goings-on at Cabazon with a larger clandestine project known as "Yellow Lodge" that operated on Cabazon land and other Indian reservations, and in specific an outpost known as "D6" located on the Jicarilla reservation, near Dulce.

Notes discovered in Casolaro's suicide hotel room mentioned "MJ 12—extraterrestrial," and "Area #51." The apparent source of Casolaro's UFO info appeared to be Riconosciuto, who was among the first to promote a story about two warring intelligence agency factions, Aquarius vs. COM-12. At one time or another, Riconosciuto even claimed he had witnessed an alien autopsy.

Younger and the other speakers at the Need To Know Conference Part 2 reflected a growing trend within the UFO and conspiracy research communities, where those on the left side of the conspiratorial-political spectrum—such as a Mae Brussell, or a Dick Gregory, for instance— could find common ground with conspiracy theorists on the far right, like a Bill Cooper, who around this time had aligned himself with the militia movement and fringe elements that considered the federal government a corrupt racket in bed with a New World Order Agenda orchestrated by the Clintons and NATO and the UN and the Council of Foreign Relations and the Bilderbergers and you name it—the ultimate goal of which was to enslave us all—not to mention directing Wackenhut security forces to cover up what was really going on at Area 51.

In the summer of 1994—less than a year before the bombing of the Murrah Federal Building in Oklahoma City—Timothy McVeigh visited Area 51 to protest restrictions on public access, concerns that had been brought to light by Norio Hayakawa's group. During this period, McVeigh seemed to be making the rounds of battlegrounds staked out by the growing militia movement, having shown up at Waco during the Branch Davidian standoff to protest against the government's actions. It was later reported that McVeigh was a regular listener to Bill Cooper's *Hour of the Time*, and that he even visited Cooper in Arizona, and gifted him a copy of the anti-government bible, *The Turner Diaries*.

Researcher Richard Sarradet suspected that Michael Younger was "psychically gifted. He may have even developed his own sort of remote viewing techniques." Sarradet met with Younger on several occasions, and it soon became evident that Younger was under constant surveillance, in particular by a tan-colored van that always seemed to show up when he was around. Sarradet recalled being followed by this tan van whenever he was on the way to meet Younger:

> One night [Younger and I] came out of a restaurant where we'd been talking and this tan van cruised past us. We were sitting behind Mike's pickup truck talking for about an hour outside, and finally this van that had been watching us parked down in a parking lot near the restaurant, backs out then cruises past us

very slowly and takes pictures...I looked at Mike and said, 'What the fuck is that?' and he said, 'If he comes around again, walk up and talk to him.' I said, 'Do you have any idea who that is?' He said, 'Yeah, I think I know who that is...David Morehouse.' This was about two years before Morehouse was ever heard of.[91]

David Morehouse (mentioned in Chapter 19) was a co-founder of the remote viewing firm PSI-TECH. This supposed I.D. of Morehouse was just one among a number of curiosities that swirled around Michael Younger, as once again remote viewing seems to be a constant theme in this over-arching saga of secret projects, UFOs, and counter-intelligence operations.

In 1994, Younger disappeared amid rumors he had contracted some type of mystery illness. Just before his sudden disappearance, Younger revealed to Richard Sarradet that his real name was Vincent Rotharmel, and as time passed it became clear that Younger/Rotharmel had never actually served as a Navy Seal, or as a liaison (or whatever function he supposedly performed) for COM-12, which probably never existed, either. Nonetheless, Sarradet was convinced that Younger "was on somebody's leash."

Apparently, Younger's wife had been unaware of her husband's double life; to the best of her knowledge, he'd just been a simple housepainter who, at some point, must have become delusional. One odd twist to this double-life angle concerned a mysterious satellite phone Younger had in his possession—which really wasn't the easiest thing to lay your hands on back in the early 1990s—and the only time his wife saw him use it was when he'd received periodic phone calls from an unidentified source. After receiving these calls, Younger would then disappear for days or weeks at a time.

The mysterious life of Michael Younger (aka Vincent Rotharmel) ended on December 31, 2001, when he died of a massive heart attack in Anaheim, California.[92]

Chapter 35

The Dulce War boiler plate

In 1979, according to legend, some disgruntled Dulce Base workers formed an alliance with a group of renegade ETs intent on freeing the human prisoners there that were being subjected to ghastly medical experimentation. In response, the reptilians running the show alerted their human co-conspirators who sent in a Delta Force team to deal with the renegade riff-raff. When the smoke cleared, the resistance was all but mowed down—except for a couple of security workers among the group who were toting flashguns, one of whom was our man, the late, great Tom Castello.

The first documented reference to the Dulce War firefight appeared in a December 2, 1981 letter Paul Bennewitz sent to Senator Pete Dominici stating that "sometime late 79 or first of 80 an argument insued [sic] over weapons and the military abandoned [Dulce base]; the final circumstance of the men unknown…" In a September 11, 1984 interview, Bennewitz informed researcher McCampbell that in 1979 "something happened and the base was closed. There was an argument over weapons and our people were chased out, more than 100 people involved…"[93] Although Bennewitz didn't implicitly state that there was an actual battle between humans and aliens at Dulce, his comments about some type of conflict, or of the humans abandoning the base, appeared to have been enough to plant the seed that later blossomed into a full-scale "Dulce fire-fight."

Certain elements of the Dulce Base story can be traced to the influence of Tal's friend, Richard Shaver. Tal, it appears, recycled certain threads of the "Shaver Mystery," as it was called, and updated them for an *X-Files* generation by inserting ET reptilians into the story and incorporating his own experiences and those of others—such as Paul

Bennewitz—who likewise believed in a dark menace dwelling seven levels deep in Dulce.

Shaver's "I Remember Lemuria" tells the story of two groups of ETs—the Titans and Atlans—that colonized Earth (in the distant past), but soon discovered that the sun's rays were detrimental to their physical wellbeing. Most of the Titans/Atlans fled Earth, but some remained behind and took up residence in the inner earth, namely the Deros, a race of degenerated and deformed beings that used negative "ray machines" to manipulate the human surface dwellers.

The Deros (before they descended) created human-animal hybrids not unlike the tall tales associated with Dulce, all of which can be traced back to the allegorical tales of Lemuria and a period in Earth's forgotten history when technology ran amuck and the Lemurians (in the aftermath of creating these strange creatures) subsequently blew themselves to smithereens.

Presented as factual accounts, Shaver's tales resonated with fans of *Amazing Stories* who started sending in their own accounts of encounters with these evil underground dwellers, including one curious encounter from a Mr. Fred Lee Crisman of Tacoma, Washington, who claimed that during World War II he and another soldier had engaged in a firefight with the Deros and that his companion soldier had been shot with a ray gun that left a dime-size hole in his hand. Crisman's supposed clash with the Deros may have contributed to the recurring Dulce-related theme (with a little twist here or there) about a confrontation between underground entities and human soldiers.

The Dulce firefight angle was also embroidered upon by Bob Lazar, who had allegedly,

> ...read about the incident in a briefing paper at S-4, a Gray alien being was giving instruction of some type to 44 scientists at Dulce. Apparently a security guard with Delta Force, who helped patrol and provide security for the Dulce base, entered the room

with a side arm of some type. It was known by all Dulce personnel that no firearms of any kind were allowed anywhere near the
Grays. Whatever the reason for the security guard's mistake, the
Gray immediately killed him and the 44 scientists. Seeing the
disaster taking place on the security cameras, other Delta Force
personnel came for revenge but the alien killed them also. Both
Castello's account and the account read by Lazar at S-4 said all
66 deaths were caused by 'head wounds.'"[94]

A similar underground base battle was recounted by an occasional caller to *The Billy Goodman Happening* who identified himself as
"Yellow Fruit," which was the codename for a top secret security
division at Area 51. According to Yellow Fruit, there was an underground base at the facility, and one of his fellow security workers there
was an alien who he referred to as the "benevolent one." According
to the "benevolent one," at some point grey aliens had taken over the
base and "the benevolent ones" waged a war against the greys and
were ultimately victorious, returning command of the base back over
to their human counterparts.

During our breakfast meeting of the minds, Tal mentioned that,
on occasion, he had phoned into *The Billy Goodman Happening*, which
came as a bit of a surprise, as I was an avid *Happening* listener back in
the day and hadn't recalled ever hearing Tal on the show. I was recently
re-listening to some old episodes and stumbled upon a couple of shows
featuring Yellow Fruit. Listening to these episodes, it suddenly dawned
on me that Yellow Fruit sounded a hell of a lot like Tal Levesque—and
the more I listened, the more convinced I became that, indeed, Yellow
Fruit was, most likely, my pal Tal.

Yellow Fruit was also featured in the writings of Branton, who
as previously noted was clearly associated with Tal, which provides
further fodder that Tal and Yellow Fruit were one and the same—or
more correctly, Yellow Fruit was another Tal literary construct, much

in the same vein as Tom Castello. One of the shows featuring Yellow Fruit included Bill Cooper, which isn't too surprising given the fact that Tal claims he hung out with Cooper a number of times during his phone-in appearances on *The Billy Goodman Happening*. Branton also published an alleged interview with Tom Castello, which from all appearances was most likely authored by Tal. In this interview, Castello mentions "Yellow Fruit."

Tal informed me that around the same time the Dulce War supposedly went down, a prison riot occurred in Santa Fe, New Mexico. When the dust settled—or more accurately, when the blood dried—thirty-three inmates had been killed and several were injured. Somehow Tal learned that this riot was induced by a brain-wave transmission experiment that apparently caused some of the inmates to go ape-shit. Newspaper accounts from the period confirm that a riot did indeed go down at the Penitentiary of New Mexico in Santa Fe on February 2–3, 1980.

Around the time of this prison riot, Tal was working as a security guard when he was summoned by his supervisor one night and directed to the abandoned St Vincent's Hospital in old town Santa Fe. Tal was instructed to dress in black and at midnight open the back door of the building, then stand aside. As Tal told me:

> A couple of black SUVs showed up, full of guys in all black, heavily armed. I let them in. They did NOT come back out. The SUVs left. I knew for a fact that a wall in the basement could slide to the side. There was a hallway behind it. I was told NEVER to go in there.
>
> I know for a FACT—having been in the connecting tunnels under Santa Fe and my other locations that I protected—that a vast network of tunnels is under the city. I would guide VIPs to secret meeting locations under certain hotels in town.

In email correspondence, Tal informed me the Dulce War victims were transported to St. Vincent's Hospital. What I think Tal suspects (assuming I've correctly read between the lines of his mind) is that the prison riot causalities were shuttled to St. Vincent's on the same night he interfaced with the Black Ops commando dudes.

According to Dulce War legend, sixty-six renegade workers were killed when the shit hit the proverbial fan, which was twice the number that died during the Santa Fe prison riot. 33 at Santa Fe and 66 at Dulce—both of which are mystical numbers in Masonry and the Kabbalah—none of which I'm sure was lost on Tal, who is hip to all things esoteric.

It could be conjectured that the Dulce War victims (allegedly transported to St. Vincent's) served as a metaphor for the Santa Fe inmates subjected to human experimentation—not unlike the alleged Dulce War victims—which was perhaps Tal's underlying message: that these underground facilities exist, and that these rumors of horrendous human experimentation actually go on there.

Chapter 36

Composite characters

It's entirely possible Tal Levesque fleshed out the Dulce Base story that Cherry Hinkle laid on John Lear in the late 1980s. Or—conversely—it might have been Tal who originally presented the Dulce Base story to Hinkle when the two met in Santa Fe in 1979, and then a decade later Hinkle passed the story on to Lear. Whatever the case, I suspect that Hinkle's alleged meetings in Santa Fe with both Tal and Thomas Castello were actually just with Tal alone and from this meeting the Castello character was conceived as a means for Tal to distance himself as the primary source of the Dulce Base revelations.

Tal moved to Albuquerque in the early 1980s and became acquainted with Bennewitz at this time, which suggests the possibility that Castello was a literary composite based not only on Tal himself, but Bennewitz, as well. To extend the theory further, Tal claimed intimate knowledge of Deep Underground Military Bases (DUMBs) where bio-genetic experiments were allegedly being conducted (or he suspected as much) and mashed-up his experiences with the heroically unhinged Bennewitz character to cobble together the Thomas Castello/Dulce Base story. In Santa Fe, Tal claimed he lived a couple blocks from Castello. Similarly, Tal told me he lived a couple of blocks from Bennewitz during the period he resided in Albuquerque. In the early '90s, Gabe Valdez devoted a considerable amount of time attempting to confirm the various Dulce Base stories making the rounds, one of which was determining if a fellow named Thomas Castello actually ever existed. Since it was reported that Castello lived in Santa Fe at the time of the reported Dulce War, Valdez reviewed county assessor records for the area but turned up zero evidence that anyone named

Castello had lived there during the period in question. It was also alleged that Castello had a young son, but Valdez also ran a check of the local schools for Castello's son's attendance and again couldn't find any evidence to support this allegation.

Some may think I'm giving Tal Levesque way too much credit— that he was simply one among many who jumped aboard the Dulce Base bandwagon. While I admit that my theory is speculation, it does seem to coalesce in a coherent (though convoluted) fashion. It's awfully convenient that Thomas Castello disappeared and no one can prove that he actually existed—except for Tal and Cherry Hinkle, that is, who claim they knew Castello, but provide no evidence to corroborate their claims.

Tal informed me that in the early 1990s, he and John Lear tracked down Castello's Social Security number and discovered it had been reissued to a fellow with the last name of Keller who currently resides in Bradley, Illinois. According to Tal, Lear called the Keller residence and got Mrs. Keller on the line, who apparently acted funny ('strange' funny, not 'ha-ha' funny), although she didn't deny that the Social Security number in question had, at one time, belonged to someone else prior to it being issued to her husband.

Tal shared Castello's supposed Social Security number with me for what reason I'm not clear. Perhaps as confirmation that Castello had been a real person. Afterwards, I ran a check on the Social Security number in question and it did indeed track back to a Mr. Homer G. Keller, age 70, of Bradley, Illinois, although there's no evidence that the number had ever been reissued or, for that matter, belonged to a Thomas Castello. This Social Security number was first issued in 1962, which was probably the year Keller applied for it when he got his first job, at around age twelve or thirteen.

According to Dulce Base history, Thomas Castello was born in Wheaton, Illinois, on April 23, 1941, which would have made him 80 at the time of this writing. Tal Levesque would now be 70, roughly the same age as Homer Keller. What all of this means, I'm not really sure.

In 1961—once again according to Dulce legend—Castello was stationed at Nellis Air Force Base as a military photographer with top secret clearance. Not long afterwards, he was transferred to West Virginia where he received top secret training in advanced intelligence photography at an undisclosed underground facility.

Castello remained with the Air Force until 1971 (once again according to Dulce lore) at which time he accepted a Security Technician position with the Rand Corporation in Santa Monica, California. In 1977, he was transferred to the Dulce facility, which was connected via underground shuttle system to Santa Fe where he and other Dulce workers lived and commuted from each day. After the Dulce War went down (in late '79 or early '80), Castello went underground (no pun intended) and his last known whereabouts, according to Cherry Hinkle, was Costa Rica.

Tal informed me that in the latter half of the 1960s he'd been stationed in West Virginia at an underground facility where he received some sort of super-secret training, which dovetails with the Tom Castello timeline. When Tal laid this West Virginia info on me, it was not more than a passing mention, and the details were probably intentionally vague as to whether the location was a military or civilian installation.

Like Tom Castello, Tal lived in Southern California during the late 1960s and '70s. In the late '70s, he moved to Santa Fe during the period that Castello allegedly lived there. In Santa Fe, Tal claimed that he worked as a private security contractor for the same firm that employed Castello, although Tal insists he never worked at Dulce Base for the Rand Corporation.

The Rand Corporation connection to underground bases (once again from the world according to Tal) began in 1946 when Rand Co. became involved in a research project funded by the U.S. Air Force to develop the "Planetran," a high-speed floating train that would theoretically travel from Los Angeles to New York City in under two hours. Although the Planetran was never officially constructed (as far as we know!), Tal claimed that early Planetran patents produced by Rand included atomic-powered boring machines that were used to create tunnel systems connecting a series of secret underground bases. This tube shuttle system ran from Kirtland Base to Santa Fe to Dulce Base to Los Alamos, and was serviced originally by a steam train (similar to the proposed Planetran), and then later replaced with a "Mag-Lev Tube Shuttle."

David Perkins recalled conversations in the late 1970s in which Tal mentioned having worked for Motorola, and that the company, at the time, was allegedly involved in top secret mind-control research. This was during the period when rumors were running rampant through the conspiracy research community that the government could watch you through your TV set. National Director of MUFON Walt Andrus, it should be noted, worked for many years as an executive with Motorola, which once again illustrates a curious overlap between prominent figures in ufology and the corporate sector, most particularly within the aviation industry and Skunk Work projects.

It was in a dumpster at a Motorola facility, Tal told David Perkins, that he came across the Rand blueprints for tunnel-boring machines and tube shuttles. On the down-low, Tal then shared these blueprints with other researchers, including Richard Sauder, who brought the existence of these materials to a wider audience with the release of his book, *Underground Bases and Tunnels* (1995).

Chapter 37

Jumping the Dulce shark

You need a scorecard to keep track of the different players who have promoted the Dulce Base mythos. Among those who skyrocketed to sudden yet fleeting Dulce Base stardom was Christa Tilton, a buxom blonde bombshell who exploded on to the saucer scene in the late 1980s with a tale that mirrored, in many respects, Myrna Hansen's underground alien base experience.

In the mid 1980s, Tilton reportedly tied the matrimonial knot with long time UFO raconteur Col. Wendelle Stevens at the same time Stevens was finishing up a five-year sentence at the State Prison in Douglas, Arizona for "Child Molesting, Furnishing Obscene Matter to a Minor, and Films and Pictures of Minors in Sex Act."[95] Stevens told *Spin Magazine* that the charges against him had been a CIA setup to discredit his work with the Swiss saucer contactee, Billy Meier.

In 2007, Bill Moore's early '80s correspondence with Bob Pratt was released, including this tantalizing tidbit:

> Lt. Col. Wendelle C. Stevens (USAF ostensibly retired) is in reality an active agent for AF Intelligence. He is part of the government's 'disinformation' program with respect to UFOs and civilian efforts. Doty advised me in strong terms to 'Forget about it and leave him alone!' He says he has known this for some time, but waited to see how much I knew before telling me.

More recently, during an appearance on Jimmy Church's *Fade to Black*,[96] Richard Doty confirmed that Wendelle Stevens had "cooperated" with the AFOSI's counter-intelligence operation. If true, might Christa Tilton have been targeted in the same manner as Paul Bennewitz? Was Wendelle Stevens to Christa Tilton as Bill Moore was to Paul Bennewitz?

Stevens and Tilton's whirlwind romance and subsequent marriage was documented, more or less, in a privately circulated manuscript entitled *UFO Abductions of Women: The Triad Experiment* co-authored by the Stevens-Tilton tag team. *The Triad Experiment* included Tilton's account of a 1972 abduction by promiscuous Pleadians who purportedly impregnated her with a human-alien hybrid daughter. When Billy Meier caught wind of Tilton's claims of this alleged Pleadian impregnation he called BS on her story, an irony not lost on anyone who has examined Meier's own implausible Pleadian claims.

Christa Tilton in the early 1990s

A good portion of *The Triad Experiment* covers a period in the summer of 1987 when an extraterrestrial presumably directed Tilton to travel to Arizona to hook-up with Wendelle Stevens. As mentioned, Stevens was then serving a prison stint, and Tilton visited him on several occasions in lock-up while at the same time staying at his house in Tucson. It was there that Tilton claimed she first encountered a mysterious military intelligence man who warned her against marrying Wendelle Stevens.

Another player in the Tilton-Stevens matrimonial saga was Clifford Stone. In a letter Tilton wrote to Stevens dated July 27, 1987, she encouraged Wendelle to "make contact with Sgt. Stone for I believe he can help us all. I really feel things are going strong…Honey, my ears are giving me fits so I'm going to go on…" At that point in the letter, Stevens noted:

I understood the reference to her ears giving her fits to mean she was hearing beeps and the undulating hum that precedes a contact. I was familiar with this from earlier discussions with her. This was the last line of the page. The last three words looked weak. She numbers her pages as she writes, and that was the end of page 6.

The next page started off boldly in an entirely different hand, a different way of forming the words and smaller in size. Even the slope of the letters was different throughout the new pages. There were no strikeouts and no corrections in the new part as opposed to her older familiar style. The words were obviously written at a faster pace. This is what the new part of the letter said:

> "This transmittal to your investigating team —
>
> "It is to your advantage that contact be made with this individual man [Clifford Stone] whom we have been in contact with for many of your years. You know how to approach these special ones. Sensitivity is a quality experience not known by us as you. Feelings — possessing these emotions cannot be interpreted until our experiments are transposed neuro-genetically by our accelerated process of what you know to be tachyon velocity. When tachyons were discovered thousands upon thousands of your years ago, many of your scientists lost control of their meaning—in a sense—to explain to you simply—everything ceased to exist in our realm of existence. Your friend, little Christa, sees our tachyon velocities in the realm in which we transmigrate our energy particles. This co-exists in a realm of space and time unknown to any human at this time. These tachyons are a major part of our ability to maneuver out craft in such an erratic manner to you..."

Suffice it to say, the apparent ET channeled in Christa's letter continued rambling on (as channeled ETs are often wont to do), but the gist of the alien message seemed to be that Clifford Stone was a pivotal player in this unfolding story of ET contact. The letter concluded with:

> "I am MAIJAN — your emissary for this time you give to me."

In a second letter, dated July 29, 1987, Christa mentioned to Stevens "a telephone conversation with Clifford E. Stone presently of Roswell, New Mexico. She said she had some strange experience he needed to share with me, and would I mind dropping him a line, and she furnished me his postal address…"

A month later, on August 20, Tilton bumped into cattle mute researcher Tom Adams at a Food Giant supermarket in Tucson. The reason that Adams, who lived in Paris, Texas, had shown up in Tucson was unclear, but whatever the case, he indicated to Christa that he was staying at a nearby Motel 6. Christa invited Adams back to her place, although there was nothing romantic suggested in the invitation; however, that aspect of their relationship was soon to change.

As they were in separate cars, Adams agreed to follow Christa back home, but when she made a turn at an intersection, he kept on going, and disappeared, which of course puzzled her, and she thought that perhaps Adams had missed the turn and had gone back to the Motel 6. When Christa arrived home, she called the Motel 6 asking for Tom Adams, but the desk clerk informed her that there was no Tom Adams registered there. Christa then dialed Adam's home number and got his answering machine, but "not wanting to alarm him, [she] left no message." Christa next called Clifford Stone to tell him about this curious turn of events. After their conversation, Stone was apparently able to get through to Adams, as right after that, Adams called Christa. As Christa recounted in *The Triad Experiment*:

> The real Tom Adams, who voice I recognized immediately, said, 'I hear you had a visitor in Tucson.' And playing it cool, I said, 'What do you mean?' I just wasn't sure whether I should elaborate on it or not, so I said, 'I had a visitor…' and then I explained what had happened. He said, 'Christa, you are just pulling my leg,' or words to that effect, and I said, 'Yes, I had a visitor who said he was you, and you know I have never seen you, and you

have not sent me a picture, but when I recovered from the shock, I realized that this man did not have your Texas drawl. And how did he know that I have never seen you and don't know what you look like. How did he know he could pull this off? How did he know I was going to that store, and at that time?'

Left unmentioned in *The Triad Experiment* was the fact that only one week after taking their wedding vows, Stevens annulled his marriage to Tilton. Whether the annulment was due to pressure coming from this mysterious military man is unknown. Shortly after, in December 1987, Tilton married Tom Adams.[97]

It was through Tom Adams that Tilton gained access to Dulce veterans like Gabe Valdez and Richard Doty—not to mention the dean of Dulce himself, Paul Bennewitz, who by the late '80s was still somewhat active in the field. This was around the time that Bennewitz reported ETs walking through his walls and shooting him up with drugs. Both Bill Moore and Richard Doty, on separate occasions, witnessed first-hand Bennewitz's mounting paranoia, describing him as spun out and barricaded inside his house chain-smoking cigarettes, waiting in fevered anticipation for the final ET showdown. In *Project Beta*, Greg Bishop recounted: "Bennewitz told Moore that after the aliens injected him, they would make him drive his car into the desert in the middle of the night, but he couldn't remember what he did after he got there."[98] Around this time, Bennewitz's family committed him to a mental health facility for nervous exhaustion. After a month in treatment, Bennewitz was released and afterwards all but disappeared from ufology, not a surprising development given the fact that his UFO research had played a major role in delivering him to the edge of madness.

During the period Tilton hooked up with Tom Adams is when she first started talking about being abducted in July 1987 and transported by alien greys to an underground facility. It was there she was handed over to a man in a red military-like jumpsuit with a serpent insignia. Tilton recalled being led through a tunnel with computerized check points and stepping on a platform and being scanned, after which the computer issued an identification card. Tilton was told by her jump-suited guide that:

> ...they had entered Level One of a seven-level underground facility. Christa goes on relating how she was eventually taken down to Level Five, where she reports having seen alien craft and little grey alien entities in some of the areas that she passed through.
>
> In one large room she saw computerized gauges hooked to large tanks and large arms that extended from some tubing down into the tanks. She noticed a humming sound, smelled formaldehyde, and had the impression that a liquid was being stirred into the tanks. She was not shown the contents of these tanks. Christa made a drawing of much of what she claims to have witnessed during her abduction.[99]

Due to Tilton's association with Tom Adams and Paul Bennewitz — and the ufological street cred it afforded—she earned the reputation, for at least a bright shining moment, as the Dulce Base go-to-gal. In 1990, Norio Hayakawa assisted in the production of a Nippon Television documentary about Dulce Base and Area 51 that included interviews with Tilton, Bob Lazar and another anonymous whistle blower filmed in the shadows, none other than our old pal Tal Levesque. Like any good UFO documentary, Nippon Television rented a helicopter and flew Christa around the general Dulce area searching for an entrance to the rumored underground base. During the production of the documentary, Tilton tried to persuade Paul Bennewitz to participate. Bennewitz responded with the following letter:

Dear Christa,
    Relative to your letter concerning getting together with the Japanese and yourself; I am afraid I will have to say no at this

time; I just do not have the time to spare nor do I want to go public in any way be it here or in Japan. I really have nothing to tell them or yourself except to rehash the same old thing which with the writing of my book has become unimportant to me. The book takes a completely different slant and I am just not ready to talk about it to anyone. Vallee wanted to come and talk with me yet I put him off also, at least to another day.

A fee to give an interview is not of interest either as I have no need for any money. One does not know what the final tape will look like after cutting; they can make it say anything that they want it to say, so I am just not interested. Sorry to take this approach however I have grown tired of the distortions and untruths that have seemed rampant; it is certainly doing no one any good.

Please do not be angry with me; I am just being candid and saying how it is. Maybe someday the book will be published and

The enigmatic Tal Levesque during the filming of the Japanese documentary on alien underground bases

then the true story will be revealed. Give my regrets to your Japanese contacts and let me hear from you once in a while.

Best Regards,
Paul F. Bennewitz

By the time Bennewitz composed this letter he had long gotten over any desire to do any more Dulce fly-overs. The last time he'd been involved in just such a stunt, Bennewitz organized a helicopter flight for a CBS news crew during which they encountered those same ubiquitous "lights in the sky" often witnessed over Mount Archuleta, and at the same time had a run-in with some military helicopters. Greg Valdez recalled a ride-along with his dad, Gabe, when they observed a Jet Ranger land at the Dulce airport:

> We were just driving around town and a Jet Ranger lands right in town, and my dad says this aircraft is not from around here, let's go see if they need help. So guess who jumps out of the helicopter? It's Paul Bennewitz, and he's freaking out! As soon as he lands, two Chinook helicopters landed and one of them was having mechanical problems. My dad attempted to board one of the Chinooks and was met by armed Delta Forces. You could see the Delta Force insignia on their flight suits. They finally fixed whatever was wrong with the helicopter and then took off."[100]

Greg Valdez believes (as did his father) that Mount Archuleta/ Redding Ranch was an offsite military testing facility, and that the two Chinooks that chased off Bennewitz had been on security duty that day to keep prying eyes away. This theory, of course, runs counter to the story Doty has promoted: that he set up props at Mount Archuleta (such as tubes planted in the ground to resemble ventilation shafts) to fool Bennewitz into believing there was actually an alien base there, a ruse intended to throw him off the scent of the secret testing going on Kirtland. This is the switch and bait method of UFO disinformation: Watch what this hand is doing—don't pay attention to the other. As Greg Valdez recalled:

We found the ventilation shafts. They were not props. Paul never hiked into Mount Archuleta with us because he was a two day a pack smoker (laughs). He flew it in an aircraft. So a lot of the stuff that has been called props, such as the crash site—those were not props. You couldn't find some of this stuff unless you hiked—you had to crawl through scrub oak, up and down canyons. So Doty was kind of bullshitting on that, because it was not props. He was trying to deflect because he shouldn't have told people there was an operation going on at the [Dulce] site. Are they going to dig a ventilation hole in the side of a mountain when Paul Bennewitz was just flying overhead in a Cessna? I don't think so—Doty was just trying to spin it to other researchers saying it was just props out there and there was nothing to worry about—A lot of things called props you couldn't see from the air, and we had a hard time finding them [on the ground]."[101]

Chapter 38

The Bennewitz Papers

In 1991, Christa Tilton privately published *The Bennewitz Papers*, a chronicle of her research, and alleged experiences, concerning the Dulce underground base and interactions with Paul Bennewitz. It can be assumed that much of the source material for *The Bennewitz Papers* came to Tilton through her then husband Tom Adams, who was one of the initial recipients of the Bennewitz/Dulce materials in the mid 1980s. *The Bennewitz Papers* predated other seminal works on the subject, among them Greg Bishop's *Project Beta* and Christian Lambright's *X Descending*. Unlike these later efforts, Tilton's book depicted Richard Doty in the exact manner that Doty, no doubt, preferred himself to be portrayed—as a whistle-blowing patriot do-gooder trying to get to the bottom of the UFO mystery who was unjustly scape-goated as a fall guy in the Bennewitz affair.

In *The Bennewitz Papers,* Tilton provided some of the same information Doty later passed along to Greg Bishop. Unlike Tilton, Bishop used additional sources to corroborate or refute Doty's claims, whereas Tilton seems to have taken Doty at face value. As Tilton noted in the intro to *The Bennewitz Papers*: "Many of the actual participants in the 'Bennewitz Affair' refused interviews with the author except AFOSI Agent Richard Doty (Ret.) His correspondence by mail gave me much insight on how the counter-intelligence agents do their job..."[102]

Conversely, Tilton cast Bill Moore as a malevolent actor in the Bennewitz psychodrama, which of course was the fashionable thing to do in the aftermath of the '89 MUFON Symposium when Moore burned as many bridges as humanly possible during his presentation. Tilton claimed that she approached Moore for an interview but he declined, although she said he replied with some "nasty letters," which wouldn't have been all that surprising as by this time Moore had pretty much washed his hands of ufology, as ufology likewise had of him.

Prior to the publication of *The Bennewitz Papers*, Tilton published an article called "Going Underground" in which she related her Dulce Base experience as well as citing similar stories, such as those of Myrna Hansen. Shortly after this article appeared, Myrna Hansen contacted Tilton apparently out of the blue surprised to see her name again in print again after so many years. Hansen told Tilton she had much more of a story to share than was publicly known and that perhaps one day she would tell all. That was basically the gist of their conversation as related in *The Bennewitz Papers*. Of course, Tilton made many curious claims, as well as some outright fabrications along the way, and I suspect her alleged conversations with Myrna Hansen may have been just such a construct—not only to enhance Tilton's ufological street cred, but to reinforce the narrative that she was a serious researcher with serious contacts, digging deep into the Dulce depths.

On page 17 of *The Bennewitz Papers*, Tilton asks a provocative question:

> What about the possibility of a government-sponsored abduction of Myrna Hansen? Could our government somehow beam alien images in our minds from some type of implant? Could the aliens really be our own government agents carefully manipulating us into believing we are being abducted by extraterrestrials?"

At the time Tilton wrote these words, she was corresponding with Martin Cannon, who in his monograph *The Controllers: A New Theory of Alien Abductions* had put forth this very same theory: that alien abductions were a cover for U.S. government mind-control operations. This theory would soon expand into what became known as MILABS (an acronym for military abductions), which added an extra layer to Cannon's theory to the effect that alien abductions themselves were real, and that government agents were kidnapping abductees, and using them as "deep black operatives" in military intelligence operations. Some MILAB scenarios even suggested that the military and the aliens were working in cahoots, which brings us back full circle to the Dulce base legend and similar stories of a secret pact between our government and White Draco reptilians from the Zeta Reticuli star system.

Elsewhere in *The Bennewitz Papers*, Christa recounts a conversation with Richard Doty which oozes with MILAB-like implications. Tilton said that Doty:

> ...told me that Myrna and her son had a very real encounter with something very strange. What she did state made Doty believe she was somehow describing an underground area that he felt fit the description of an underground weapons facility. He stated he was quite taken aback upon hearing her describe this area because the information he had would seem to definitely indicate she had been taken to 'the underground weapons STORAGE AREA.' He also stated that Myrna and her son may have accidentally encountered a highly classified government project and was legally detained until she could be possibly drugged and then removed from this area. So in essence, Doty is stating that abductions such as these types could happen. But what struck me as odd is his description to me. It seemed like Doty was telling me something he had knowledge of in this particular case. I could be wrong, but it is just a hunch...

While Tilton's claimed contact with Myrna Hansen has not been independently verified, Christa did indeed befriend Cherry Hinkle not long after Hinkle began sharing her Dulce Base revelations. The two women later had a falling out when Tilton went on record stating that the Tom Castello story had most likely been fabricated. Hinkle shot back that Tilton also made up a bunch of stuff and so the two women ultimately agreed on not much more than the existence of a secret underground base located somewhere near Dulce.

Tal informed me that, in recent years, Cherry Hinkle had become some type of disinformation agent, although my interactions with her led me to believe she was a kind-hearted, though perhaps semi-delu-sional lady still sticking to her story that Tom Castello was the real-deal Dulce base flashgun hero. As for Tilton, Tal claims he was on to her from the start and warned others to steer clear of those same charms that apparently beguiled Wendelle Stevens and later Tom Adams. Tilton's ultimate gambit—according to Tal—was that of an agent provocateur sent in to vacuum up information and disrupt the UFO research community. Regardless of her actual intent, it certainly seems that she accomplished that goal.

What Tal was referring to—in regards to Tilton performing the role of "agent provocateur"—concerned a salacious rumor that found its way to the nexus of Dulce Base "researchers" we've previously mentioned: Tal Levesque, Bill Hamilton and John Grace. The rumor in this instance concerned Christa dumping Tom Adams to run off on a romantic romp with a mysterious intelligence agent named John Wallis, who was serving the role as Christa's "handler."

Tilton's purported lover/handler, John Wallis, was first mentioned in an interview with Christa that appeared in *Crux* issue #4, Spring of 1989, that included this lead in:

UFO ABDUCTEE TRACKED BY GOVERNMENT AGENT

...CHRISTA TILTON HAS HAD COMMUNICATION BY PHONE AND IN PERSON WITH A MAN WHO NOT ONLY EXHIBITS INTIMATE KNOWLEDGE OF HER EXPERI-ENCES AND HER LIFE IN GENERAL – HE IS ALSO AN AGENT OF THE FEDERAL GOVERNMENT. CHRISTA

WAS INTERVIEWED REGARDING HER CONTACTS
WITH THIS MYSTERIOUS INDIVIDUAL...

In said interview, Tilton recounted her first meeting in August of 1987 (just one month after her alleged Dulce Base abduction experience) with John Wallis (referred to in the interview as "W.C."), who appeared on Tilton's doorstep flashing an identification card with "DIS" on it. During this meeting, Wallis warned Christa not to marry Wendelle Stevens, apparently because of his research into UFOs and abductees. Wallis also informed Christa that he knew about her history as an alien abductee, and was aware of a recent visit she had made to Dulce, warning her to stay away from there, and that it wasn't a safe place to visit. Later in the interview, Tilton stated:

> At the time of that Tulsa visit, [Wallis] proceeded to tell me about an abduction experience that I had had in Tucson in July of 1987. The only people who knew the details of that particular experience had been Budd Hopkins, who had hypnotized me, and me. I have no reason to think that this man ever had contact with Budd Hopkins. He claimed that he was there with others to view this abduction, and that there were photos and videotapes to prove it...They removed a fetus from me...I don't know if it was staged or what. But it appears that the government has a great deal of interest in my case and in the genetic experiments that are going on...
>
> [Wallis] feels it is his duty to keep these secrets. He is a very patriotic man. But he has told me that there are several alien factions on earth and that some of them can pass for human. The man is cautious. He knows that I am going public with my story; but he wants me to be cautious, too, about what I say...
>
> I spoke for a UFO group in Dallas and he was there in the audience. He was simply monitoring what information I was

giving out to the public. He asked me some questions from the audience. There was about seven minutes between his first question and his last. We received the 'official' audio tapes of that meeting and that entire seven minutes had been deleted; he was not on the tape at all. How did we know about the missing 7 minutes? Because we had made our own tape of the presentation. So I definitely feel he was in contact with someone in that group and was maybe calling some shots. He will not put his voice on tape, not even on an answering machine, and he will not allow himself to be photographed...

Around the time of Tilton's *Crux* interview, Martin Cannon caught wind of the rumor that Tilton had ran off with the enigmatic Mr. Wallis. According to a June 1989 letter, Cannon reached out to:

...another researcher, an odd fellow named Tal Levesque, to see if he knew any more about Christa. Turns out he knew a lot...He'd heard that Christa had left her husband; apparently, this Wallis fellow had taken off with her, telling her that Uncle Sam was going to use her as the "channel" through which the government would reveal the grim fact of alien abduction to the general populace. Until the day of Grand Revelation, she was to be kept under the watchful eye of the military; presumably in one of those underground bases Christa claims to have visited.

Quite a story. I didn't accept it at face value, obviously; everything Tal says should, if possible, be checked against. A few days later, Christa sent me a very strange and disturbing letter, which I enclose...[103]

Below is Tilton's response, dated May 20, 1989:

Dear Mr. Cannon,

I understand that you have inquired about me and my relationship with a certain military man. First of all, I understand that you wrote for CAUFO [*California UFO*] magazine. No, I was not aware that anything about me or my relationship (which was totally blown out of proportion) would be in the most recent issue. So it came as quite a surprise to me and my husband and to Wallis. I supposed what concerns me most of all is what has concerned Tom and I since our marriage almost two years ago. There were many people who decided to take Tom under their wing and try to persuade him that he should dump me because I was nothing but an evil witch. This only made us cling closer together because as you must know, there are vicious people among the ranks of UFOLOGY. If I had known what I know now I would have never gone public with my story.

So my concern is for the other evening when you called my husband and he returned your call. Of course we were curious about your interest because unfortunately you got caught in the middle of a small wager we we're having with some others. You see, my supposed elopement with Wallis was deliberately fabricated by we three to see just how far the rumor would go and who would spread it. So far we have nailed it down in your area to Tal LeVesque, Bill Hamilton (who I led to believe this story) and Capt. John Grace of NAR. You see, I knew Bill was calling me quite a lot and we were unsure of his intentions toward me. Also John Grace. When we received your call we couldn't believe it. First of all, you did not know either me or my husband or our personal lives. So when you asked Tom if his wife had run off with Wallis, Tom was at a loss for words. Whether I had or hadn't isn't anyone's business, but many think it is their place to take matters into their own hands, You see, just because I told Bill about my visit to Vegas and my problems at home (again which were a fabrication) I, [Wallis] and Tom wanted to see how far the rumor would go before it exploded. I am sorry you got caught in the middle...

I also understand you wanted to speak to me about mind control in my situation. Funny, John Grace said the same thing. Anyway, since my husband and I got married and suffered all these attacks in UFOLOGY we decided to bone up on the subject of mind control because we are convinced a lot of these people are under such a spell and so I will mention just a few books we have studied:

1.   The Manipulated Mind-Denise Winn
2.   The Mind Stealers-Samuel Chavkin
3.   Operation Mind Control-Bowart
4.   In Search for the Manchurian Candidate

We have a full library of these types of books, all of which I have read. You see Mr. Cannon, I am not under any mind control techniques...In fact a lot of people are not aware of my own families connections to high-ranking military officials in which they worked with for quite a number of years. My whole family is military and so it would be alright for me to say that my connections with Wallis are simply for information and protection and to label him a over-the-shoulder "Big Brother" only made us all laugh. So I guess the last laugh is with all of us. I do not rule out the possibility that mind control techniques are rampant in UFOLOGY and we must do all we can to stop these CIA dis-informants that lurk at all our conventions and join all our UFO organizations! They are not only bumbling idiots, but they are harming our UFO abductees. These people are very fragile and to hear that they have been taken over by a fluid-sucking grey alien makes me very angry.

We not only have two years before the evil aliens invade, but we have rampant dis-information campaigns to scare the daylights out of us all. I would like you to read CRUX #4 over and see if you couldn't get something positive out of it. Dr. Thomas Bullard wrote and said he was so impressed with the way I turned what could be a devastating experience into a positive one and it will give all abductees hope. Well, that is my plan. I am here only to serve in positive ways. I am not the evil bitch people make me out to be. I think you will find, if you question enough of these people, that most, if any at all, have never laid eyes on me. So I hope nothing anyone has said to you has tainted me in your eyes. I would love to believe that statement, but Tom and I are realists. We have been the source of devastating rumors for months and months.

As far as Wallis, that is not his real name. He is a high-ranking AF man at Nellis AFB. He is a kind family man and knows a lot about my underground experience. He is not in control of my mind…

Tom and I wish you luck. And again, if you hear anything personal about someone's relationship, it is best not to get involved. Tom and I never get involved in anyone's personal life. We just want to live our lives in peace. We wish you the same.

Christa Tilton Adams

It's interesting to note that Christa referred to her Air Force handler, John Wallis, as "a very patriotic man. But he has told me that there are several alien factions on earth…" It seems plausible—if indeed Christa's story can be believed—that John Wallis might have been our old friend Richard Doty. As previously noted, both Bill Moore and Doty have gone on record stating that Wendelle Stevens was an AFOSI asset, and so Tilton's short-lived marriage to Stevens would have conceivably placed her in the same orbit as Doty and other AFOSI operatives. Also of note is that Doty was a key source for *The Bennewitz Papers*, so there was evidently some contact between Tilton and Doty, although to what extent is unclear. Tilton described her interactions with Doty as strictly correspondence and phone conversations. At one point, according to *The Bennewitz Papers*, Christa attempted to set up a face-to-face meeting, but Doty ended up being a no-show. Clifford Stone, like Doty, was also a key source for *The Bennewitz Papers*, which included excerpts of Bennewitz's rambling letters to Stone concerning the alien hierarchy living at Dulce Base. Stone also provided Christa with chapters from a book Bennewitz was working on which apparently was never completed entitled *The Cyanon Gauntlet*.

There are those who suspected that Tilton had been playing the role of a honey-pot with her sudden marriage to Tom Adams in December of 1987. It can't be emphasized enough how key a role Adams played in the UFO and cattle mute research communities of the '70s and '80s. In this regard, his research into mystery helicopters and mutilations would obviously have been of great interest to AFOSI, and other sectors of the intelligence community, particularly if they suspected that he'd happened upon sensitive information related to national security and secret projects.

As we learned from the Bennewitz Affair, one method to derail a UFO researcher is to feed them wild stories from supposed government sources that the researcher then regurgitates and in the process discredits themselves when the story falls apart—which may have been the ultimate design behind the John Wallis episode, a rumor Christa claimed was something she and Adams had concocted to see how disinformation spread in the UFO research community. However, the suggestion that Adams was involved in such machinations runs counter to anything he'd ever been involved with in the past. Although Adams was certainly open to the prospect that UFOs were piloted by visitors from other planets, he was nonetheless a careful and thorough researcher not prone to jumping to conclusions or making outlandish claims, and we really don't know how much he actually knew about this Wallis affair, or the possibility that Tilton was simply messing with his head by spreading these rumors.

Another consequence of his marriage to Tilton was that it drove a fatal wedge between Adams and the many researchers he'd long worked with and considered friends, most specifically his long-time running mate Gary Massey, who felt that Christa had intentionally poisoned his relationship with Adams, as after the marriage communications basically ceased between those two old buddies who had spent so much time roaming the high desert on the cattle mute trail.

Tom and Christa were divorced on April 22, 1991. In the fallout from their ill-fated marriage, Adams removed himself from the UFO and cattle mute research fields, spending his final days as a clerk at a Dollar General Store in Tulsa, Oklahoma. He passed away on August 20, 2014.

As for Christa, she remained active in ufology until the mid 1990s, occasionally appearing as a speaker at UFO conferences, as well as turning up now and then in the always-entertaining letters section of Jim Moseley's *Saucer Smear*, where you could find her trading barbs with such ufological gadflies as Bill Moore and the litigiously minded Dr. Harley Byrd.

One of these *Saucer Smear* exchanges featured a dispute Christa engaged in with the aforementioned Dr. Byrd, who claimed to be the grandson of Admiral Byrd. Harley was fond of repeating the rumor that his grandfather the Admiral actually discovered an entryway into the inner earth during his exploration of the North Pole, which was apparently Harley's claim to fame by association and provided his bonafides as a UFO promoter and Hollow Earth devotee. Whether he was actually related to Admiral Byrd is another matter entirely.

Christa's kerfuffle with Byrd resulted in a twenty-five page booklet she authored entitled *Going 2 Extremes: An Expose of Harley Byrd Compiled by Christa Tilton and Other Victims of Harley Byrd in the UFO Field*. According to Jim Moseley, in the December 5, 1994 issue of *Saucer Smear*:

Christa is quite understandably mad at Inner Earth advocate Harley Byrd for having lifted large parts of her book 'The Bennewitz Papers' together with other material, and he now offers this material for sale for his own profit, in a book called 'The Dulce Papers'. Christa's exposé includes a series of letters to her from Byrd. First there were love letters, when [Byrd] thought she would come into town and lecture at his recent Los Angeles convention. Then came the hate letters, when she didn't show up and when she also threatened to sue him for the above-mentioned lifting of material.

Also included in this tome are a number of fake threatening legal forms & letters that Harley has a habit of writing, and misspelling; and there is a copy of a real legal paper indicating that Harley was convicted of indecent exposure in 1991.

Christa is charging a mere five dollars for this priceless gem of non-UFO non-research, and she can be reached at: 2163 S. 78th, Tulsa, Oklahoma 74129-2421...

By the late 1990s, Christa had all but disappeared from ufology, and according to the social security death index, she officially exited the earth plane on July 17, 2012, a mere 60 years of age.[104]

Chapter 39

Just another flash Gun hero

In the mid-1990s, a fellow named Phil Schneider picked up the Tom Castello torch, presenting himself as a whistle-blowing former Dulce Base worker with a laser scar on his chest to prove it. Schneider had been on the fringes of ufology for a number of years, and along with his pal, Ron Rummel (aka 'Crestor'), produced a 'zine called *The Alien Digest* that ran the gamut of the UFO-conspiratorial smorgasbord: alien bases on the moon, Alternative 3, MJ-12, Richard Shaver's Deros, Dr. Teller's Anti-Gravity research, etc., etc. Rummel and Schneider took occasional UFO-themed road trips, including a jaunt in December 1989 to the outskirts of Area 51 where they claimed to have filmed a flying saucer from the parking lot of the "Little A-Le-Inn".[105]

It was through these ufological endeavors that Schneider networked with Tal Levesque, and it was Tal (at least according to Tal) who first turned him on to the Dulce Base-Tom Castello material. John Lear also had a role in promoting Schneider's story, so all of these confluences helped elevate him in the field of conspiratorial ufology.

Schneider stated that the reason he decided to blow the Dulce Base whistle was due to the passing of his 'zinester pal, Rummel, who Schneider identified as a former Air Force intelligence officer. Rummel's body was discovered in Macleay Park in Portland, Oregon, in August 1993, the apparent victim of suicide, having shot himself in the mouth with a handgun. Schneider claimed that Rummel's death was actually an assassination orchestrated by Deep State bad actors to silence his research into the Reagan-era Star Wars program, and its alleged connections to mind control, brain implants and the "accidental deaths" of over thirty British scientists. This was information Rummel planned to release in a forthcoming book that apparently would have shocked the world had it not been for his untimely demise.

Not long after Rummel's passing, Schneider rolled out his version of the Dulce Base story, and soon became a rising star on the UFO-Patriot lecture circuit with tales about how he'd worked at Dulce and apparently even had some laser scars on his chest which he'd show-off as proof that he was a survivor of the Dulce fire-fight.[106] According to Schneider:

Back in 1954, under the Eisenhower administration, the federal government decided to circumvent the Constitution of the United States and form a treaty with alien entities. It was called the 1954 Greada Treaty, which basically made the agreement that the aliens involved could take a few cows and test their implanting techniques on a few human beings, but that they had to give details about the people involved. Slowly, the aliens altered the bargain until they decided they wouldn't abide by it at all. Back in 1979, this was the reality, and the firefight at Dulce occurred quite by accident.

I was involved in building an addition to the deep underground military base at Dulce, which is probably the deepest base. It goes down seven levels and over 2.5 miles deep. At that particular time, we had drilled four distinct holes in the desert, and we were going to link them together and blow out large sections at a time. My job was to go down the holes and check the rock samples, and recommend the explosive to deal with the particular rock. As I was headed down there, we found ourselves amidst a large cavern that was full of outer-space aliens, otherwise known as large Greys. I shot two of them. At that time, there were 30 people down there. About 40 more came down after this started, and all of them got killed. We had surprised a whole underground base of existing aliens. Later, we found out that they had been living on our planet for a long time, perhaps a million years. This could explain a lot of what is behind the theory of ancient astronauts. Anyway, I got shot in the chest with one of their weapons, which was a box on their body, that blew a hole in me and gave me a nasty dose of cobalt radiation. I have had cancer because of that...

After barely making it out of Dulce with this life, Schneider allegedly landed a gig at Area 51 where he witnessed Bob Lazar-type scientists reverse-engineering ET craft and ultimately decided that enough was enough, he was going to blow the whistle on this whole rotten government-working-with-the-ETs-deal as well as everything else going on at Area 51 that included a mash-up of Montauk and Philadelphia Experiment conspiracies.

Phil Schneider's family background was chock full of paranormal intrigue, including claims that his father, Otto Schneider, had fought for both sides during World War II, first as a German U-Boat Commander and then later as a repatriated (à la Operation Paperclip) U.S. Naval Captain who was involved in nuclear testing programs as well as serving on the *U.S.S. Eldridge* during the fabled Philadelphia Experiment disappearing act. While Schneider's father did indeed serve as a captain in the Navy, the German U-Boat story was a complete fabrication, along with Schneider's other fanciful Philadelphia Experiment and Montauk Project yarns.[107]

According to Norio Hayakawa, the official-looking Navy documents Schneider passed off as evidence of his dad's connection to the Philadelphia Experiment were actually forgeries Phil created on blank Navy stationery that had been absconded from his father's estate. These spurious letters—allegedly written by Otto Schneider during the 1940s and '50s—conveniently name-dropped many of the purported MJ-12 members like Admiral Roscoe Hillenkoetter and Lt. Gen. Nathan Twining. Even Nikola Tesla and J. Edgar Hoover appeared in some of these letters, as it was evident Schneider had steeped himself in

MJ-12 and Philadelphia Experiment lore as a means to further embroider his fantasy world.

Schneider claimed he had worked as a government contractor until 1993 after which he started his Dulce Base whistle-blower career. Gabe Valdez investigated many of the claims associated with the Dulce Base story, including those of Schneider. Valdez obtained copies of Schneider's Social Security benefits statement, which showed that he'd received disability payments starting in 1981 at the same time he was supposedly working on secret government projects. These statements also showed that during the period Schneider was allegedly working at Dulce and/or Area 51, he was employed for a at Brown's Shoe Store in Portland. When confronted with these discrepancies, Schneider countered that he actually had two Social Security numbers, although he provided zero evidence to support this seemingly spurious claim.

As for his disability, Schneider reportedly suffered from mental illness and was a self-mutilator, which explained the chest scars and missing fingers he claimed were a result of some ET laser weapon that purportedly zapped him during the Dulce War shoot 'em-up. These allegations of self-mutilation were recently confirmed by a FBI-FOIA release:

> Schneider was a former patient of Dammasch State Hospital, Wilsonville, Oregon from July 30 1968 to January 29, 1969. While at Dammasch, Schneider was characterized as schizophrenic with chronic and differentiated traits. Under stress Schneider would mutilate himself for self attention and had amputated two fingers and a thumb...

Easily the strangest nugget in these FOIA files was the fact that Schneider had acquired a sizable quantity of radioactive material in December 1974 from a fellow named George Meyer. According to an FBI report, Meyer took Schneider to a house in Portland where:

Schneider removed approximately 300 pounds of material...
since then [Schneider] claims to have suffered from nausea,
hemorrhaging and soreness in his extremities. He had kept the
material under a bed in his room...some of it was given or sold
to unknown individuals in Portland...

On 3/22/75, a Portland source advised that he had been
in the house of one Philip Schneider...at which time Schneider
displayed a quantity of material that he [Schneider] described as
being material he was going to use to make a 'nuclear device'...
[Schneider] lives in Portland in a very dilapidated house alone
and is allegedly conducting unknown-type experiments in an
adjacent building. Source claims he is keeping the material
under his bed and supposedly had to get rid of the bed because it
had become contaminated with radioactivity.

[FBI Special Agent] O'Rourke advised they were unable
to locate subject's father who is a retired Navy captain but they
were able to locate the subject's uncle who is a medical doctor
in the Portland area. The doctor was interviewed and stated that
his nephew had given him two chunks of the material which the
doctor readily produced from his office. After checking with
Energy Research and Development Administration (ERDA)...
they contacted the State Health facility in Portland and, under
secure conditions, transported the above material to their laboratory for examination. The material was examined and our Agents
were advised that the material was indeed radioactive and at least
one piece was identified as thorium...The doctor advised our
Agents that subject claimed to have 80 pounds of this material.

According to the FBI's March 26, 1975 interview with Schneider:

On advice from Dr. Schneider [Phil's uncle] and Philip's landla-
dy, most of the material was discarded in the trash. Some of it

was given or sold to unknown individuals in Portland. Philip stated he had no idea possession of this material might violate federal statute or present a health hazard. He had no intention or capability to manufacture a 'nuclear device.'

Like his pal Ron Rummel, Schneider's death became fodder for the New World Order conspiracy crowd due to claims that he'd been assassinated by government agents keen on keeping a lid on the Dulce Base story. This theory was first floated by Schneider's widow, Cynthia Drayer, who enlisted Gabe Valdez to look into her husband's death, meanwhile attempting to solicit Gabe for funds to support her cause to bring the supposed shocking truth of Schneider's death to the public.

As for Schneider's death, the officers who responded apparently overlooked a catheter wrapped around Phil's neck which was only discovered during his autopsy. This fact helped feed into the rumor mill that Schneider had been assassinated by the same secret government goons who supposedly did-in his pal, Ron Rummel. Gabe Valdez was able to acquire the autopsy report from Phil Schneider's brother who worked as a police officer in Clackamas County, which revealed that the coroner's office concluded that Phil's death was indeed a suicide. But, of course, that's what *They* would want you to believe…

Chapter 40

Bob Bigelow's spooky squad

Founded in 1995 by Robert Bigelow (of Bigelow Aerospace), the National Institute of Discovery Science (NIDS) was established to investigate reports of unexplained phenomena using a science-based methodology. Key players on NIDS' staff included purported Aviary members Kit Green, Col. John Alexander and Hal Puthoff. There were also rumors circulating that, at one time or another, Richard Doty had also been involved with NIDS.

Due to the presence of such former government intelligence agency insiders, NIDS gained the reputation in some circles as a spooky squad. NIDS' two main focus areas were cattle mutilations and those mysterious black triangle aircraft that first materialized around the time that the Bennewitz affair and Dulce Base stories were making the ufological rounds. Prior to forming NIDS, Bigelow briefly funded Bob Lazar's research through an LLC called the *Zeta Reticuli Corporation*.

Shortly after launching NIDS, Bigelow entered into an agreement with MUFON to provide financial backing for its volunteer field investigators (a project dubbed the "STAR Team"), the intent of which was to form rapid response teams for deployment to UFO sightings. In return, MUFON provided Bigelow access to its backlog of case files, an agreement that later led to accusations that some of these files had disappeared from the MUFON tracking system.

Among other notables brought into the NIDS stable (cattle mute pun intended) was Gabe Valdez. For Valdez, NIDS seemed a golden opportunity to explore the cattle mutilation phenomenon to a greater depth (and with deeper pockets) than he'd been able to while working as a New Mexico state trooper where the cattle mutes were a sideline. According to Greg Valdez, much of what his father uncovered about the cattle mutes was never publicly revealed due to a non-disclosure agreement with NIDS, although Gabe would occasionally share some tantalizing tidbits. In a 2009 *UFO Hunters* episode, Gabe was asked by host Bill Birnes what he thought was the most anomalous cattle mute evidence he'd uncovered:

> Gabe Valdez: "They mutilated this animal…they didn't complete the whole process, and they left a fetus inside the animal that looked like a human, a monkey and a frog. It didn't have any bones in the head, it was all full of water. It was probably about forty-two inches long. But something went wrong with whatever they were doing."
>
> Bill Birnes: "What you're implying is that the cow was being used as an incubation chamber for a cloned creature."
>
> Gabe Valdez: "Exactly. We took it and had it analyzed. It was very confusing to the veterinarian.

In *Dulce Base: The Truth and Evidence*, Greg Valdez explores the theory that there were two secret labs and/or bases involved in the Dulce area cattle mutes, the first located at Los Alamos—approximately seventy-seven air miles from Dulce—and a second, more remote lab, at what's known as the Redding Ranch, located in the same general vicinity of the alleged Dulce Base. The Mundo Ridge mountain range provides a straight line between these two locations (Los Alamos Labs and Redding Ranch) and mysterious aircraft would frequently travel down Mundo Ridge on a flight path leading directly to Los Alamos.

Col. John Alexander—it should be noted—was a prominent figure at Los Alamos during the late 1980s where he was involved in the development of non-lethal weaponry, some of which sounded quite similar to what may have been employed on poor Paul Bennewitz, such as the mysterious orbs that appeared to have been monitoring his activities, and the "alien beams" he suspected were scanning his brainwaves.

In the mid '90s, Bob Bigelow purchased the Skinwalker Ranch in Utah and deployed a NIDS team there to collect evidence of reported high weirdness, some of which mirrored Dulce stories featuring UFOs, cattle mutilations, orbs, etc., in addition to the type of shapeshifting critters that inhabit Native American lore. There are those who have theorized that Skinwalker Ranch was utilized in a similar fashion as Dulce: partly as a form of disinformation, but also as a site to conduct secret government projects.

James Carrion—MUFON director from 2006-2009—reportedly uncovered evidence suggesting that NIDS representatives had embellished, or misrepresented, certain claims associated with Skinwalker Ranch. All of these stories surrounding Skinwalker, NIDS, and secret government projects have created an aura of secrecy around Bigelow, who over the years has held his cards exceedingly close to the vest.

Chapter 41

At the top of the Aviary birdhouse

ndless conjecture has surrounded the identity of the mystery man referred to as Falcon, who sat at the top of the Aviary birdhouse, flapping his shadowy wings. The unmasking of Falcon became one of the favorite guessing games at UFO conferences and on internet bulletin boards during the 1990s, and it seems nearly everyone had their own Falcon theory that disagreed with the next person's Falcon theory. Some have suggested Col. Barry Hennessey as a probable candidate for Falcon-hood. Conversely, Richard Doty has gone on record claiming that former CIA director Richard Helms was Falcon. Of course, anything uttered by Doty should be taken with an inordinate amount of salt.

Over several years, Greg Bishop prodded his pal Bill Moore to reveal the identity of this enigmatic bird. At the time that Bishop was writing *Project Beta*—in the early 2000s—Moore was unwilling to flip the lid on Falcon's identity, but a couple years later—after Falcon had presumably flapped away to that big birdhouse in the sky—Moore finally revealed that Falcon was a former high-ranking CIA official named Heinrich August Rositzke, better known as Harry, who served as the chief of military intelligence in London, Paris and Germany during World War II. After the war, Rositzke served as the CIA's Soviet division chief. Rositzke "retired" from The Company in 1970...but as the old adage goes, you never actually "retire." It was later claimed by Bill Moore that during the airing of *UFO Cover-up Live!*, Rositzke sat in the studio audience in Gulf Breeze quietly observing his counterintelligence masterpiece unfold.

According to Nick Redfern in *Flying Saucers from the Kremlin: UFOs, Russian Meddling, Soviet Spies & Cold War Secrets*:

...U.S. Intelligence learned to its consternation during both the 1970s and the 1980s, an unclear number of unnamed UFO researchers, with important links to the U.S. defense industry, had been compromised by Soviet agents. It went like this: those saucer-seekers who worked in the field of defense, and who had been caught tightly in a Kremlin web, would secretly provide the Russians with top secret data on the likes of the F-117 Nighthawk 'stealth fighter' and the B-2 Spirit 'stealth bomber' - which, at the time, were still highly classified and in test-stage out at the likes of the notorious Area 51. In return, the KGB would provide those same American researchers with sensational documents on crashed UFOs and dead aliens. The plan that Moscow had in mind was for the Russians to get their eager hands on real top secret U.S. documents that could be used to advance Russian military aviation programs; but those hapless UFO investigators would receive nothing but faked garbage from their Soviet handlers...

This infiltration of UFO groups was highlighted by Todd Zechel in the August 1978 edition of the *Just Cause* newsletter:

CAUS has developed reliable information that a KGB officer or agent thought to be Gennadiy I. Fedosov, First Secretary for Public Cultural Exchanges, Soviet Embassy offices, Washington, D.C., attempted to recruit NICAP [National Investigations on Aerial Phenomenon] President John L. "Jack" Acuff in May 1977. The purpose of the operation is not clear at present: One theory is that the Soviets noticed NICAP had developed confidential sources who were providing the group with classified UFO reports, such as the NORAD message about the 1975 flap and the Iranian, Moroccan, and Tunisian UFO reports of 1976—parts of which were published in the NICAP newsletter, *UFO Investiga-*

tor. In that case, the Soviets either were interested in the sources of the classified data or in the UFO data, or both.

Another theory contends NICAP was targeted because of certain covert CIA employees who hold or held important positions in the organization. Still another theory explains the attempted recruitment as a continuation of the KGB operations aimed at the Society of Photographic Scientists and Engineers (SPSE) from 1967 to 1970, when Jack Acuff was its Executive Director.

The KGB operations against SPSE began rather innocuously: The Soviets ordered books about—presumably—photometry and photogrammetry for SPSE, sending checks for them through the mail. The FBI intercepted the checks and/or monitored the bank accounts, then phoned Acuff to inquire as to their purpose. From then on, Acuff made a point of notifying one particular FBI agent whenever Soviet checks came in. Eventually, Acuff's relationship with the Bureau reached the point where he would meet Soviet personnel at the secret request and guidance of the FBI. The Special Agent-in-Charge of the Washington office told Acuff he thought the KGB was trying to "get through to some of the people who are doing classified work" in the SPSE.

In May 1970, Acuff became President of NICAP, and left SPSE. This made no difference to the FBI, but it did to Acuff: The FBI asked him to initiate new contacts with the Soviets, but Acuff declined. Apparently, there was no further communication with the Soviets until May 1977, when Fedosov phoned Acuff to try to arrange a meeting. Fedosov said he was interested in UFOs personally and he wanted to discuss the subject with Acuff.

The NICAP head cleared the meeting with the FBI and met Fedosov for lunch in a downtown Washington restaurant. The Soviet never once mentioned UFOs, despite his earlier professed interest. Instead, Fedosov made a rather intriguing offer to Acuff, one that could be interpreted as part of a cultural exchange, or as part of something more ominous: "You will have a lot of money soon. You'll have a lot more space. You're going to have to learn a foreign language because you'll be traveling abroad."

Afterward, Acuff dutifully reported the Soviet offer to the FBI. The agent told Acuff, "We think they will offer you money; what we want to know is what the strings are." Evidently, Acuff never did learn what were the "strings," since Fedosov never contacted Acuff again, as far as CAUS can determine. The Soviets did attempt to recontact Acuff in late July or August 1978, when another KGB officer or agent came to NICAP headquarters in Kensington, Md., but Acuff was out of the office at the time.

Though the reasons for the KGB interest in NICAP are not yet clear, it is known that the founder and original Chief of the CIA's Psychological and Political Warfare Staff, Colonel Joseph Bryan, 3rd, (USAF-Ret.), is a prominent member of the NICAP Board of Governors... Some observers suspect the CIA's interest in NICAP stemmed from the Agency's concern about the dangers of Soviet psychological exploitation of NICAP's vociferous charges of government coverup, which Donald Keyhoe and others hurled repeatedly throughout the late 1950s and early/mid 1960s. Whether or not Bryan's involvement with NICAP was related to this CIA concern, and whether or not he took part in some sort of plot to neutralize the organization, is not yet known...

This U.S.-Soviet spy vs. spy game appeared to be the focus of the AFOSI's counter-intelligence operation, which would explain Harry Rositzke's involvement, but according to Greg Bishop to refer to these machinations as simply an 'AFOSI operation' presents a limited view of what was actually a far larger counterintelligence operation, with UFO disinformation comprising but a small sliver of a much larger pie.

What may seem curious to some is that *UFO Cover-up Live!* was a joint Soviet/US broadcast, which in itself was unprecedented at the time, and would have required a high level of cooperation between both governments to coordinate. Although there had been an easing of Soviet-U.S. tensions during this period, the walls around the Cold War didn't officially fall until 1991 with the dissolution of the Soviet Union.

According to Richard Doty, it wasn't UFOs that initially brought Bill Moore to the attention of the AFOSI: "Bill Moore spoke Russian. He had contacts with Soviet researchers. He had a contact with somebody inside Moscow who he corresponded with. [AFOSI] knew about that, and when we approached Bill, we wanted him to report to us what this scientist was saying and, expanding that, to allow us to make contact with this person inside the Soviet Union, which began our operation."[108] As Doty stated, Moore indeed was fluent in Russian, and prior to jumping head-first into the world of ufology he taught French and Russian in the Pennsylvania public school system from 1966-1978.[109]

One segment of *UFO Cover Up Live!* featured an unnamed Soviet scientist, so it's not a leap to suspect that this might have been one of the Soviet researchers who Bill Moore was interacting with that brought him to the attention of AFOSI. Another *UFO Cover Up Live!* segment featured a reporter from the Soviet news agency TASS, who described himself as a "UFO investigator." TASS has long been identified by U.S. Intelligence as a conduit, or front, for Soviet (now Russian) spy operations.

One of the earliest mentions of Area 51 appeared on *UFO Cover-up Live!*, and it could be assumed that Bill Moore might have had a hand in introducing this material to the program. According to Area 51 aficionado Norio Hayakawa: "What got me first interested in Area 51 in 1987 was when I received from a Los Angeles-based writer named Bill Moore a copy of a satellite photo of Groom Lake taken by the Russians ..."[110]

Chapter 42

Step right up for the SERPO circus!

On November 1, 2005—on a UFO email list in a galaxy far, far away—the following cryptic lines were posted:

My name is Request Anonymous. I am a retired employee of the U.S. Government. I won't go into any great details about my past, but I was involved in a special program...

In the days to follow, Request Anonymous (an apparent government insider privy to top secret UFO poop) would go into exhaustive detail about a joint ET-U.S. government exchange program code-named Project SERPO that started in 1965, when entities from Zeta-Reticuli landed at the Nevada Test Site and turned over the keys of their craft to twelve of our planet's best and brightest who got a quick lesson on how to steer a saucer and then traveled to Planet SERPO for an extended stay.

One of the ETs enlisted in the program was referred to as EBE-1 (the same name mentioned by Falcon on *UFO Cover-up Live!*) who unloaded a vast amount of mind-blowing info on his human hosts concerning planet SERPO, their culture, how their spaceships operated, etc.—all of which sounded straight out of Rick Doty's old UFO disinfo playbook.

The private email list circulating the SERPO info was maintained by a mild-mannered UFO enthusiast named Victor Martinez, who suddenly found himself thrust into the spotlight. To share these revelations with a larger audience, Martinez launched a website (serpo.org) and before you knew it ufology was all abuzz with the

SERPO story that further spread out over social media forums and UFO message boards.

Before posting some of the SERPO material online, Martinez took it upon himself to correct misspellings and other obvious errors, which apparently didn't sit well with "Request Anonymous" who had previously cautioned him not to alter the material in any way. One of these attempted corrections concerned the mission to SERPO. According to Request Anonymous:

> The 12 remained until 1978, when they were returned to the same location in Nevada. Seven men and one woman returned. Two died on the alien's home planet. Four others decided to remain, according to the returnees. Of that eight that returned, all have died. The last survivor died in 2002.

For those with basic math skills, Request Anonymous' numbers didn't add up. As Greg Bishop observed:

> The math is wrong. How could eight people return to Earth out of twelve when two died on the planet and four decided to remain? My contention is that this was a deliberate mistake designed as a calling card or message that would be recognized as such by those who were supposed to know where to look for more information elsewhere in the text. Martinez was dropped because he was garbling the message. Meanwhile, UFO fans and radio hosts were busy deciphering their own meanings from the latest craze that flattered their prejudices and helped to spread the SERPO meme in cyberspace, on the airwaves, and in UFO publications. 'Mistakes' like these sometimes hide in plain sight, but many UFO investigators are too busy looking at the finger to realize where it's pointing. The disinformers used a story that had been circulating for at least 20 years and built on it to lend credence to the campaign.[111]

Due to his typographical transgressions, Martinez soon found himself on the outs with Mr. Request Anonymous and the SERPO torch was passed to an Englishman named Bill Ryan. (Ryan and his gal-pal Kerry Cassidy went on to create a niche for themselves with "Project Camelot," a website dedicated to an emerging subculture of time-traveling "super soldiers" who use "star gates" as their preferred method of teleportation.)

As the SERPO story progressed, it became increasingly preposterous. Mark Pilkington observed:

> The stories started getting wilder...[Request Anonymous] started promising photographs from SERPO of the extraterrestrials playing American football...Images started to appear of the architecture on SERPO, and someone pointed out that the kind of images that were being released were being created using standard stencil sets you could buy in a stationary store.[112]

Nine months before the first Project SERPO email surfaced, Greg Bishop was scheduled to appear on *Coast to Coast AM* to promote *Project Beta: The Story of Paul Bennewitz, National Security, and the Creation of a Modern UFO Myth*. During a pre-interview chat, Bishop got Art Bell up to speed on the Bennewitz affair, and the involvement therein of Richard Doty. On the spur of the moment, Bishop suggested he might be able to persuade Doty to come on the show that night, a suggestion Art heartily encouraged.

So it came to pass that after an extended period of ufological semi-retirement, Richard Doty returned center stage. During his *Coast to Coast AM* appearance, Doty acknowledged his role in the Bennewitz affair with the caveat that he'd never actually intended to cause any harm, and in fact considered Bennewitz a "close friend." Doty said he regretted his past actions, explaining he'd taken an oath of allegiance (to the good ol' US of A) and had simply been "following orders." Doty went on to say that he'd seen the error of his ways while at the same time trotting out many of the same claims from his old AFOSI days, including revelations about a secret U.S. government exchange program courtesy of Zeta Reticuli—basically the same story soon to be recycled as Project SERPO. Doty even doubled down on his claim that the ETs possessed a fondness for strawberry ice cream, and further clarified that the disinformation he'd previously spread had actually contained a mix of fact *and* fiction.

Afterwards, Greg Bishop grew to suspect that Doty's *Coast to Coast AM* appearance "was some sort of preparation for the SERPO project. I think that Doty was briefed before the interview on what he could and could not say, as well as how he could subtly lay the groundwork for the later SERPO story. Most likely, the Air Force Office of Special Investigations (AFOSI) and other interested agencies monitored the reaction publicly as well as in the UFO community."

In December 2005, Doty returned to the *Coast to Coast AM* airwaves, joining SERPO spokesman Bill Ryan and the ever-popular abductee-author Whitley Strieber, who had likewise jumped aboard the SERPO saucer spinning madly out of control. Strieber now seemed convinced that SERPO was the real deal based on a distant memory of attending a UFO conference in the 1990s when he was approached by a former military man who claimed he'd traveled to another planet with a name that sounded something like "Serpico." Meanwhile, Linda Howe was waving around photos of a semi-strange looking craft (most likely a drone) which she was passing off as an actual alien spaceship that somehow along the way became associated with SERPO. Strieber didn't help matters by saying that when he'd first laid eyes on these images of the drone-like thing, he intuitively felt—via his Whitley Strieber spidey sense—that they were indeed of extraterrestrial origin! (It was later rumored that Richard Doty was the source of these spurious photos of spaceships from SERPO.)

The February 2006 edition of *UFO Magazine* featured a special issue dedicated to the hottest topic going at the time, which of course was you know what, and included articles by Bill Ryan, Victor Martinez, Mark Pilkington, and lo and behold, none other than our recurring character in this UFO dog and pony show, Richard Doty, who wrote:

> My name is Richard Doty retired special agent, Air Force Office of Special Investigations (AFOSI), and now a private citizen living in New Mexico...
>
> In early 1979, after arriving at Kirtland Air Force Base as a young special agent with AFOSI, I was assigned to the counter-intelligence division of AFOSI District 17. I was briefed into a special compartmented program. This program dealt with United States government involvement with extraterrestrial biological entities. During my initial briefing I was given the complete background of our government's involvement with EBEs. This background included information on the Roswell incident...basically, this was exactly the same information that Mr. Anonymous released.

In March 2006—just as the Project SERPO craze had become all the rage—Bill Ryan was invited to deliver the keynote speech at the annual International UFO Congress in Laughlin, Nevada. According to Mark Pilkington—who filmed the event for inclusion in his film *Mirage Men*—Ryan seemed out of sorts to suddenly find himself swept up into the center of this SERPO cyclone, as on a daily basis more internet posters were coming forward with stunning new revelations. It was like a runaway train that continued gathering more steam, destined for an inevitable wreck.

During the course of the UFO Congress, an anonymous envelope mysteriously arrived, addressed to Bill Ryan, containing "three sheets of word processed text...a new section of the SERPO astronauts' journal, describing the difficulties communicating with the Ebens after being taken to their planet. With it was a page of small, hand written [with a green sharpie], squiggly glyphs, forming a wobbly grid of sixteen lines."[113] These "squiggly glyphs" were presumed to be an ET script.

About the same time this mystery envelope materialized, so did that old ufological trickster, Rick Doty, making one of his rare public appearances. At the time, Doty had become an advisor to Bill Ryan on all matters SERPO-related, and it was Doty who helped "validate" many of Request Anonymous' claims. Doty's involvement with Ryan immediately raised a red flag with old ufological hands, who had seen this game play out before: a new UFO Disclosure hero is suddenly thrust into the spotlight with promises of amazing revelations soon to unfold in the days and weeks to come. But with this mantle often comes a creeping paranoia that overcomes our hero—in this case, Bill Ryan—who by this time had convinced himself that he was now under constant surveillance, and was exhibiting the same sort of mania that got Paul Bennewitz so spun out that he ended up in a psych ward. As Mark Pilkington recalled:

> We were a little worried about Bill [Ryan], actually. He was getting very anxious and paranoid and, to be honest, delusional. And we were worried he was going to crack in some way…he was clearly being played, but he refused to accept that possibility, because by that point he'd invested so much time and energy of himself into the story, and here he was as the keynote speaker at the biggest UFO conference in the world."[114]

Greg Bishop also attended the UFO Congress, and when he became aware that Doty had shown up and was "advising" Bill Ryan, he offered these words of caution: "Be very careful, Bill. If Rick is involved I wouldn't let yourself be drawn in too deep. You know what happened to Bennewitz. One way or another you've got to make sure you don't end up fried like Paul.[115]

Mark Pilkington, who was a firsthand witness to these Doty-Ryan interactions, observed:

The whole thing was a kind of circus show, really. Again the question is to what end? I'm not suggesting it was a counterintelligence related operation. But if it was, it shows that they will spend a lot of time and money just for one very simple operation, to one simple end. I was just reading an article that talked about how in the early or late 70s, the CIA actually organized a huge nuclear fission conference and invited all the world's leading nuclear fission scientists from around the world and funded the whole thing...and the entire reason was to draw the Iranian physicists to the conference who they wanted to defect. So they will go to extreme lengths for just one thing that they need. But one thing that was curious at the Laughlin conference was there was a big contingent of Chinese UFO researchers there, so I did wonder if the Chinese connection was important in some way. And as we know well, UFOs are a very good way to get information about clandestine aviation technology or satellites or space technologies. That was one of the things in the back of my mind: Was the whole thing set up just to find out if there was some Chinese industrial espionage going on? The point being: If there was a counterintelligence or disinformation purpose to the SERPO papers it's still not impossible that they would have used someone like Rick Doty, even if he'd been previously exposed and discredited, he still may have been someone they would go to as having experience in the UFO field and someone who might know how to get the information into the right hands, for whatever reason.[116]

As this SERPO psychodrama played out at UFO conferences and over the internet, a couple of former (alleged) intelligence officers named Paul McGovern and Greg Lakes came forward with SERPO forum posts that seemed to confirm the claims of Request Anonymous. McGovern identified himself as a former Area 51 security chief, and

Lakes, a former Defense Intelligence Agency official. Not long after, in March 2006, a group of internet sleuths associated with www.realityuncovered.com were able to get their hands on the original emails sent by Request Anonymous, Paul McGovern and Greg Lakes, and traced their IP addresses back to one single source: Richard Doty. Doty, of course, denied any direct association with Request Anonymous or any of the others, which is probably the best confirmation you could receive that he'd indeed masterminded the whole crazy caper.

In February 2007, at the UFOMystic blog, Greg Bishop suggested that SERPO was "...very likely a disinformation operation designed to ensnare unsuspecting UFO researchers, and all those interested in UFO information, in order to track connections and interests. This is remarkably similar to the events which surrounded Paul Bennewitz and the UFO community in the 1980s. The fact is less remarkable when we consider that some of the same people, notably Richard Doty (and other "Aviary" members) came out of retirement to lend support to the project."

Chapter 43

What happened to Jaime Shandera?

Jaime Shandera remains among the more enigmatic figures associated with the MJ-12 saga. Shandera's last media appearance was the July 2, 1997 edition of *Coast to Coast AM* where in the intro to the show Art Bell introduced him as "a director, producer and investigative journalist for 30 years. He has worked behind the scenes guiding productions in news documentaries, political campaigns, national and international commercials and thousands of shows of every variety…"

Although he was said to have been a film producer/director, there's no record of any productions credited to Shandera in the IMDB database, or elsewhere on the web. IMDB lists Shandera as a member of the crew of "The Devil's Rain," a 1975 occult film that featured a star-studded cast including Ernest Borgnine, Eddie Albert, William Shatner and John Travolta. However, it's unknown what role Shandera played in the production. Who knows if "Jaime Shandera" was even his real name?

The circumstances of how Bill Moore and Shandera first hooked-up are as equally mysterious, and it's entirely possible that Shandera was an intelligence agency asset sent to keep tabs on Moore. As Greg Bishop recalled:

Moore said he went to a meeting with Shandera once, at some Air Force base, and after the meeting somebody from one of those alphabet soup agencies came up to both of them, and pointed to Bill, and said, 'You're new.' And then they pointed at Shandera, and said, 'You we've seen before and worked with.' And Bill Moore is like, 'Whaaat?'

The only thing Moore would tell me—and I believe Shande-ra confirmed this—was that Jaime provided testimony in a court martial case when the government had to determine wheth-er a recording was an actual recording of somebody's voice, or if it was edited together, and since he was technically efficient at post-production, I guess, that's the story: that he testified in some trial in the early '70s. And from what I can tell, he's one of those people like Bob Emenegger. They did their thing, but they agreed to do other things for certain agencies when it was useful. Whether for pay or not, I don't know.[117]

In the mid-1980s, Moore and Shandera began receiving the "Bird Code," a series of postcards from American intelligence contacts stationed in the Soviet Union, New Zealand and other countries. These messages were coded breadcrumbs, or pieces of a puzzle, that Moore and Shandera began attempting to decode.

Robert Collins suggested that this "Bird Code"—when finally pieced together—gave directions to a safe house, or "Bird Sanctuary," in Washington, D.C., where a female ET "ambassador" was in residence.[118]

Sometime in the 1990s, the ET ambassador was apparently shipped back to her home planet. Shandera had decoded enough of the "Bird Code" by this time that he felt it warranted a trip to D.C in the summer of 1995. It was there that he met with a mysterious "Mr. X" at the National Mall. Mr. X escorted Shandera to a building where he was shown a top secret vault reportedly containing "volumes" of ET-related materials. At least this was Robert Collins' version of the story. This was similar to something that Shandera told Greg Bishop:

I was communicating with Shandera in 1999. At that point I think he'd gotten a divorce and moved out of the house and also the last thing he did, strangely enough, he told me about going to the National Mall in Washington D.C., and meeting some guy who showed him something that made Shandera realize there really were aliens here. And he told me if I guessed it, he'd tell me if I was right. And I never did. And I'd thought I'd gone through everything...I guessed film, video, pictures, a document, an actual encounter with an alien...but none of those were the correct answer. He said he was going to do an interview for my magazine [*The Excluded Middle*] in December of '99 after he got back from a trip to New York, and by January of the next year I called his house and a woman's voice came on an answering machine and says that Shandera is no longer at this phone number, and that she didn't know his new number. This was very strange because usually it takes months for the phone company to switch a number over. They did it very quickly within a couple of weeks. [119]

In February 2018, Richard Doty called in to Jimmy Church's *Fade to Black* and made some curious comments regarding Shandera:

In 2006 [Shandera] showed up at the UFO conference in Laughlin...with Bill Ryan and Kerry Cassidy...and I knew, you could just look at him, that he was on some kind of prescription drugs, or illegal drugs. He would rant about things that had happened to him, and he had marks on his body where he claimed that he'd been at a beach in California, and the Navy Seals landed and took him in a helicopter to Coronado Island and put him in a brig and beat him because he saw them training aliens...and that was just one of the many stories he told...that was the last time I saw him.

Doty's claim that Shandera attended the 2006 UFO Congress appeared to be yet another red herring tossed into a swirling sea of UFO disinformation—but to what end? Both Mark Pilkington and

Greg Bishop were hanging out with—or in close proximity—to Bill Ryan and Rick Doty the entire weekend of the UFO Congress, and if Shandera had shown up, it certainly would not have gone unnoticed.

Chapter 44

Sifting through the Roswell wreckage

"Disinformation, as the Soviet term *desinformatsiya* was quickly anglicized by admiring Western intelligence agencies, is the propagation of false, incomplete, or misleading information to targeted individuals. But for a disinformation campaign to be truly successful, it must accomplish two related goals. One, the target must act on these new 'facts.' And two, the target must be irrevocably diverted from the more fruitful path he had previously been following."

– Howard Blum, *Out There*

A fresh batch of MJ-12 papers surfaced in the mid-1990s, courtesy of a researcher named Timothy Cooper who claimed he'd received the documents from a retired CIA agent identifying himself as "Thomas Cantwheel." This material, which consisted of thousands of pages, not only included previously unseen MJ-12 material, but documents related to manufactured viruses and biological weapons. Also in this batch of documents was a purported CIA memo dated August 3, 1962, that summarized a wiretapped conversation that journalist Dorothy Kilgallen had with celebrity columnist Howard Rothberg concerning pillow talk that took place between then Attorney General Robert Kennedy and Marilyn Monroe. The document contained revelations about JFK's planned inspection of "things from space" located at a "secret air base." The memo was stamped Top Secret and titled Project Moondust, signed by James Jesus Angleton, CIA Chief for Counterintelligence.

Cooper shared the Moondust memo with Milo Speriglio, a Hollywood private detective and author of a number of tabloid books about Marilyn Monroe. Afterwards, Speriglio held a press conference announcing the existence of this bombshell memo, claiming it had been authenticated by his contacts in the intelligence community. In the years to follow, the Moondust memo would inspire a smattering of books claiming that JFK had been assassinated due to dangerous knowledge he possessed about crashed saucers and dead ETs. The Moondust memo ultimately turned out to be a fake, although Project Moondust was indeed a bonafide U.S. military program dating back to the 1950s relating to UFOs—but not so much little green men or ET spacecraft. According to Nick Redfern, "when the military was referring to 'UFOs' in their files they were *not* talking about alien spacecraft. Rather, they were referencing probable space debris that originated with the former Soviet Union."

Later, allegations surfaced that Cooper had forged the Moondust memo and other MJ-12 documents in his possession. Researchers noted typewriter anomalies that matched those found in other documents that passed through Cooper. In response, Cooper swore out an affidavit in which he denied any involvement in a hoax.

In the late 1990s, a retired engineer formerly employed at McDonnell Douglas named Dr. Robert Wood, along with his son Ryan, began researching and attempting to validate Cooper's MJ-12 material. In 2001, Cooper sold his files to the Woods, and a short time later the Woods hired Nick Redfern to review and index the documents. During his review, Redfern came across correspondence relating to a series of incidents witnessed by a nurse named Marian Earhart who worked at Los Alamos Labs in the aftermath of World War II. During this period, Earhart observed some odd-looking bodies apparently with genetic deformities that had been wheeled into the facility to be used in "experiments for biological and nuclear medicine research." In Cooper's notes related to this correspondence, he stated his suspicion that the bodies might be related to the Roswell crash. According to Redfern, it was at this point in Cooper's research that he was "flooded with mountains of controversial and likely bogus UFO-themed files that, time-wise, far-too-conveniently emphasized the E.T. angle."[120] This suggested to Redfern that Cooper may have been getting too close to a terrestrial answer for the Roswell crash, and in specific that it was related to human experimentation research, which may have been the reason he was inundated with these forged MJ-12 documents that seemed designed to lead him astray and discredit his work.

Not long after his review of the Cooper/MJ-12 materials, Redfern was approached by a whistle-blower he identified as the "Black Widow," a former nurse who had worked at the Oak Ridge, Tennessee atomic energy facility during the 1940s and '50s. According to the Black Widow, she witnessed unusual bodies being brought into the facility during the summer of 1947. A month after the Roswell crash, the Black Widow observed a new batch of bodies brought in, many that had suffered fatal injuries, apparent victims of some sort of high-speed collision. The rumor among the nursing staff was that these subjects had been used in top secret high-altitude experiments in New Mexico. Some of the victims appeared to be of Japanese descent, while others displayed signs of a condition known as progeria, with oversized craniums, bulging eyes and an absence of body hair. Redfern obtained FOIA documents which confirmed human experimentation had indeed been conducted at Oak Ridge on subjects with progeria.

According to Redfern's research, these clandestine experiments may have played a part in a top secret program overseen by General Curtis LeMay to test the effects of radiation on human subjects, some of whom were Japanese POWs. This project utilized experimental aircraft designs based, in part, on captured Axis technologies secreted to the U.S. in the aftermath of the war, part of Project Paperclip, a program designed to import German scientists and intelligence officers into the U.S.

Concurrent with Project Paperclip, Major General Charles Willoughby launched a clandestine operation to seize the files of a Japanese secret project known as Unit 731, which was similar to the Nazi human experiments that Dr. Mengele conducted at Auschwitz.

Both of these operations (Paperclip and Unit 731) were a race against the Russians to acquire secret Axis technologies.

In 1991, researcher Kathy Kasten uncovered information concerning a team of military remote-viewers that had been tasked with remote viewing the Roswell crash. According to Nick Redfern: "Kathy's records show that, according to the results of the Army's quest for the truth of Roswell, and in Kathy's own handwritten words, 'It began and ended at Fort Stanton.'" Through FOIA requests, Kasten acquired a number of files on Fort Stanton – which, it happens, was located not far from the Foster Ranch, site of the Roswell crash.

During World War II, Fort Stanton served as a relocation center for Japanese internees, physically handicapped people, and German and Japanese POWs. It was from Fort Stanton, Kasten theorized, that the military secured test subjects used in their experimental aircraft test flights.

Kasten's research eventually led her to William Randolph "Randy" Lovelace II, a military physician in charge of aviation biology at Wright Field, Ohio (later renamed Wright-Patterson Air Force Base) during the 1940s. Lovelace's research included tests on the effects of high-altitude exposure to the human body and nervous system. After the war, Lovelace established the Lovelace Foundation for Medical Education and Research in Albuquerque that was involved in projects to evaluate the effects of radiation on animals, all of which weirdly worms its way into the Dulce Base/cattle mute mythos.

One of the Lovelace-related documents Kasten came across concerned the story of an experimental test subject that survived one of the purported New Mexico saucer crashes, and was transported to Fort Stanton for examination. The victim apparently died a few days later, and was buried in the Fort Stanton cemetery. There are those who speculate that this "test subject" helped evolve the dead alien story that was part of a medical examination à la *Alien Autopsy*.

In a 2017 interview with Midnight Rider News, John Lear claimed that:

Part of the [Roswell saucer] wreckage went to Los Alamos, part of it went to Wright Patterson Air Force Base, and at Wright Patterson there was an Air Force surgeon named Randy Lovelace, who was from Albuquerque, and they sent him back to Albuquerque to build the Lovelace clinic, which was going to be a very advanced state of the art hospital, and it was going to be a cover for where the aliens, dead or alive, were sent and where they could be autopsied and held.

In 1947 – '48 they built a huge underground facility there in the Manzano Weapons Storage area, just to the east of Kirtland Air Force base and that's where for years they kept the alien bodies. They had different access hallways and routes to get into there...and they had a series of keypads that you would have to press numbers and you got three tries and the third one, if it was wrong, the room was immediately filled with poisonous gas and you were instantly dead. They were very serious about keeping it quiet...[121]

How seriously one wants to take anything John Lear says I'll leave to the reader's discretion, but the fact that he was advancing these Lovelace/Kirtland stories as recent as 2017 speaks to this enduring mythology and endless cast of oddball characters who have promoted its various permutations.

In this same interview, Lear recounted a crash he'd been involved in that occurred in the summer of 1961, when he was piloting a Bucker Jungmann biplane that went down near Geneva, Switzerland. Apparently, Lear got racked up pretty bad, breaking bones all over his body, and barely survived. After spending six weeks in a hospital in Geneva, Lear was sent home to finish his recovery at his family's ranch in the nearby town of Onex. According to Lear, the doctors handling his case had failed to notice that he'd come down with gangrene. Concerned that there weren't proper facilities in Switzerland to treat his son's condition, William Lear arranged to have John flown back to the states where he was put under the care of none other than Randy Lovelace in Albuquerque, who John Lear later credited with saving his leg from amputation.

Bill Klass, who wrote for Aviation Week, knew William Lear quite well, and had been a frequent guest at his homes in Santa Monica, California and Geneva, Switzerland. Klass described Lear's son John as:

> ...an oddball. When he was a teenager in Switzerland, he rented an aerobatic airplane and was doing stunts over his family's estate on the outskirts of Geneva and cracked-up. I've heard that he broke every bone in his body; probably an exaggeration, but they didn't expect him to live. In fact, if you see John Lear walk today, he walks like an eighty-year old man, instead of a forty-five year old man. I have wondered, when I see some of the strange things he has said and done, I've wondered if there might have been some brain-damage...[122]

Richard Sauder—author of *Underground Bases and Tunnels*—uncovered information that the Lovelace Foundation ran an auxiliary animal research lab at Kirtland AFB. This lab purportedly conducted tests on terminally ill patients who had consented to experimental therapies. During a 1964 visit to this Kirtland-Lovelace facility, Aviary member Ernie Kellerstrauss allegedly observed ET body parts that had been exposed to radiation. Kellerstrauss was told that these body parts were on loan from Wright-Patterson.[123]

According to Greg Bishop's research, the Lovelace animal lab at Kirtland was connected to the Bennewitz affair:

> At Bennewitz's request, Doty arranged for [Myrna] Hansen to be X-rayed at the Lovelace center [at Kirtland] to locate the implant that Bennewitz was sure was embedded near the base of her skull along the spinal cord. The object did in fact show up on the ultrasensitive X-ray exposure, but Air Force doctors were

satisfied that it was a natural growth and pursued it no further. During his meetings with Base Security and other intelligence personnel, Bennewitz told of underground rooms and tunnels that Myrna Hansen visited during her abduction. Doty recalls that while under hypnosis with an Air Force psychologist, she described and drew one of the facilities at Manzano in great detail. 'She even knew what the elevator looked like,' he says. How she was able to do this was a priority concern to the intelligence detachments charged with security of this area.[124]

In light of the above passage, it's entirely possible that Myrna Hansen's hypnosis session at Kirtland morphed into an imagined alien abduction. Or, more ominously, the proposition that an AFOSI hypnotist intentionally inserted false memories into Hansen's subconscious mind that were later confabulated into her Dulce Base experience. While the timeline of these events places Hansen's hypnotic regressions with Sprinkle and Bennewitz has having occurred before the Lovelace facility sessions, we are left to ponder what sort of tinkering AFOSI may have been involved in that could have conceivably led Hansen to conflate her experiences.

It's also worth entertaining the theory that Hansen herself might have been a witting participant in the AFOSI disinformation campaign: in essence, an actress playing a role; a spy embedded in the Bennewitz operation to gather information and seed a narrative of UFOs, cattle mutes, and secret underground alien bases. As Greg Valdez has observed:

It is a possibility that the Myrna Hansen story was also part of the disinformation campaign. Paul [Bennewitz] claimed that several individuals would show up at his house unannounced and show him scars and evidence of implants, and then they would simply leave. I will go out on a limb here and say that the story of Myrna Hansen was probably a well-orchestrated hoax because of a very important fact: the listening devices found in my dad's house. The government heard all the conversations on the phone between my dad and [Bennewitz], so such a hoax would be relatively easy to accomplish...Myrna Hansen came into the picture in May of 1980 and the Air Force did not even acknowledge contact with Paul until November of 1980... Although this evidence can barely be viewed as even circumstantial, it would explain a lot of things and how and why they transpired during the 1980s based on what we currently know.

The same also applies to the false stories of Thomas Castello and Phil Schneider. These stories have one common denominator: John Lear. According to Chris Lambright's research, Lear and Doty were at the same location in Laos during the Vietnam war. There is a very high likelihood Doty and Lear worked together to produce the Dulce Papers and the Castello story because the stories are all intertwined with each other. The Myrna Hansen story coincides with the Dulce Papers. The Castello Story is similar to the Schneider story, which deals with underground levels and a war between aliens and the government. Bennewitz started the story of an underground alien/government war at Dulce, yet it was passed around in a big circle. That circle includes Bennewitz, Lear, and Doty. The three supposedly separate stories all share attributes from each other and they were started by the Air Force. They were eventually passed off as truth through Lear, which ultimately came from information provided to Bennewitz. Bennewitz and Lear were involved in a disagreement and had a falling out around the time the Dulce Papers were released, and no one other than Lear knows what happened to cause the argument. There is suspicion from several investigators that Lear stole some of Bennewitz's evidence but it has never been verified...

If this scenario is true, it would explain a lot... Lear was an Air America pilot for the CIA. Former CIA employees tend to keep in touch with each other, from all the evidence that I've seen. There is an organization for former Area 51 employees who call themselves the Roadrunners. The Roadrunners website organizes and coordinates routine conferences and get-to-gethers so former Area 51 employees can keep in touch. John Lear's father William Lear was affiliated with this Roadrunner group and John is also a member, and his dad has ties to Area 51 in regard to work he conducted for the military. It appears the Lear family has a long non-alien presence and history at Area 51. Based on the secret aircraft development and the false cover stories of aliens and UFOs that have come out of Area 51, I don't find it very difficult to see why John Lear may have become so involved in the UFO community, based on his and his families ties to the CIA. Do I really need to say more about what this might entail if it were true? A family with ties to the CIA, Area 51 and high-dollar military contracts is facilitating tales about aliens. Think about that for a second before you count the Thomas Castello story as fact...."[125]

Although Greg Valdez has left us a lot to unpack here, the theory that Myrna Hansen was a knowing participant in the AFOSI's counter-intelligence operation certainly ties together many of the loose threads dangling in the Bennewitz affair. When the AFOSI (or other alphabet soup spooks) listened in on Bennewitz's phone conversations with Gabe Valdez, they most likely caught wind of the claims that Myrna Hansen had been implanted with an extraterrestrial monitoring device. Presumably, Bennewitz based these implant theories partly on scars and/or scoop marks discovered on Hansen's body, which he felt were indicative of alien medical procedures. Afterwards, as Valdez notes, strangers appeared unannounced on Bennewitz's door-step, showing him scars and other purported physical evidence that appeared to be the product of this perceived alien invasion.

It's always been a bit of a mystery as to how Hansen ended up being "treated" at the Kirtland-Lovelace facility. The scenario that makes the most sense is that AFOSI was pretending to take Bennewitz's claims seriously and offered up their assistance with x-rays to determine if there was actually some sort of implant lodged in Hansen's skull. In this regard, Tal informed me that John Lear provided him with the original Hansen x-rays, which theoretically provided evidence—at least to those who choose to believe in such things—that whatever was lodged in her head was of extraterrestrial origin.

During the production of the underground base episode of *UFO Hunters,* Tal stated that he handed over Hansen's x-rays to Bill Birnes for safekeeping. Birnes recently confirmed to me that Tal did indeed provide him with these x-rays, in addition to other rare Dulce Base-related materials. So the chain of custody would seem to be Bennewitz → Lear → Tal → Bill Birnes. Once again, these x-rays don't necessarily prove anything other than adding to the other spurious stories that have become part and parcel of Dulce Base lore.

Chapter 45

The MJ-12 Papers ride again

In the run up to the 70th anniversary of the Roswell crash, in July 2017, yet another batch of MJ-12 documents made their way into the public domain courtesy of Heather Wade, host of *Midnight in the Desert*. Wade claimed that she received 47 pages of "new" MJ-12 documents from "a trusted source." These documents included "Condensed Conversations with the Aztec, New Mexico Extraterrestrial Biological Entity," which was basically a sit-down chit-chat with an ET named Sentimus that reads like sci-fi fan fiction. Apparently Sentimus survived a saucer crash and lived to tell about it. When asked what had brought him to planet Earth, Sentimus informed his U.S. military hosts that he and his fellow ETs were awfully fond of Earth-trees, which was one of the reasons they had traveled all the way across the cosmos: to save our trees from atomic bombs!

This new slew of MJ-12 papers contained several grammatical errors, which some might suspect came straight out of the old Richard Doty playbook. Was our old friend at it again? Was Rick Doty the "trusted source" who had provided the MJ-12 materials to Heather Wade? Such details as the mention of Aztec as the crash site—for those who were paying attention—were obvious clues showing that this latest edition of the MJ-12 papers contradicted previous iterations.

Another curiosity concerning the Wade MJ-12 papers is a reference to a secret base in Flat Rock, Nevada; the only problem with this—as Nick Redfern pointed out—is that Flat Rock is a completely fictional location that was lifted from Michael Crichton's *The Andromeda Strain*, which is the story of an alien virus that attempts to wreak havoc on the human race. In *Flying Saucers from the Kremlin: UFOs, Russian Meddling, Soviet Spies & Cold War Secrets*, Redfern speculates that this latest batch of MJ-12 papers were quite possibly produced by the same hidden hand behind the Timothy Cooper materials.

For ease of discussion, I'll refer to the different iterations of the MJ-12 papers as 1) "Moore/Shandera" – 2) "Cooper" – 3) "Wade." And if that wasn't convoluted enough to follow, Nick Redfern further speculates that the Cooper and Wade MJ-12 iterations were quite possibly an outgrowth, or continuation, of an infamous KGB disinformation campaign known as "Operation InfeKtion," a fictitious story planted in July 1983 in the English language newspaper *The Patriot* published in New Delhi, India. The article in *The Patriot* claimed that the Human Immunodeficiency Virus (HIV) had been concocted in a clandestine lab at Fort Detrick, Maryland by diabolical government scientists to be used as a biological weapon targeting gays and people of color in the U.S. and third world countries.

After planting the "Operation Infektion" time-bomb, the KGB let the story go dormant, which is often the long game played when seeding disinformation—plant a seed here, and another there, let them germinate and see what eventually sprouts. As the spread of HIV continued on into the 1980s and eventually become an international health crisis, the KGB decided to jump back into the Operation "Infektion" game in 1986. The cut-out the KGB used, in this instance, was a Soviet newspaper that, in turn, recycled The Patriot news story as their source. Soon after, a "scientific" study was published by a pair of East German biologists—the husband and wife team of Drs. Lilli and Jakob Segal—in which the doctorly duo claimed to have discovered that HIV had been cooked up in the good ol' USA. The KGB then went to work spreading the Segal's sketchy study to journalists around the globe, and in no time flat it went old school viral, appearing in numerous newspaper articles around the world.

In March 1987, Operation Infektion found its way to the *CBS Evening News* with Dan Rather, who reported that "a Soviet military publication claimed the virus that causes AIDS leaked from a U.S. Army laboratory conducting experiments in biological warfare..."

Following this broadcast, Operation Infektion went ever more viral and in time injected itself into the American bloodstream to remain there indefinitely, a permanent fixture in conspiracy culture.

The Cooper/MJ-12 materials emerged in the early 1990s and included a document entitled *Majestic Twelve Project: 1st Annual Report* detailing a purported UFO crash-retrieval that occurred in New Mexico in 1947 which let loose a dangerous alien virus and eventually led to the spread of AIDS.

Nick Redfern suspects that the MJ-12 materials passed along to Tim Cooper in the 1990s were a follow up, or alternative attempt, to resurrect Operation Infektion, but with a new twist in the form of an alien virus that has been unleashed, the facts of which are then covered up by the U.S. government and used to nefarious ends.

As noted earlier, the alleged former intelligence officer who passed along the MJ-12 documents to Cooper went by the name of "Cantwheel," which—as Nick Redfern discovered—is not a real name at all, although it's quite similar to "Cantwell", the last name of Dr. Alan Cantwell, author of *AIDS and the Doctors of Death: An Inquiry into the Origin of the AIDS Epidemic* (1987).

Redfern further theorizes that the Wade/MJ-12 materials may have also been part of this same saucer-themed "Operation Infektion" spin-off. A continuing theme in the Wade/MJ-12 materials is that the ETs are hypercritical of race relations in the United States, observing that blacks and Native Americans have been harshly mistreated, often victims of genocide at the hands of The Man. While these sentiments certainly have historical resonance, they are exactly the type of anti-U.S. rhetoric that the Kremlin has propagated since the Cold War era in their attempts to sow discord and create fractures in American society.[126]

Chapter 46

The song remains the same

A pattern has repeated itself over the last 40+ years that started back in 1975 when film producers Robert Emenegger and Alan Sandler were approached by Air Force officials offering supposed UFO footage of real ETs! At the time, the prospect of UFO Disclosure seemed just within reach…and then suddenly the rug was pulled out from under Emenegger and Sandler's feet. A few years later, Linda Moulton Howe received a similar dose of the same bad medicine, the same old song and dance promising the Holy Grail of UFO footage.

Bill Moore, it appears, got strung along farther than the others, and perhaps learned a lot more, at least in terms of the inner-workings of U.S. (and Russian) intelligence and its penetration into the wild and wooly world of American ufology. But, in the end, the carrot at the end of stick seems to have been the same poison pill (to mix metaphors) that was dangled before Emenegger, Sandler, Howe, et al. This began with the book project Moore was working on with Bob Pratt; a fictional account of flying saucers and government secrets, and of the brave, young intelligence officer, Richard Doty, who wanted to enlighten the world about the shocking truth of ETs visiting our planet.

For whatever reasons, the Moore-Pratt book project never panned out, and the two men eventually went their separate ways. Moore next teamed up with film producer Jaime Shandera. It was during this period that the heavens opened and the MJ-12 papers were conveniently deposited on Shandera's doorstep, a gift from the ufological gods. Over time, the consensus formed that the documents had most likely been faked, although most who cast their lot with the Roswell crash religion were loathe to admit it—or accept the reality when the truth came crashing down—much like their beloved Roswell saucer. Even some of the more conservative old school Roswologists—like Stan Friedman—maintained that MJ-12 and Roswell were the real deal. Of course, when someone gets invested in something, and stakes their reputation on Roswell or Bigfoot—or fill-in-the-blank—it's hard to take a step back and admit the possibility that they've been duped.

The Roswell crash mythos further spun into popular consciousness with *UFO Cover-up Live!* that also introduced into the mix Area 51, and a secret exchange program with an alien race from Zeta Reticuli. Shortly after, Bill Moore blew everything up at the '89 MUFON Symposium, and it seemed like this house of Roswell cards might suddenly collapse—or at the very least, run out of steam.

Roswell enthusiasts shortly after were able to pick up the pieces, and out of the ashes arose the *X Files* Generation that combined all these past elements (Roswell crash, Area 51 and Dulce Base) into a hip sociological stew to be consumed by an eager young Gen X audience.

In 1994, *Roswell: The UFO Cover-Up* starring Kyle MacLachlan and Martin Sheen premiered, further reinforcing these tales of a government cover up orchestrated to bury the "horrible truth" about crashed alien craft and the little people who fly them.

And if that wasn't enough to keep the Roswell drum beating, yet another MJ-12 related document surfaced in April of that same year when UFO researcher Don Berliner received an anonymously sent package that contained a roll of undeveloped 35 mm film. (Sound familiar?) Once developed, the film in question revealed a 29-page document entitled SOM 1-01, Majestic-12 Group Special Operations Manual, which purported to be a guide instructing an elite military team on the do's and don'ts of flying saucer crash retrievals.

The father and son team of Robert and Ryan Wood eventually acquired the rights to SOM 1-01 and added them to their ever-growing cache of MJ-12 oddities. Along the way, the Wood's claimed they had authenticated SOM 1-01, although others in the UFO research community were much more skeptical, such as MUFON's Richard Hall and Thomas Deuley, who issued this joint statement:

> The SOM-01-1 manual arrived in the mail to Don Berliner as a roll of film from an anonymous source. This immediately raises suspicions, since there is no identifiable source whose veracity and reputation can be checked and no original documents that can be subjected to forensic analysis. We believe this to be a hoax document, a deliberate fake designed to mislead the public and to plant a false information in the UFO research community.[127]

SOM-01-1 also included a reference to "Kirtland Air Force Base, New Mexico" which some suspected was a wink and a nod that this seemingly spurious document may have been another Richard Doty snow-job. Nonetheless, it has continued to be embraced by some of the more prominent voices in ufology, such as Linda Howe, who at the Citizens Hearing on Disclosure (a pretend congressional hearing held at the National Press Club in 2013), claimed that SOM-01-1 had "stood the test of time"[128]—when of course it had done nothing of the sort, and only added to the stack of spurious MJ-12 related documents that have littered ufology with what researcher Robert Hastings refers to as "bird droppings" deposited by individuals associated with the Aviary.

In 1995—as *The X-Files* was starting to gain traction in pop culture—FOX, the same network that brought us Mulder and Scully, treated saucer buffs far and wide to an epic hype-fest that became known in the annals of u-fool-ology as the "Alien Autopsy" film.

Roswell remained on the top of the ufological charts well into the '90s with the release of retired U.S. Army Lieutenant Colonel Philip Corso's *The Day after Roswell*, that just so happened to coincide with the Roswell 50th anniversary in 1997. Co-authored with *UFO Hunter* Bill Birnes, *The Day after Roswell* was received as the latest and greatest chapter of UFO Disclosure, coming from an actual former intelligence officer who had worked at the U.S. Army's Foreign Technology Division. Corso claimed to have firsthand knowledge of the Roswell crash debris, and even witnessed one of the supposed Roswell bodies at Fort Riley, Kansas in the summer of 1947. Corso, it so happens, was involved in counterintelligence work and disinformation operations during his military service, thus suspicions arose—among the conspiratorial-minded—that *The Day After Roswell* was a similar sort of disinformation.

In April of 1996, Art Bell got in on the Roswell action when he received a letter from a military man pseudonymously identifying himself as "A. Friend." The mystery military man explained that he wasn't at liberty to reveal his real name because he currently held a security clearance and didn't want to jeopardize his career by going public with "information related to the Roswell UFO crash."

According to A. Friend, his grandfather—who had been a member of a UFO crash retrieval team—passed away in 1974, "but not before he had sat down with some of us, and talked about the [Roswell] incident..." Enclosed with the letter were "metal samples" described as "pure extract aluminum" that A. Friend's granddad had "appropriated" from "a large batch subsequently sent to Wright-Patterson AFB in Ohio from New Mexico." According to "A Friend", his granddad stated that when his team arrived at the Roswell crash site:

[T]hey found two dead occupants, hurled free of the Disc. A lone surviving occupant was found within the Disc, and it was apparent its left leg was broken. There was a minimal radiation contamination, and it was quickly dispersed with a water/solvent wash, and soon the occupant was dispatched for medical assistance and isolation. The bodies were sent to the Wright-Patterson AFB, for dispersal. The debris was also loaded onto three trucks which finished the on-load just before sunset.

Granddad was part of the Team that went with the surviving occupant. The occupant communicated via telepathic means...

Granddad spent a total of 26 weeks in the Team that examined and debriefed the lone survivor of the Roswell crash. Granddad's affiliation with the 'project' ended when the occupant was to be transported to a long-term facility. He was placed on-board a USAF Transport aircraft that was to be sent to Washington, D.C. The aircraft and all aboard disappeared under mysterious and disturbing circumstances, en route to Washington, D.C.

It may interest you that three Fighter aircraft, dispatched to investigate a distress call from the Transport experienced many electrical malfunctioning systems failures, as they entered the airspace of the transports last reported location. No crash or debris of the Transport was ever found. The Team was disbanded...

This letter and the contents of the package are given to you with the hope that it helps contribute to discussion on the subject of UFO Phenomena.

I agree with Neil Armstrong, a good friend of mine, who dared to say, at the WHITE HOUSE no less, that there are things "out there", which boggle the mind and are far beyond our ability to comprehend.

Signed
A. Friend

Chapter 47

The rock and roll UFO show

In 2016, former Blink 182 front man Tom DeLonge revealed his role as a supposed conduit for top secret UFO intel courtesy of "sources within the aerospace industry and the Department of Defense and NASA...Former high-level officials and scientists with deep black experience who have always remained in the shadows are now stepping into the light."[129]

By now, a claim of this type is old hat for those of us who have taken this particular saucer for a spin before, and are hip to UFO history and its recurring themes. But with each new decade, it seems inevitable that these themes and memes will get trotted out again, with a cosmetic tweak here or there, dressed up in new clothes, but still "the same old story, the same old song and dance"—new lipstick on a pig that never flies; only flaps its wings and squeals, but never actually leaves the ground.

A rock and roll UFO tie-in makes perfect sense from a marketing standpoint—utilizing a hipster millennial to reach a youthful audience—'cause let's face it folks, if you've been to a UFO conference recently, for the most part the fan base has grown a bit long in the tooth. And if you're going to roll out variations on this same tired tune, then you need a fresh hook to grab and grow your audience, and bring in new butts to fill the seats. For the most part, promoters of MJ-12 and the Roswell crash, over the years, have been squares—the old school suit and tie, nut and bolt ufologists—many now well into their autumn years, repeating basically the same things they were saying thirty odd years ago, although now without the energy and passion of their youth.

Then along comes Tom DeLonge, who twenty years ago was probably an eager dope-smoking skate boarder who couldn't wait for his latest *X-Files* fix. In the years to follow, DeLonge would wade into the ufological waters at the same time he was pursuing a music career, so this transition from rock star to ufologist seemed a natural progression. If you look at rock and roll history, there have been any number of musicians who've experienced UFO sightings, including Hendrix, Bowie, and Lennon. Rock music has always been about escape, ascendance and discovery.

In February 2017, at the annual International UFO Congress, DeLonge was named "UFO Researcher of the Year," a title that doesn't necessarily mean much other than the sponsors of the event probably figured it would be good to curry favor with this new UFO sugar daddy, who was in the process of setting up his own prospective ufological empire called To The Stars Academy of Arts and Science (TTS/AAS, or TTSA for short). According to reports, TTSA would utilize a two-pronged approach: one prong would consist of a multimedia operation with plans to release a series of books, feature films, and television productions; the second TTSA prong would be a research group, kind of like a new and more overt version of the Aviary, comprised of former intelligence officers and scientists. UFO journalist/enthusiast Leslie Kean learned that "important unclassified data and documentation is expected to be released through the Academy's on-line Community of Interest (COI) in collaboration with the US government, which will be set up soon."

In certain respects, TTSA harkens back to Bill Moore's plan to produce a series of books and films based on info he'd received from whistle-blowers and insider sources, the ultimate goal to reveal the truth about UFOs. Running parallel with Moore's activities was the Aviary—a similar two-pronged approach—although the Aviary was a more decentralized research group than what DeLonge and his crew have proposed. Granted, Moore and DeLonge are totally different animals, but each, it seems, served a similar purpose, as point men for UFO disclosure...or disinformation.

Although it was sometimes difficult to pin down Bill Moore's motives—and how much he was, or was not, manipulated—he was nonetheless a competent researcher, who (for good or ill) left an indelible mark on ufology. In contrast, DeLonge appears to be what many in the Intelligence Community might refer to as a "useful idiot"; someone recruited to play a role that, at least in his own mind, is full of excitement and intrigue, even potentially heroic, all in the interests of bringing UFO Disclosure to the public.

DeLonge comes across as a dyed-in-the-wool believer, although there's no hiding the fact that TTSA was designed as a money-making enterprise. Part of the TTSA arrangement states that DeLonge is guaranteed a $100,000 royalty each calendar year, which in the low rent world of ufology is some serious scratch. This royalty payment, it appeared, was for attaching his name to the project and performing the role of a pseudo spokesman. (It should also be noted though that DeLonge sank $400,000 of his own money to get the starship TTSA off the ground.)

DeLonge's bonafides include a meeting with John Podesta, who has long been viewed in ufological circles as a potentially key figure in finally busting down the doors of UFO secrecy. DeLonge, it should be noted, views the Deep State as the good guys, a premise that runs contrary to the Alex Jones-Infowars conspiracy crowd who believe that Podesta is a dastardly pizza-chomping pedophile involved in satanic rituals orchestrated by the diabolical tag team of Hillary Clinton and George Soros. Conversely, DeLonge and his throng think the Deep State has got a bad rap, and that UFO secrecy (of the past) was actually for the greater good—which is why the Deep State good guys of yore kept UFOs under wraps, in the interests of National Security, but the time has come at last for the figurative saucer hatch to open, and for the truth to finally emerge like the ET disembarking the mothership in the final scene of Close Encounters of the Third Kind. This sentiment, in essence, is what members in the Aviary were long ago promoting, among them super-spook Rick Doty, who at times has presented himself in this same vein, as a Deep State UFO whistle-blowing do-gooder who always had our best interests at heart.

The national spotlight suddenly intensified on DeLonge when his name surfaced in the hacked Podesta emails drip-drip-dripped by Wikileaks during the 2016 Presidential campaign. One of DeLonge's TTSA collaborators, author Peter Levenda, told radio host Jimmy Church that the…

> …hack of the emails was unfortunate for those of us working very hard to get some information out there, and to protect people we worked with and to protect what we were doing and our sources and methods, you might say, and so that was a bit of a problem. None of us ever suspected we would be suddenly thrust into this connection suddenly with a Russian hack, you know. I mean this whole thing was just absolutely unbelievable, so it made everybody batten down the hatches a little bit and take some additional steps for us to make sure that we were still fulfilling our mission and at the same time maintaining deeper levels of security.

Although DeLonge made heavy weather about his Wikileaks exposure, I suspect he and his TTSA associates were probably spinning cartwheels from all the free publicity it afforded. Supposedly, plans for the TTSA rollout had been stalled after these leaked emails surfaced, as if some super-secret project had been revealed to the public causing panic among the TTSA ranks. DeLonge even went offline and supposedly into semi-hiding for a while due to the possible repercussions of how this leak would ultimately compromise the TTSA mission.

By and large though, the DeLonge-Podesta emails seemed rather benign: basically press releases for forthcoming TTSA projects, with a little supposed insider knowledge thrown in to presumably impress UFO buff Podesta. In an October 26, 2015 email DeLonge wrote: "I would like to bring two very 'important' people out to meet you in DC. I think you will find them very interesting, as they were principal leadership relating to our sensitive topic. Both were in charge of most fragile divisions, as it relates to Classified Science and DOD topics." Elsewhere in the Podesta emails, DeLonge was trying to get the word out that *VICE News* was on board to:

...produce, finance and distribute the Sekret Machines Docu-Series charting my personal journey on how I met important people and how they are guiding my effort to communicate difficult themes to the youth. All the while keeping the names and identities of my Advisory council private. This is huge. VICE is the single biggest, most credible and progressive news source out there. It's international, and it's all aimed at the youth. They feed directly into HBO and just launched their own news channel...I hope you get my emails and I hope I am not bugging you. I am currently updating the Advisors, as well. Rolling Stone will break the story on April 8th. The novel is in stores April 7th. VICE series launches immediately following, and we are placing the Scripted TV series now...

DeLonge emailed Podesta on January 25, 2016, with the subject line, "General McCasland," which was a reference to a former Air Force official who was supposedly privy to Roswell-related intel:

When Roswell crashed, they shipped it to the laboratory at Wright Patterson Air Force Base. General McCasland was in charge of that exact laboratory up to a couple years ago. He not only knows what I'm trying to achieve, he helped assemble my advisory team. He's a very important man.

Best, Tom DeLonge.

Throughout 2017, DeLonge and his TTSA crew were hinting at big news just over the horizon, some sort of earth-shattering UFO disclosure type event that was going to knock ufology's collective socks off. After months of mounting anticipation, this big announcement (sort of) came on October 11, 2017, with a live-streamed press conference featuring DeLonge and his TTSA cohorts broadcasting from what appeared to be a stage in an auditorium—as if it was being presented to a live audience— but there was no audience, nor any media present asking questions of the TTSA participants; it was all a scripted presentation. The "press conference" opened with a short dramatic trailer featuring DeLonge filmed on location at the National Mall in D.C.:

> Early this year I set out to do something pretty challenging. I wanted to shift perception on an extraordinary topic that had already over 70 years of research, opinion, and frankly quite effective disinformation. I had the rare opportunity to present my ideas to an executive with the Department of Defense who worked in the special access programs in an area called Watertown, also known as Area 51. That meeting led to multiple clandestine encounters across the United States from desert airports to vacant buildings deep within Washington DC, and from these exchanges I learned three things: one, there are certain things that should never have been secret; two, there are secrets that were justifiable at the time which should now be disclosed. And three, there are things that are so unimaginable that certain interests feel that they should never ever be made public. After this you might even agree...

Other TTSA members attending the press conference came equipped with lofty titles, such as former CIA/DoD officials Jim Semivan (Vice President of TTSA Operations), Luis Elizondo (TTSA Chief of Security and Special Programs) and Chris Mellon (National Security Affairs Advisor). Also included in the TTSA lineup was none other than Dr. Hal Puthoff (Vice President of Science and Technology). Puthoff has turned up repeatedly in previous iterations of these types of pseudo-clandestine civilian research organizations, starting way back with Project Stargate, then on to the Aviary, NIDs, and now TTSA.

Rather than being some sort of a big reveal, the press conference came across as a hard sales pitch, a good portion of which was devoted to promoting the entertainment aspect of TTSA as a means to bring the "big ideas" of space exploration and potential ET contact to the public. During the press conference, TTSA member Chris Mellon described video footage in TTSA's possession that had been "captured by a U.S. Navy F/A-18 Super Hornet using the Raytheon ATFLIR Pod that was being operated by a highly trained aerial observer and weapons system operator whom the government has spent millions of dollars to train. 'Go Fast' reveals a Navy encounter that occurred off the East Coast of the United States in 2015 and the object in view remains unidentified."[130]

For some reason, Mellon neglected to show the actual video, which has been referred to as "Go Fast." Meanwhile, a slideshow was projected on a screen behind him that displayed, among other images, a photo of a purported UFO first posted to Rense.com in July of 2005. This photo was later revealed to be a mylar party balloon.[131] TTSA announced that "Go Fast" was just one among several previously classified videos they were planning to roll out in the days and weeks to come, supposedly in collaboration with the Department of Defense.

After the TTSA launch party, DeLonge followed up with a somewhat awkward appearance on *The Joe Rogan Experience*. The consensus of many armchair pundits who viewed this episode (present armchair company included) was that DeLonge came off as a bit of a flake. This narrative changed somewhat when a story broke in the December 16, 2017 edition of the *New York Times* entitled, "Glowing Auras and 'Black Money': The Pentagon's Mysterious U.F.O. Program," that many in ufology were now heralding as a UFO Disclosure game-changer. Due to this article, DeLonge and TTSA fans—after receiving a fair amount of flak over DeLonge's appearance on Joe Rogan's show—were now suddenly dancing in the ufological aisles.

This *New York Times* article didn't so much focus on DeLonge as it did TTSA member Luis "Lue" Elizondo, who revealed details about a secret Pentagon project he claimed to have supervised called the Advanced Aerospace Threat Identification Programme (AATIP), a 16 million dollar "black money" operation, the skids of which had apparently been greased in 2007 by Senator Harry Reid.

Reid's support of this secret project is where a Las Vegas connection enters the picture in the form of Robert Bigelow, formerly of the already-discussed NIDS, who, it appears, received the bulk of the $16 million appropriated for AATIP. Apparently, Reid and Bigelow had some history together, which should come as no surprise given the fact that Bigelow Aerospace is headquartered in Reid's former congressional district in North Las Vegas.

It turns out that a private organization operated by Bigelow called BAASS (Bigelow Aerospace Advanced Space Studies) had been contracted by the government to collect and analyze UFO files for AATIP. This association—when it was revealed—sent red flares into the air for many in ufological circles who had long ago pegged Bigelow as a shady character of sorts, at least in terms of the secrecy surrounding the many UFO and paranormal projects he's been involved with.

Strangely, some months before these TTSA revelations hit the pages of the *Washington Post* and *New York Times*, Bigelow had appeared seemingly out of the blue in a *60 Minutes* episode where he stated that he was "absolutely convinced" aliens exist and have visited Earth. It's unclear why Bigelow chose this particular time to issue his "ETs exist" statement, although in retrospect it seemed part of a larger campaign orchestrated by the TTSA—or possibly even shadow elements of the government, or a mish-mash of both—that wished to advance the UFO Disclosure narrative using Bigelow and/or TTSA as proxies.

It's also possible that Bigelow himself is the secret hand behind TTSA. As stated during the TTSA press conference, one of their main goals is to raise funds to ultimately build spacecraft that would propel mankind to the stars, and for this to happen TTSA would have to partner with somebody in the aerospace industry, such as Bigelow. In furtherance of their agenda, a public stock offering for TTSA was announced:

> TTS/AAS hopes to raise enough money through its public offering and through expected profits from its entertainment and aerospace divisions to fund research into the Phenomenon and related exotic technologies for global consumption. Imagine a global, transparent, research organization tackling ideas that most scientists today will not entertain for fear of ridicule, involving young scientists from around the globe.

The TTSA launch party in October 2017—and the follow-up news stories in the *New York Times, Washington Post* and *CNN*—came across like a well-oiled rollout and marketing campaign. TTSA wasn't actually mentioned in these news reports, as the focus shifted to the defunct AATIP program, and from all appearances DeLonge had been eased out of his lead spokesperson role and replaced by Elizondo.

The TTSA-AATIP amalgam found one of their biggest media champions in Tucker Carlson, the hyperbolic *Fox News* host. Carlson, a cross between infotainment meets Trump cheerleader/propagandist, has been known to occasionally delve into oddball stories, including Lue Elizondo and TTSA-related guests on a number of occasions throughout early 2018.

In media interviews, Elizondo was careful to avoid mentioning the existence of ETs, and for the most part stayed on script in terms of being all about "science," and not so much "speculation." Like Tom DeLonge the year before him, Elizondo was named "UFO Researcher of the Year" at the 2018 annual UFO Congress. During his keynote speech, Elizondo was oddly enough wearing a bullet-proof vest, which suggested to some that he was perhaps bringing some showmanship and intrigue to his presentation—or on the other hand suffering from delusions of grandeur—or perhaps the third item on the menu: that the very same Deep State actors that Elizondo had previously worked for might have targeted him for revealing "too much, too soon." Elizondo, for what it's worth, has remained a bit of an enigma. His online bio states:

> [He] is a career intelligence officer whose experience includes working with the U.S. Army, the Department of Defense, the National Counterintelligence Executive, and the Director of National Intelligence. As a former Special Agent In-Charge, Luis conducted and supervised highly sensitive espionage and terrorism investigations around the world. As an intelligence Case Officer, he ran clandestine source operations throughout Latin America and the Middle East.
>
> Most recently, Luis managed the security for certain sensitive portfolios for the US government as the Director for the National Programs Special Management staff. For nearly the last decade, Luis also ran a sensitive aerospace threat identification program focusing on unidentified aerial technologies. Luis' academic background includes microbiology, immunology and parasitology, with research experience in tropical diseases. Luis is also an inventor who holds several patents.

While impressive, Elizondo's bio seemed intentionally vague on details, offering no specific dates of service or position titles, other than that he was an intelligence officer with the DoD, and possibly other government entities. This vagueness, however, should come as no surprise given the sensitive nature and national security concerns involved in Elizondo's claimed work history.

Although his bio noted he was "a former Special Agent In-Charge" it didn't indicate "Special Agent In-Charge" of what, or with which agency. Working under the "Director of National Intelligence" also sounded impressive, although by extension anyone who works in any branch of intelligence would theoretically fall under the umbrella of the "Director of National Intelligence."

Elizondo's most noteworthy biographical claim was his participation in a "sensitive aerospace threat identification program focusing on unidentified aerial technologies." One could logically presume this is a reference to the defunct AATIP program.

Due to the *New York Times* article, Lue Elizondo soon found himself thrust squarely into the ufological spotlight. The key evidence the *New York Times* pointed to was a video of an encounter between two Navy F/A-18F fighters with Unidentified Aerial Phenomena (UAP) that occurred off the coast of San Diego, California in 2004. The pilot, Commander David "Sex" Fravor (apparently 'Sex' was his fly-boy call sign), described the UAP as resembling a white tic-tac—roughly 40' in diameter—that "zipped away at speeds, turn rates and accelerations faster than any known friendly or threat aircraft." It appeared the "tic tac" had been video-recorded using FLIR thermal imaging that captured the heat signature of this unexplained something.

While mildly intriguing, the video was really no more compelling than a lot of other blurry examples of UFO porn that litter the Internet. Granted, the pilot testimony added some contextual weight, but it really didn't bring us any closer to solving the Eternal Mystery. It was afterwards discovered that the footage in question—identified by TTSA as the "Gimbal" video—had been posted to the FighterSweep. com website several years prior, then subsequently removed in 2014. In total, TTSA has thus far released three videos, described as:

...official USG footage brought to you exclusively by To The Stars Academy of Art and Science...Gimbal is the first of three

U.S. military videos of an unidentified aerial phenomena (UAP) that has been through the official USG declassification review process and approved for public release.

In addition to supposedly declassified UFO videos, TTSA claimed knowledge of "metal alloys" containing properties "unknown to science" that were in some way associated with UFOs (or UAPs as the cool kids are calling them nowadays.) For those of a Roswellian bent, "metal alloys" sounds a bit like "memory metal." According to reports, this is where Robert Bigelow again re-enters our story, as it was Bigelow's company that reportedly "modified" a facility in Las Vegas to store these materials. Or at least that was the inference made by TTSA members and amplified by social media cheerleaders.

In the 1990s Bigelow was "...investigating alleged ET energy technology and titanium aluminide metallurgy for their investment potential." Could the 1990s "titanium aluminide metallurgy" be the vaunted "metal alloys" of 2017? Others have suggested that these so-called "metal alloys" are in reality the supposedly exotic materials that Art Bell received in 1996—dubbed "Art's Parts"—some of which were subsequently passed on to Linda Howe, who in turn has shared them not only with Bob Bigelow, but also members of TTSA.

Over time, TTSA eased off the claim that the "metal alloys"— or "meta-materials" as Hal Puthoff referred to them—were of otherworldly origin, and eventually the chatter trailed off into a non-committal posture that maybe they weren't necessarily of alien origin after all. Of course, it's possible the mystery material alluded to in the TTSA video may have actually been a purported alien implant that caused a bit of a stir when it was revealed by MUFON's Chase Kloetzke that she had handed over some type of 'artifact' to "Lue Elizondo with the production company from A&E" and it was never seen again. Or at least that's where things stood as of early 2019.[132]

Just when it appeared that the TTSA hype was starting to fizzle out, a story broke in the May 22, 2019 edition of The *New York Post* courtesy of reporter/filmmaker Stephen Greenstreet, bearing the bold title of "The Pentagon finally admits it investigates UFOs." In the article, Greenstreet quoted Pentagon spokesperson Christopher Sherwood, who confirmed that a secret government program called AATIP pursued "research and investigation into unidentified aerial phenomena."[133]

The Pentagon's simple, yet seemingly significant statement soon sent TTSA fandom into a state of ecstasy with this revelation that AATIP had indeed been investigating UFOs.

Unfortunately, Stephen Greenstreet (the author of the *New York Post* article) then turned around and seemingly jumped the shark—or the saucer, as the case may be—by reporting that "while the DOD says it shut down the AATIP in 2012, spokesman Christopher Sherwood acknowledged that the department still investigates claimed sightings of alien spacecraft." Of course, the *New York Post* has always straddled the line between straight journalism and tabloid sensationalism, so it could be assumed that Greenstreet was simply spicing up his article by using the term "alien spacecraft" — a combination of words that a Pentagon spokesperson would probably never use unless on background after loosening themselves up with a few adult beverages.

Not long after the *New York Post* article, a reporter for *The Intercept*, Keith Kloor, threw a wet blanket over the party when he contacted the same Pentagon spokesperson, Christopher Sherwood, who re-confirmed that AATIP had indeed pursued "research and investigation into unidentified aerial phenomena," but added that: "Mr. Elizondo had no responsibilities with regard to the AATIP program while he worked in OUSDI [the Office of Under Secretary of Defense for Intelligence], up until the time he resigned effective 10/4/2017."[134]

Aside from these unresolved issues concerning Lue Elizondo—and if indeed he was actually ever involved in AATIP—another area of murkiness arose around TTSA's financial disclosures, revelations of which surfaced in late 2018 in the form of Federal Exchange Commission (FEC) filings that revealed TTSA was $37 million in the red. This was initially reported by *Ars Technica* reporter Eric Berger as a $37 million debt accrued from "stock-based compensation."[135]

Not long after, DeLonge went on the offensive with the following Instagram post:

> The approximate $37 million stockholders' deficit is NOT DEBT as he characterized it but is attributable to stock-based compensation expense. This article is highly misleading and grossly mischaracterizes statements in an SEC filing.
>
> BLATENT LIE — APPARENTLY, THIS WRITER CAN'T READ. BTW- TTSA never even raised $37m!!? So how in the hell did we spend it?! Lord. I ask all of you that believe in the @tothestarsacademymission to go write a complaint on their website RIGHT NOW for trying to hurt an admirable effort to help humanity by using negative attacks and—-> lies.
>
> Dear Ars Technica— I am writing you regarding the article posted to Ars Technica this morning titled 'All the dumb things? Blink 182 front man's UFO project $37 million in debt' by Eric Berger. We were surprised Ars Technica would allow Mr. Berger to post such an article without asking either Mr. DeLonge or To The Stars Academy of Arts and Science for comment. This article is highly misleading and grossly mischaracterizes statements in an SEC filing. Had Mr. Berger bothered to reach out to us for comment this could have been prevented.[136]

Soon after, *Ars Technica* corrected the article to state that the $37 million in question had actually been a "deficit" as opposed to "debt," but for DeLonge to characterize the story as a "blatant lie" seemed overwrought hyperbole. Long time UFO skeptic Robert Sheaffer took an even deeper dive—"following the money" as they say—and discovered a paper trail for a couple of loans totaling $600,000 that TTSA received in 2016 and 2017 from the LLC called "Our Two Dogs, Inc."

With an annual revenue of $403,119, Our Two Dogs, Inc. employs a twelve-person staff and is listed in Dun & Bradstreet as a "Retail Hot Dog Stand." After poking around a bit, Sheaffer discovered that the phone number for Our Two Dogs, Inc. was the same number listed for "Louis Tommasino, CPA & Associates." Tommasino also serves as TTSA's Chief Financial Officer.

When Sheaffer searched Yelp for reviews of "Our Two Dogs" he came up empty handed, although he was able to track down a physical location—6265 Greenwich Drive, San Diego, California—which happened to be not far from where he lives, so Sheaffer decided to pay a visit and presumably treat himself to a hot dog. The location turned out to be in a business park area of the Sorrento Valley, the suite number listed as *Our Two Dogs - 210*. Sheaffer waltzed into the office armed with a copy of Dun & Bradstreet and inquired of the receptionist if this was the whereabouts of the purported hot dog stand.

As soon as the words "hot dog" popped out of Sheaffer's mouth, he was approached by a fellow who informed him that "Dun and Bradstreet is garbage, everyone knows they are garbage…You insult me by bringing that in here!" The fellow with a surly attitude about Dun and Bradstreet turned out to be the aforementioned Louis Tommasino, who informed Sheaffer: "Our Two Dogs is a management company, a highly respected management company that I have operated for many years…If you have any other questions, you can ask my attorney. And my attorney will sue you if you write that this is a hot dog business!"[137]

Afterword

Adventures in Chapel Perilous

The hazards of hurling yourself head-first into the wooly worlds of ufology and conspiracy research present the same pitfalls that any number of researchers have fallen prey to over the years—including those who knew "too much about flying saucers" like Albert K. Bender.

In the early 1950s, Bender founded the International Flying Saucer Bureau (IFSB), based out of Bridgeport, Connecticut. In March of 1953, the IFSB conducted a group mental telepathy experiment by transmitting the following mental message:

THE MESSAGE
(To Be Memorized)

Calling occupants of interplanetary craft. Calling occupants of interplanetary craft that have been observing our planet EARTH. We of IFSB wish to make contact with you. We are your friends, and would like you to make an appearance here on EARTH. Your presence before us will be welcomed with the utmost friendship. We will do all in our power to promote mutual understanding between your people and the people of EARTH. Please come in peace and help us in our EARTHLY problems. Give us some sign that you have received our message. Be responsible for creating a miracle here on our planet to wake up the ignorant ones to reality. Let us hear from you. We are your friends.

In early September 1953, Bender announced that he had solved the flying saucer mystery, the details of which would be revealed in the

October issue of the IFSB newsletter, *Space Review*—but before he could do so, Bender claimed he was visited by three mysterious Men-in-Black (MIBs) who spooked him into silence. Bender delivered the following portentous message in *Space Review* for his fellow IFSB members to ponder:

> The mystery of the flying saucers is no longer a mystery. The source is already known, but any information about this is being withheld by orders from a higher source. We would like to print the full story in *Space Review*, but because of the nature of the information we are sorry that we have been advised in the negative. We advise those engaged in saucer work to please be very cautious.

Afterwards, Bender ceased publication of *Space Review*, closed down IFSB, and retired from ufology, one of the very first (alleged) victims of the notorious MIBs. Others have speculated that Bender cooked up the whole crazy caper as a convenient excuse to leave ufology, as the pressures of overseeing IFSB had become too much for him, perhaps even leading to a psychological breakdown.

An overlooked aspect of the Bender saga was his longstanding fascination with the occult. Due to these peculiar interests, Bender transformed an upstairs room in his house into a "chamber of horrors", as he called it. He painted the walls with depictions of grotesque scenes from the works of Shelley, Stoker and Poe, and adorned it with "macabre items such as artificial human skulls, shrunken heads, bats, spiders, snakes." At the same time, Bender was "reading books on black magic, occult subjects, and other similar works...[he] even tried to hold some séances."

In recent years, UFO researcher Allen Greenfield discovered—among old photos of Bender's "chamber of horrors"—that in one corner of the room an altar had been erected, ostensibly used for magic rites.

From this, it could be conjectured, Bender's occult dabblings might have awakened some ancient force that later paid him a visit in the form of those dreaded MIBs. Likewise, the IFSB group telepathy experiment might have similarly opened a door to a negative psychic influence.

This would become a repeating pattern in the decades to follow for many who took the deep dive down ufological and conspiratorial rabbit holes. Some fared better than Bender, others far worse—such as poor Paul Bennewitz, the poster child of a certain sort of paranoia, who was given a gentle nudge into the Abyss by shadowy characters in and out of the U.S. government. An element of Bennewitz's delusion took shape in the form of Dulce Base, which in years to come would grow large in the minds of those who wed themselves to the mythos, such as Phil Schneider, another Dulce Base casualty.

Like ufology, the conspiracy research field has suffered a steady stream of causalities, minor to major, from Kerry Thornley to Bill Cooper, to name but a few. The common denominator (linking these conspiracy-ufology casualties) is a form of paranoia that sneaks up on one gradually, the result of consuming a steady conspiratorial diet combined with a lack of filters in place that typically keep one from going off the rails. Add to this equation a certain amount of self-delusion (or confirmation bias) where every coincidence becomes a momentous synchronicity; part of a larger pattern in which our hero finds himself smack dab in the middle of the greatest conspiracy of all time.

With that being said, there are pros and (obvious) cons that come with this terrain—or as Charles Manson once allegedly raved: "Total paranoia is total awareness." Manson's words were true in some respects, but there's a line one needs to draw that often falls between sanity and madness—in that mystical domain known as Chapel Perilous— where one tackles their innermost demons, and comes out at the end of the journey either completely shattered, or at last whole.

Many have lost themselves on their journey through Chapel Perilous, taking the deep dive into what Robert Anton Wilson (RAW) referred to as "reality tunnels"; an ontological game RAW played where he adopted a given set of beliefs, or indulged a certain theory—such as Dulce Base, for instance, or some variation of the Kennedy assassination—to see where it may lead; an exercise to open the mind to possibilities, "alternative facts" and shifting realities. A reality tunnel could even be a sexual kink, or an extreme political view – basically a way of viewing the world through a different lens.

RAW picked up this practice (of exploring reality tunnels) from the writings of Aleister Crowley, who was fond of adopting alternative personas and mindsets as a means of consciousness expansion; to climb into a reality tunnel for a while and poke around, dip your toes into different waters to see what there is to learn. It's a way of stretching your brain...as long as you can stay sane. The key is to know when to hit the eject button, at that point when a reality tunnel becomes no longer beneficial—when you've stopped learning anything useful, and find yourself trapped in a particular belief system, and start spinning in circles, lost in Chapel Perilous forever.

In *Cosmic Trigger Vol. 1: The Final Secret of the Illuminati*, RAW recounted his Chapel Perilous trip, featuring psychedelic adventures with strange green men and ritual magick communications with the Sirius star system—all of this amid a swirling sea of synchronicities. ('Tis an ill wind that blows no minds!) It was a high and wild time that came crashing down around RAW with the tragic death of his fifteen-year-old daughter, Patricia, on October 3rd, 1976—a tipping point that made RAW question his life's course as a freelance author-adventurer. Had it all been mere folly? All this chasing after higher consciousness that ultimately led to the depths of despair? Did a cruel-hearted cabal of secret masters send him on this merry chase only to pull the magic carpet out from under his feet and send him hurtling into the Great Abyss?

The natural reaction to the brutal murder of one's child elicits, in most of us, a sense of rage and vengeance, however robotic these emotions may seem. RAW wisely learned somewhere along the way that cages exist not only in the physical realm, but also in our minds, and that the only way to truly free ourselves from these self-imposed prisons, is to let them go.

At this figurative fork in the Chapel Perilous road, RAW was left with one of two choices: either continue down a path of despair and anger over the death of his daughter—what RAW referred to as the "loser script"—or choose instead to free his mind from the chains of the past using the "winner script" where you create your own reality; or, more precisely, a model of the world that is positive and loving. One way of doing this is through the practice of forgiveness, a sentiment RAW expressed frequently throughout his final years. In retrospect, I now understand why he placed such importance on the practice of forgiveness: RAW realized that the more we can do to unchain those ghosts of the past that haunt us, the freer we can be to live, love and learn.

A proponent of space exploration, life extension and cryogenics, RAW made the bold leap—in the aftermath of Patricia's death—to have her brain cryonically preserved. As he told the *San Francisco Examiner*: "We thought that if we could make a contribution to science something good could come out of this tragedy...We feel it is a long shot, but it's our way of expressing our belief in life and our rejection of the casual acceptance of murder and death in our society."

Conversely, RAW's friend Kerry Thornley was the poster child for Chapel Perilous gone south. Thornley first entered Chapel Perilous in 1958 (even though he didn't know it at the time) when he and his teenage pal Greg Hill invoked the Greek Goddess of Chaos and Discord, more commonly known as Eris, in a bowling alley in Whittier, California, and soon after launched the "spoof" religion, Discordianism. At the time, this was nothing more than an in-joke between Thornley and Hill, although in the decades to follow Discordianism would become a countercultural phenomenon of sorts, inspiring such classics as RAW and Shea's *Illuminatus!*

Two short years after co-founding Discordianism, Thornley encountered none other than Lee Harvey Oswald while serving in the Marines, and for a short period the two became friends, a couple of outfit oddballs with mutual oddball interests. Afterwards, Thornley began working on a novel titled *Idle Warriors* about the misadventures of a soldier during the Cold War period. Initially, the lead character of *Idle Warriors*—Johnny Shellburn—was a composite character that Thornley based on himself and other Marines he had served with, including Oswald. In early 1960, while stationed in Japan, Thornley learned that Oswald had defected to Russia, and it was from that point forward he decided to base his novel entirely on Oswald. So, in essence, Thornley was writing a book about his old Marine pal, and future JFK assassin, three years before the Kennedy assassination. Thornley's story grew progressively stranger from there.

In 1967—as Thornley was embracing psychedelia and the Summer of Love—he became a target of New Orleans District Attorney Jim Garrison's JFK assassination probe. Garrison alleged that Thornley was part of a conspiracy based out of New Orleans, and that he had played the role of an Oswald double, masquerading as his old Marine pal to ostensibly set him up as an assassination fall guy.

During the '60s, Thornley had been cynical and dismissive of conspiracy theories, particularly those of the John Birch Society variety, and so he found it particularly preposterous when one of Garrison's independent investigators—a John Birch Society member named Allan Chapman—suggested that the Bavarian Illuminati not only orchestrated JFK's assassination, but had also taken over all the major TV networks!

After catching wind of Chapman's Illuminati-JFK assassination theory, Thornley—along with some of his fellow Discordian conspirators—initiated what became known as Operation Mindfuck (OM), a campaign designed to screw with Garrison's head by sending out spurious announcements suggesting that he (Thornley) was an agent of the Illuminati. Among the culprits who helped perpetrate this hoax was none other than RAW. As Thornley recalled:

> Wilson and I founded the Anarchist Bavarian Illuminati to give Jim Garrison a hard time, one of whose supporters believed that the Illuminati owned all the major TV networks, the Conspiring Bavarian Seers (CBS), the Ancient Bavarian Conspiracy (ABC) and the Nefarious Bavarian Conspirators (NBC).

In 1973, Thornley came across a copy of *Coup d'Etat in America* by A.J. Weberman and Michael Canfield, which presented the theory that the three mystery tramps picked up by Dallas police in Dealey Plaza following JFK's assassination were actually "spies in disguise" acting as a hit team. To bolster their theory, the authors presented a series of photographic overlays comparing the profiles of certain notorious individuals to those of the tramps, one of whom was former CIA agent, and Watergate burglar, E. Howard Hunt. After comparing the photo of the old man tramp to Hunt, they discovered that their features identically aligned with one another.

After examining the old man tramp photo in *Coup d'Etat in America*, Thornley began to suspect that a shadowy character he'd met in New Orleans back in 1961 named Gary Kirstein may have actually been E. Howard Hunt in disguise. On one occasion, Kirstein had engaged Thornley in a theoretical discussion of how to kill a president, and in particular, JFK. At the time, Thornley considered this nothing more than a morbid intellectual exercise. Later this conversation would come back to haunt him.

This realization that E. Howard Hunt might have been the curious character that Thornley met in New Orleans soon after opened a floodgate of memories that, in time, led him to believe he'd been a victim of MK-ULTRA mind control as well as part of a Nazi genetic breeding experiment. As Greg Hill told an interviewer during this period:

"[Thornley] has recently been in a state of extreme discord. We were talking about Eris and confusion and he said, 'You know, if I had realized that all of this was going to come true, I would have chosen Venus [to worship instead.']"

In the intro to *The Prankster and the Conspiracy: The Story of Kerry Thornley and How he met Oswald and Inspired the Counterculture*, RAW quoted from a work that Thornley had written in the late 1960s entitled "Epistle to the Paranoids":

> Ye have locked yerselves up in cages of fear—and, behold, do ye now complain that ye lack FREEDOM! Ye have cast out yer brothers for devils and now complain ye, lamenting, that ye've been left to fight alone.

RAW further commented:

> Kerry Thornley wrote those words [*Epistle to the Paranoids*] in the mid-1960s and within 10 years he had become a clinical paranoid himself, in the judgment of almost all of his friends, including Dr. Robert Newport, a psychiatrist who had known Kerry since high school. The moral of this seems to me: take great care which nut cases you dare to mock, for you may become one of them.
>
> I do not write in any spirit of smugness or superiority. I became somewhat paranoid myself, for a while there, or at least experienced acute anxiety attacks. For several months I literally could not leave my house without looking around to see if Kerry crouched behind a bush waiting to shoot me. You see, he had become convinced that I worked for the CIA and served as one of his "managers" or "brainwashers," but I thought I worked as a freelance writer and considered myself his friend.
>
> As his letters to me grew increasingly hostile and denunciatory, I began to fear that he might have graduated from "weirded

out" to "dangerous." This now seems silly to me—an overreaction—but the violence and paranoia of the Nixon years made everybody in this country feel a bit jumpy. A Black Panther leader in my part of Chicago seemed to have gotten shot by the local police while sedated; the extreme Right and extreme Left both had wild conspiracy theories about everybody else; anti-war meetings, anti-segregation meetings, even pot-legalization meetings all had people making nervous jokes about who among us the government had infiltrated to report on our Thoughtcrimes. The government not only appeared irrational and out of control, but so did a large part of the population. I finally moved to Ireland to start a new life as an expatriate, and my worries about Kerry executing me for "brainwashing" him made up only a microscopic part of my motive. The whole country seemed a bit funny in the head and I had to hide out and lie low for a while. Silence, exile, and cunning, as Joyce had advised. Looking back, I feel amused and humbled. Like Kerry, I had satirized the paranoids before the sheer number of them frightened me into acting just like one of them.

I remember my last phone conversation with Kerry, during which he announced that just a week earlier I had come to Atlanta, argued with him about my alleged CIA connections, spiked his drink with LSD, and brainwashed him again. I told him that I had not left San Francisco in months, and that if he had a bad trip the previous week then somebody else gave him the acid, not me. I insisted on this as persuasively as I could. Finally, Kerry relented—a bit. "Well, maybe you believe that," he said. "But that means your bosses have been fucking with your head and implanting false memories in you too!"

How do you argue that you haven't had your head altered? "Look," I said, "I'll put my wife Arlen on. She'll tell you I haven't left here in months." "That won't prove anything," he said with the calm certitude of a Grand Master announcing checkmate. "They probably fixed her head too." I don't remember the rest of the conversation. I felt lost in an Escher painting...

During the mid 1990s, IllumiNet Press became one of the go-to publishers for conspiracy books, and it was IllumiNet's publisher—Ron Bonds—who provided Thornley a platform for material he'd never been successful in getting published, such as *Idle Warriors* and *Zenarchy*. Unfortunately, Kerry didn't have a lot of time to enjoy his literary revival due to a rare kidney disease he contracted in the early '90s, a condition that ultimately led to his death on November 28, 1998. (Thornley suspected that this disease had been part of a decades-old conspiracy to finally shut him up for good.)

One of the last projects Thornley and Bonds were working on was *Dreadlock Recollections*, which would encapsulate all of Thornley's theories and supposed involvement in the JFK assassination, including meetings with the shadowy figure, Gary Kirstein, who he believed to be E. Howard Hunt. Hunt—it so happens—was still alive at the time, and ultimately Bonds got cold feet about the project, fearing a lawsuit or worse from Hunt, who was not only a litigious type, but had also garnered a reputation of almost James Bond villain type proportions.

IllumiNet's most prolific writer was Jim Keith, author of numerous conspiracy-related titles including *Black Helicopters Over America*, *Casebook of the Men in Black* and *Saucers of the Illuminati*. By the late 1990s, Keith had become Bond's partner at IllumiNet, and the pair had plans to release many more conspiracy titles in the years to come. Less than a year after Thornley's passing, Keith met his own untimely demise. On September 3, 1999, Keith injured his knee falling from a stage at the Burning Man Festival, and the next morning was transported to a medical facility in Reno, Nevada, where kidney problems developed that prevented immediate surgery. Three days later, on September 7 when surgery was finally performed, Keith died as the result of a fatal blood clot that was released from his leg, traveling into his lungs.

These developments came as a big blow to Ron Bonds, losing his two most prolific authors over the span of two short years. Unfortunately, Bonds met an equally untimely death—in April, 2001—due to food poisoning. So—within less than three years—the main players at what was the premiere publisher of conspiracy books, IllumiNet Press, had all passed away in what some considered curious circumstances.

Kenn Thomas suspected something sinister attributed to the deaths of IllumiNet's holy trinity—Keith, Bonds and Thornley—that was perhaps part of a larger plot designed to silence voices in the conspiracy research field. In particular, some were pointing to the last article Keith had written for a short-lived internet magazine, *Nitro News*, about Princess Diana's death. Keith had contacted Diana's physician, who claimed that—at the time of her passing—she was pregnant with the child of Dodi Fayed, and due to this fact had been targeted for murder by British elites working in cahoots in MI6.

In 1997, Thomas and Keith co-authored *The Octopus: Secret Government and the Death of Danny Casolaro*, which concerned another suspect death, that of investigative journalist Danny Casolaro that occurred on August 10, 1991, in Martinsburg, West Virginia. The coroner's report stated that Casolaro died in a very messy manner after slashing his wrists, although Casolaro family members claimed that Danny was deathly afraid of razor blades. Before leaving for Martinsburg for a clandestine meeting with his secret "Octopus" source, Casolaro made a cryptic remark to the effect that he feared his life might be in danger.

The term "Octopus" was a catch-all for what Casolaro had purportedly uncovered that connected damn near everything in the 1980s conspiratorial kitchen sink: the October Surprise, Iran-Contra drug and gun running, and in particular the so-called Inslaw Affair/ Promis software scandal. At the center of this many-tentacled monster was Michael Riconosciuto (aka "Danger Man"), a scientific whiz-kid who in the early 1980s had worked for the Wackenhut Corporation on a secret version of the Promis software. At the time, Wackenhut had set up a secret compound at the Cabazon Indian reservation in Indio, California where—in cahoots with Danger Man—they were developing a wide range of biological and chemical warfare weapons to be used by CIA-funded mercenaries in the jungles of Nicaragua and other South American garden spots.

Casolaro's research linked the goings on at Cabazon with a larger clandestine project known as "Yellow Lodge" that operated on Cabazon land and other Indian reservations, and in specific an outpost known as "D6" located on the Jicarilla reservation, near Dulce, which of course brings us full circle to where our story began.

Notes discovered in Casolaro's "suicide" hotel room mentioned "MJ 12—extraterrestrial," and "Area #51." The apparent source of Casolaro's UFO info appeared to be Riconosciuto, who was among the first to promote a story (later picked up by Michael Younger, see Chapter 28) about two warring intelligence agency factions, Aquarius vs. COM-12. At one time or another, Riconosciuto even claimed he had witnessed an alien autopsy.

* * *

My own journey through the looking glass (UFOs and conspiracy research) was "initiated" (and I don't use that word lightly!) with a psychedelic UFO encounter that I've spoken about ad nauseam over the years, so skip ahead a few paragraphs if you've heard this tale before.

In a nutshell, a stoner colleague and I were at a party one mid summer's eve in the late '70s (in a central California town that shall remain unnamed!) when we both dropped a hit of some righteous acid called Red Dragon. Soon after, the walls started doing their wavy dance and closing in on us—it was all becoming too much—so we decided to get away from the cacophony of the party, take in some fresh air and check out the night's sky. We walked to a nearby ditch-bank where we'd be able to get off the city streets, away from humans and houses. Along the way, one of us asked the other, "What if we saw some UFOs right now? No one would believe us because of the state we're in!" And then the two of us started laughing (somewhat uncontrollably) at this prospect.

It wasn't more than fifteen minutes later that we were treated to a crazy UFO show that transpired over the course of an hour and a half or so, as one after another—whatever these things were—danced across the sky and blew our minds. The first craft we witnessed was of the classic saucer variety, followed by progressively weirder ones in various shapes and sizes, including an almost cartoonish-looking contraption with a multicolor propeller.

In retrospect, our psychedelic UFO experience (at least for me) was an introductory phase of Chapel Perilous, the first steps through that crazy door. Once inside, part of the process was trying to figure out exactly what we'd witnessed. ETs were the first obvious answer, the easiest conclusion to arrive at given the climate of those times with such films as *Close Encounters of the Third Kind* in the forefront of the minds of a couple of teenaged psychonauts with a deep desire to travel to other planets and experience ET contact.

As time progressed, I began to explore other possible answers for our psychedelic UFO experience and play the "reality tunnel" game (before I was even familiar with Wilson's use of the term) in an attempt to explain something that was ultimately unexplainable. One possible explanation I explored was the scenario laid out in the Christian-themed tome *UFOs: What On Earth Is Happening?* by John Weldon and Zola Levitt, which put forth the treatise that UFOs were demons in disguise sent to Earth by Satan himself to beguile and corrupt humankind—a theory I halfway believed at one time or another. I eventually came to my senses on that one—and besides, it wasn't a healthy reality tunnel to fixate on when there were scads of more sexy avenues to explore.

The theory laid out in Martin Cannon's *The Controllers* was another reality tunnel I dove into to explain our psychedelic UFO experience—that what we observed, or had been subjected to, was some sort of mind control program. Granted, this was a somewhat narrow box in which to try to cram an experience, but just the same an intriguing thought experiment—and that's the beauty of reality tunnels: immerse yourself in the journey and enjoy the ride, but don't go so far down the hole you never find your way back out.

Of all the reality tunnels I explored, the one that makes the most sense—or resonates most strongly—is the "Co-Creation Theory," a term coined (I think) by my friend Greg Bishop, which subscribes to the theory that we humans play a pivotal, or co-equal role in the UFO experience; that there's an interplay between whatever forces are behind "UFOs," coupled with our perceptions of these events.

When talking about the co-creation theory in recent years, I've framed it (at least in terms of my own experience) as an "unwitting magick ritual." As noted, my friend and I actually entertained the notion: "What if we saw some UFOs right now—no one would believe us." (Due, of course, to the psychedelized state we were in.) In retrospect, I suspect that we may have unconsciously planted some sort of psychic seed that sprouted not more than fifteen minutes later in the form of a crazy "UFO" show.

My wanderings in Chapel Perilous were put on hold for a few years as life became more mundane (in some respects) with a real job and marriage and a home to attend to, as well as raising a couple of crazy cats. But in the late '90s, Chapel Perilous re-entered my life, partly on account of my interest (some would say obsession) with mind-control conspiracies, particularly some of the terrain covered in my book *The Shadow Over Santa Susana: Black Magic, Mind Control, and the Manson Family Mythos*, and the supposition that the Manson Family had been a "military mind control experiment," as famed conspiracy sleuther Mae Brussell once upon a time theorized.

Around this time—by a matter of happenstance, synchronicity or dumb luck—I was put in contact with Ira "The Unicorn" Einhorn, the '60s activist and co-founder of Earth Day, who became a major player in ufological and paranormal circles during the 1970s, and a close associate of Dr. Andrija Puharich.

Einhorn was associated with some members of the Aviary, most notably CIA scientists Kit Green and Ron Pandolfi. In fact, Bill Moore (on an episode of Greg Bishop's *Radio Misterioso*) recalled that while on his *Roswell Incident* book tour he'd been scheduled for a radio interview hosted by Einhorn on the University of Pennsylvania campus. When Moore arrived for said interview, he was informed Einhorn had suddenly skipped bail and fled to parts unknown after being charged with the murder of his girlfriend, Holly Maddux. Einhorn would later claim that Maddux's murder was part of some sinister CIA set-up. Around this same time, Puharich fled to Mexico, claiming he was likewise being hounded by mean-spirited Deep State spooks.

It was indeed an odd set of circumstances that brought Einhorn and I together in cyber space (the particulars of which I won't go into here, mainly because it involved someone who would probably just as soon keep their role on the down-low). Einhorn had only recently re-emerged during this timeframe (circa 1997), and was living in the French countryside with his common law wife, Annika Flodin, and had yet to give any media interviews. That being the case, I decided to dive in headfirst—as I am often wont to do—and approached Einhorn for his first public interview in over two decades, to which he consented. The results of our exchange afterwards appeared in Greg Bishop's *Excluded Middle* magazine.

My interactions with Einhorn were conducted solely through email, going back and forth over the period of a couple months, as I tried to pry out of him—in as gentle a way as possible—his knowledge (or version of events) pertaining to Holly Maddux's murder, as well as his role in the UFO and paranormal research scenes of the 1970s.

At the end of the day, I don't think I was particularly successful, as Einhorn had a tendency to quickly pivot from any questions he didn't really want to answer, and then spin them into another topic.

About midway through our exchanges, I received a mystery email that included truncated text from an email Einhorn had previously sent me. The creepy thing about this email was that it hadn't come from Einhorn's address, but from another unknown email address. This mystery email led me to speculate that our exchanges were being monitored, and that this truncated email was sent as a heads-up to let me know "They" were watching, which I guess, in retrospect, I appreciate. (Thanks FBI or NSA or Interpol or whoever!) It was another one of those Chapel Perilous moments.

It was a heady time; I was working on my Manson book, interviewing Einhorn, as well as writing a slew of "high strangeness" articles for various 'zines. It was the halcyon days for what became known as the zine movement, a relatively short-lived "golden age" when copying machines had become more accessible, and anyone could go to a nearby Kinko's (or better yet, use a Xerox machine at their place of work after hours on the sly) to run off copies of their very own DIY publications.

Access to this technology provided a platform for those of us on the so-called "marginal fringe" interested in exploring where conspiracy theories, the paranormal, UFOs, psychedelics, and other seemingly disparate subjects intersected. This stew of crazy ingredients brought together a nexus of individuals who were all more or less into a lot of the same stuff: Kenn Thomas (SteamShovel Press), Joan D'Arc and Al Hiddel (Paranoia Magazine) Greg Bishop, Rob Larson, Peter Stenshoel (The Excluded Middle), Wes Nations (Crash Collusion), Tim Cridland (Off The Deep End), Jim Keith (Dharma Combat), Rob Sterling (The Konformist), Jim Martin (Flatland), Miles Lewis (Elf Infested Spaces), Ron Bonds (IllumiNet Press) and Adam Parfrey (Feral House).

The zine revolution (or zine movement) of the late 1980s and '90s formed a bridge between the old school brick and mortar publishing world to a more free form scene (in the form of zines) that soon after spilled over into the emerging currents of cyberspace that soon overtook the planet. Some of my zine colleagues now look back wistfully at those bygone days (pre-internet/social media) when our gang of conspiracy sleuthers were akin to the Book House Boys from *Twin Peaks*; a secret club of likeminded souls connected to snail mail networks where we shared rare documents like *Nomenclature of an Assassination Cabal,* or *The Gemstone Files,* or *MJ-12 Documents,* or *Alternative 3* video—all the sort of nerdy conspiracy stuff that Mae Brussell was hip to—and if you were gonna be a cool conspiracy dude (or dudette) you needed to be hip to, as well. Of course, nowadays most of these rare and arcane documents are accessible more or less through your home computer; all the secrets of the conspiratorial or ufological universe delivered right to your digital doorstep.

This transition (hard copy to digital) caused the zine scene to quickly wither on the vine, and before we knew it many zine publishers had either given up the ghost or, conversely, moved to internet forums, websites and blogs. Of course, at the time none of us really knew where the "internets" was going, but the writing on the wall was quickly becoming clear—better jump aboard this train before it left the station, and get on the ground floor to wherever this technology was taking us. One of the early sites paving the way for this digital transition was the short-lived *Nitro News*, which published Jim Keith's last article on the death of Princess Diana.

Around the time of Jim Keith's death, I'd traveled down to Los Angeles to take in a lecture by Kenn Thomas, and hang out with members of our conspiracy cabal who had converged that weekend in the City of the Angels. One evening we found ourselves at *Swingers*, a hip coffee shop in West Hollywood, our cabal consisting of Robert Larson, Peter Stenshoel, Greg Bishop, Kenn Thomas, Rob Sterling and the late Acharya S. (aka Dori Murdock), author of *The Christ Conspiracy: The Greatest Story Ever Sold* (1999).

As we huddled and shared the latest conspiratorial gossip, one of us joked (I think it was Bishop) that "They" (the infamous "They") could wipe out half of the conspiracy research community by bombing our table. (At least the hip part of the conspiracy research scene, as we perceived ourselves.) We all laughed, of course—one of those partly nervous laughs—due to a certain sense of paranoia oozing through the scene at the time. However, we didn't really exhibit our unease with the same sort of "sweaty paranoia" as a Bill Cooper or Phil Schneider, but nonetheless there was this creeping sense within our crowd that The Man was on to us—I mean, he had to be, right? —or at least was watching us, and maybe even had our table wired?

Later that night, our cabal gaggled after-hours at a secret spot in a southland industrial park—a sort of conspiratorial clubhouse—at a party hosted by Ruffin Prevost, who during this period had launched one of the early conspiracy websites, Periscope. Also in attendance was Kathy Kasten, a middle-aged, larger-than-life character, who was dealing with her own Chapel Perilous adventures, including confrontations with certain Men in Black that—at one point or another—had apparently hassled her about her Roswell crash investigations.

During how-do's, Kathy commented with a wry smile: "I wonder who's the spook in the room? There's one in every crowd, you know. Any time a bunch of conspiracy researchers get together, there's bound to be a spy there." And since Kathy didn't know me from Adam, she gave me a wry look. and said, "I bet it's you, wink-wink." I don't know how serious Kathy actually was about suspecting me to be a spook, but whatever the case we ended up getting along fairly well over the course of the evening. While swapping conspiracy yarns, and smoking big, fat stogies, Kasten dropped the bomb that (according to her sources!) John Alexander was the actual author of Martin Cannon's *The Controllers*, and that Alexander's involvement therein was part of some larger grand deception. I didn't know quite what to make of this assertion, although, as I learned, Kathy was well connected and had a number of legit sources within intelligence agency circles.

That same weekend of the Kenn Thomas lecture, I attempted to hook up with Cannon for a meeting of the minds. Previously, I'd corresponded semi-frequently with Martin, and as I recall this was around the time he had discussed meeting up with me for a Cathy O'Brien/ Mark Phillips lecture in Santa Barbara. (O'Brien was an alleged Project Monarch mind-control victim, and Phillips was her "de-programmer"). As I recall, Cannon basically wanted to go there and give the pair a hard time—which sort of sounded like fun, I must admit.

When I dialed the number Cannon had given me, someone answered who said no one by that name lived there, so I hung up and said oh well. Afterwards, I figured it was indeed Cannon who I'd spoken to, and for whatever reason he thought better about meeting up. Cannon's run-around was just more of the type of paranoia I'd witnessed on occasion that permeates the conspiracy research field; where researchers grow suspicious of other researchers because they suspect they're CIA plants or some such. Not long after, Cannon pretty much disappeared from the scene, although anonymous sources suggest he later popped up just long enough to plant the hoax-rumor that Barbara Bush was Aleister Crowley's granddaughter.

* * *

My little foray into Chapel Perilous came to a head during this late '90s period, as my paranoia (or "higher awareness" to quote Chuck Manson) went through the roof due to a series of unsettling experiences—in the form of physical sensations—that started at home one night as I was eating dinner, sitting where I always sit when dining, at one end of the sofa in our living room.

Suddenly my head started getting hot and I wondered what the hell was going on. My wife Heather looked over and commented that my head was a cherry red, and I told her I was burning up. I just sat there for a few minutes, trying to be calm about the situation, wondering if I was going to have to be rushed to the ER. After a few minutes, the heat gradually receded and things returned to normal.

A week or two later it happened again. Once again eating dinner, sitting in the exact same spot on the sofa when my head start heating up, and Heather commented again, "Hey, your head is bright red"—and then it eventually receded just like the time before. Afterwards, I tried to look for a rational answer: Was it something I had eaten? There was nothing really hot, like chilies for instance, I'd had with dinner. Nor was I ill at the time, or anything like that. Soon I started wondering if the remote microwave machines (that alleged MK-ULTRA victims talk so much about) had been trained on me, boiling my brain like soup. Whatever actually occurred, it was eerily similar to the accounts of those who've been subjected to "non-lethal" weaponry such as "Active Denial Technology."

A few weeks later it happened again when Heather and I were dining at a local Mexican restaurant. Same scenario: I got a hot head and felt like I was on fire; Heather noticed that my head was all red...you know the drill. I cooled down and everything was back to normal and I finished my meal. And then a few weeks later we were at the same Mexican restaurant—actually sitting at the same table in the same seats as the previous time—when it happened again. There was a window facing the street outside through which someone could have directed a microwave beam at me, and so the paranoia continued to simmer in my head. I was now officially a "wavie" (as they have been referred to in mind control lore).

That was my fourth and final experience with this head-on-fire phenomenon, and I have no explanation how or why it happened—nor at this point, some twenty years later, do I really care—but it all seemed very odd at the time and fed my semi-paranoia that I was somehow targeted because of my research. I never went full overboard with this premise, but it certainly was a rabbit hole I poked my head into.

Around the time I was going through my microwave Chapel Peril-ous head-on-fire phase, Greg Bishop was going through his own Chapel Perilous passage, precipitated by—among other things—his interac-tions with Michael Younger, that curious trench-coated character with dubious spy credentials who you can find out more about in Greg's book, *It Defies Language: Essays on UFOs and Other Weirdness* (2016).

It was Younger who initially approached Bishop after having "looked at [his] file." As Bishop points out in *It Defies Language,* these are the sort of cryptic come-ons that can start a conspiracy theorist's head a-spinning; the type of come-on that plays to one's personal vanity, or sense of significance in the grand conspiratorial scheme of things, much in the same manner that Bill Moore was long ago approached by "Falcon" who informed him that "you're the only person we've heard talk about this subject, who seems to know what he's talking about."

It's these sorts of recruitment ploys (used by spooks or supposed spooks) that send a shot of paranoia-tinged adrenaline into the veins of the mark; the type of drug that, more often than not, can become quite addictive, leading to delusions of grandeur and the prospect that you're now an insider privy to ufological or conspiratorial secrets of the highest order—that you've figured it all out and are sitting at the center of a conspiracy that revolves around you, and only you, like in the cases of Kerry Thornley and Paul Bennewitz, or more tragically, Bill Cooper. According to Greg Bishop:

Early on, [Younger] handed me about 500 pages of his own writings on the subject of government secrets and UFOs. The thick booklets, printed on one side of each page, discussed the secret history of spycraft, UFOs, mind control, and even biowarfare. Apparently, these were given out to only a few people. Why he (or someone else) would go to all this trouble just to rile up a few UFO researchers remains a mostly inscru-table question...

Ultimately, there was nothing provable about his UFO statements, but his method should be studied by anyone who is interested in the UFO/government angle: He told us about secret developments in the military world that later turned out to be true in order to get myself and others to listen to his UFO stories, which we really had no way of checking out. This is why I have often said that anything coming from a so-called 'inside' source should not be taken as gospel until the facts can be checked. Unfortunately, many researchers are so charmed by this attention that they immediately regurgitate the UFO info, thereby infusing the public with many crazy stories that both muddy the waters of understanding and serve the insider's agenda, which is of course ignored by the incautious researcher. Because of this experience, and those of others (credulous and otherwise) I believe that many UFO 'revelations' foisted on us in the last 50 years may have had very little to do with aliens and flying saucers. They were more likely cover stories to advance other agendas having nothing at all to do with UFOs, such as spycatching and diversionary tactics in service of counterintelligence operations. The UFO stories tend to be the wackiest of the wacky, such as those told to Paul Bennewitz in the 1980s, and which spread throughout ufology for years afterwards.[138]

Around the time Bishop was interacting with the mysterious Mr. Younger, he and his wife were surveilled on a number of occasions. Richard Sarradet reported the same scenario of being trailed during the period he was interacting with Michael Younger. Whether Younger had somehow orchestrated this surveillance, or if it was government agents keeping an eye on people associated with Younger, we'll probably never know. This is how Chapel Perilous sometimes unfolds...

Bishop became convinced that his phone was tapped, and that his mail had been tampered with, specifically targeting his correspondence with fellow UFO researchers. As Bishop recalled, these tampered letters "always turned up opened, partially destroyed, or never made it to me...Most of these letters arrived partially opened or torn and then placed in plastic bags with notes of apology from the Post Office about problems in transit or with their machinery."

Bishop ultimately took RAW's advice to follow the "winner script" (as opposed to the "loser script"), making a conscious effort to stop worrying about any supposed surveillance—or whatever seemed to be swirling around him—and just let it go. "Eventually I came out of my own room of Chapel Perilous with a higher degree of general happiness than I had before, and a mindset that looked at coincidences and synchronicities as dispassionately as possible."

As fickle fate would have it, the last time I remember having my mail (possibly) tampered with concerned a tape-recording Bishop made of an interview I conducted with RAW at his apartment in Santa Cruz, California, in the spring of 2001. This interview occurred around the same time our mutual friend Miles Lewis was organizing the annual National UFO Conference (NUFOC) scheduled for later that year in Austin, Texas.

Miles—aware of our meeting with RAW—put a bug in my ear about approaching him about speaking at the event. Afterwards, I connected RAW with Miles, and a deal was subsequently sealed for RAW to appear at that year's NUFOC. In this regard, Miles put together a stellar line-up of speakers, many of whom are mentioned in this book—or who I intersected with—including Kenn Thomas, Greg Bishop, Pamela Stonebrooke, David Perkins, James Moseley, Tom Deuley—not to mention Eugenia Macer-Story, a psychic whose work I helped shine a light on with an internet interview in the late 1990s.

Eugenia sometimes came across as brilliant; other times bat-shit crazy. I think Eugenia existed in a world where both of these realities were possible. I corresponded semi-irregularly with her during the late '90s, at the same time as I was experiencing neurological issues—

technically diagnosed as "transverse myelitis"—a fancy way of saying "inflammation of the spinal cord." During the period I was going through this "transverse myelitis" episode, I was referred to a neurologist in San Francisco. After my appointment, I returned home and was going through emails when I came across something Eugenia had sent me at the exact same time I was being examined at the San Francisco clinic. (She had no idea I was there.) In her email, Eugenia mentioned that she'd just been on a bus in upstate New York when an image of yours truly suddenly flashed in her mind and she heard the words "San Francisco!" These are the type of synchronicities one encounters visiting Chapel Perilous.

James Arthur—another slated speaker for NUFOC (whom I'd recommended to Miles) —was author of *Mushrooms and Mankind: The Impact of Mushrooms on Human Consciousness and Religion,* one of the first books to examine the influence of *Amanita muscaria* on the myth of Santa Claus and Christmas. At some point, I'd discovered that James lived nearby me, and so I contacted him and we met over coffee one morning. Given that two of my main interests were psychedelics and UFOs, our conversation inevitably gravitated to both, and Arthur mentioned that back in the 1970s he had attended the Giant Rock Spacecraft Conventions (near Joshua Tree, California) and was part of a semi-underground psychedelic-UFO scene that had infiltrated the event and turned-on such old school contactees as Gabriel Green to the wonders of d-lysergic acid. Arthur even hinted that this loose-knit group of psychonauts might have actually conjured UFOs upon occasion while under vitamin L's divine influence.

Over time, I lost contact with Arthur, and was alarmed to hear in 2004 that he'd committed suicide in the Madera County jail where he had been incarcerated on child molestation charges. The story became increasingly darker from there, the details of which I won't get into here, but suffice it to say Arthur's supporters claimed he had been the victim of some type of police state set-up, while his detractors instructed that if anyone wanted to get the real scoop on Arthur (real name James Arthur Durovic), all they had to do was visit the Megan's Law website.

Arthur's death seemed emblematic of the sort of end-of-a-crazy-millennium-start-of-an-even-crazier-one vibe that claimed not only the Twin Tower victims, but also Miles' NUFOC event, which turned out to be the greatest UFO conference that never was, given the fact that it was scheduled for the weekend of Sept 15, 2001—just a few days after 9-11—during a period when all flights within U.S. air space were grounded.

In many ways, 9-11 was Chapel Perilous for Generation X. It was the first major conspiracy that came to full bloom in the internet age; a Rorschach blot on which to overlay whatever conspiracy-reality tunnel fit within its broad outlines. To that end, 9-11 was a unifier of sorts, bringing together both sides of the conspiratorial-political spectrum—the far left and extreme right. To the left, it was a perfidious plot by warmonger George W. Bush to bring about the surveillance state in all of its Orwellian glory—and the right conspiratorial wing was pretty much on the same page, seeing Dubya as part of the globalist cabal orchestrating a New World Order false flag rat fuck that was coming after your god-given right to get drunk as a skunk and shoot up shit on your back forty.

One of the most outlandish 9-11 theories was promoted by conspiracy enthusiast Alfred Webre who claimed that it was a New World Order black op utilizing time-traveling UFOs equipped with directed energy weapons. It's not clear if Webre was suggesting actual aliens were behind the plot (actually, none of what he was suggesting was at all clear), but hey, I'm sure it must've had something to do with a secret treaty between the U.S. government and Zeta Reticuli.

9-11 was a litmus test for many in the conspiracy research community to choose up sides. It created a divide between true believers (Truthers) and skeptics—and never the 'twain would meet—you were either on the bus, or off the bus, as Ken Kesey said. There was no way to straddle the fence: You had to make a stand! The bottom line seemed to be that if you challenged 9-11 conspiracies—in whatever shape or form—then you were part of the coverup. Somehow the Man had got to you. When Art Bell of all people voiced 9-11 skepticism, many of his listeners took this as a deep betrayal that somehow Art had sold out, and even suspected that he was now part of a globalist conspiracy orchestrated by his uncle, Warren Buffet.*

* * *

In early 2003, I phoned RAW with some follow up questions for *The Prankster and the Conspiracy*, which I was then readying for publication. During this period, I was on RAW's email list and whenever he emailed anyone, he'd cc: John Poindexter, then head of the notorious Information Awareness Office, a recently formed DoD agency overseeing the government's brand-spanking-new domestic surveillance program established after 9-11.

When I asked RAW what the deal was with cc-ing Poindexter, he explained that by sending his email messages directly to Poindexter it would eliminate the need for anyone to maintain surveillance on him, thus cutting down on government waste. "Besides," RAW added, "it amuses me to think of Poindexter reading my emails."

I asked RAW if "They" had lifted the Information Awareness Office (IAO) logo from the cover of *Illuminatus!*, as the IAO logo featured the all-seeing eye in the triangle, with a light beam focused on planet Earth, indicative of an Orwellian nightmare come true, wrapped up in symbolic imagery so blatant it seemed absurd.

"I don't know what the hell's going on," RAW admitted. "I think we're being taken over by a bunch of surrealists."

---

* During a number of episodes of Coast2Coast AM, Art Bell asserted that he was Warren Buffett's nephew, which at the time I accepted as fact, because who would make up something like that? Art also claimed, at one time or another, that J.Z. Knight was his sister. Neither of these assertions appear to have been true.

Acknowledgements

Thanks to those who helped guide me on this journey into the dark, sometimes tragic, and often comical underbelly of ufology and the mysterious human creatures who inhabit that realm.

Tal Levesque and John Rhodes certainly merit a nod of gratitude for collectively (and unwittingly) propelling me on this mad odyssey oh so many years ago over bacon and eggs at a rustic rural restaurant in California's gold country. After dropping endless hints over the years, Tal finally came clean and spilled the beans (via an email in November 2015) that he'd fabricated large swaths of the Thomas Castello/Dulce Base story—which is what I'd always suspected. I include this email in the appendix.

Just a few months before finishing the first draft of this book, I was informed that Tal passed away on December 21, 2018 to his final resting place in the Inner Earth where he'll no doubt be reunited with friends and lovers like Richard Shaver and Mary Martin. As it is above, so it is below.

Thanks to those that laid the foundation with previous work and research into the Dulce Base story, MJ-12 papers and the Bennewitz affair, who were generous with their time and support, among them Greg Bishop, Norio Hayakawa, Christian Lambright, Nick Redfern, Jack Brewer, Mark Pilkington, Bill and Nancy Birnes, Greg Valdez, and last but not least David Perkins, whose enthusiasm, keen insights and detailed memories from decades past helped cheer me on through the last mile and across the finish line to whatever literary glory might await me.

Adam Gorightly
Dog Days of Sirius, 2020

Appendix A

During our multi-year correspondence, Tal repeatedly claimed that Thomas Castello was a real person, and that the Dulce Base material was authentic. Nonetheless, I continued to press him during our email exchanges, never directly calling him out on what I suspected his role was in the creation of the Dulce Base mythos, but just asking the questions again and again in different ways until at last the dam broke and Tal shared the truth, or at least something close to that.

The question I posed, that elicited Tal's final email to me, concerned an alleged interview of Thomas Edwin Castello (TEC) that surfaced in the late 1980s, an artifact which I always assumed originated with Tal. My question: "When did this interview with Castello take place...I thought he was in hiding after '89?" Tal's email response was as follows:

You still do not get it.

TEC is a creation. A MYTH.

I took rantings from a Heavily Drugged (Prescription Pills) woman (C.H.), made corrections to stuff that was really wrong, added my own REAL Research, mixed it together. That was the basis of the two original DULCE BASE articles. Literally I made 100 large envelope PACKETS with supporting material (real stuff) about Underground Bases; Genetic Research; Hidden Science (R&D); etc. And sent the material to authors and lecturers, who then mixed it into their talks, articles and books. This made it look like it was coming from MORE THAN ONE SOURCE.

You see I had a copy of the 1959 RAND Project on Deep Construction; my friend's father designed improvements on the Tube Shuttle System, he worked with Werner Van Braun. I

would go on vacations with them to Edwards [Air Force Base]...
VIP stuff; my father worked for MAJIC; I worked in Advanced
Project Development, later as counter-Intelligence and as a
SECURITY Supervisor.

I mixed stuff I was not suppose to make public into the
DULCE MYTH.

The GOAL was to Manipulate UFOLOGY into anoth-
er direction. Away from the Boring Lights in the sky stuff. To
EFFECT the "Public Imagination". So...Norio [Hayakawa] was
right. I was behind a MIND GAME. When it caught on, I could
NOT reveal what was true and what was not. I had to protect
that CH was out of her mind and keep it going.

Later, Cherry and I had a falling out when she went public
on Facebook saying SHE was the Secret Source. But, source of
WHAT? Have you read any of her Porno DULCE Revelations?

The INTERVIEW Never Happened.

It is creative writing.

I asked several people to submit questions for TEC.

Then sent them to Cherry (this was done TWICE.)

SHE answered the Question, as IF she was TEC.

I do NOT think he ever existed.

BUT...I'm NOT going public with that Opinion. Are you
kidding?

Look at how the DULCE MYTH has changed UFOLOGY
and SCI-FI.

I'm not going to fuck with it now.

And I hope you don't either.

Cherry sent back answers from TEC.

Cherry was heavy into CHANNELING TEC on the
typewriter.

Answers would APPEAR at times...She said, I don't remember typing that.

I CLEANED UP her stuff...Then sent it out to the people who asked the questions, other authors, etc.

Then, that got spread around.

As long as I did not come forward I was a big LOOP of an ever growing MYTH.

Now here is the problem...ONLY certain things CAUGHT on.

People didn't respond to certain REAL things...THEY loved the SENSATIONAL.

I gave CLUES to REAL stuff.

There is a BASE at Page (Section P) ARIZONA, so I connected it on a map to DULCE. Then started connecting more Bases. Some I knew were ALREADY connected. Others I connected were Tunnel links I wanted the DoD to create. So... the MYTH covers up the TRUTH. That is WHY, even though threatened TWICE and following THEIR instructions to stay alive, I'm still here.

Now here is the other problem...There IS a base at Mt Archuleta."Section D"...there is an entrance (two, really) IN the city of Dulce and at least two more outside of town. One is a MINE that connects to the system. Everything is linked to Los Alamos and that is tunnel connected to Santa Fe and that to Sandia Base. These are all REAL.

So, here we go again...myself and a FACTION within the hidden ALTERNATIVE military/Science Civilization...have been working on ways to reveal MAJESTIC (which is real) to the public and still protect its existence. See the problem?

We must MIX things up. NO real exact locations to the public. We can not risk ANYONE getting into the System.

I HAVE been down there in my work as a Security Officer. I have "Protected" the Physical ACCESS to CERTAIN LOCATIONS.

But...I can reveal ANYTHING (until I'm advised NOT to), anything else I want. It is part of my job to TEST SECURITY. And to locate THOSE who might be getting TOO close. This puts me in Danger to various FACTIONS who do not know what I'm up to and WHO I really am and what my Clearance Level is. I can get out of many (most) situations IF not killed first. There is a CODE...a number (let's say an AGENCY) that does its best to protect me from others and outside the SYSTEM.

WHY am I telling You?

To EXPAND your mind.

What you see around you is like DISNEYWORLD in Florida, designed by a THINK TANK and construction overseen by the Military. The control system is BELOW the Park. Same in the USA for OVER 200 years...an Alternative Civilization lives BELOW the SURFACE.

This is what the GAME is.

99% of the Surface Population are unaware about how advanced our fellow humans really are. It is ULTRA TOP SECRET....well UMBRA-TS. MAJESTIC is just the "Interface...get it ?

The GAME is in the MIND.

One Group has been Manipulating all of Humanity, for almost Forever.

This is a PRISON PLANET.

Humans do not live this way, in other Non Surface or off Planet Cultures.

WE do not die at Physical death...we existed BEFORE coming here to infiltrate and alter this HOLOGRAM (Virtual Reality).

It does NOT Exist, when you are not Looking at it.

It is an ALTER-NET. The fucked Controllers are GAMING the other PLAYERS.

We are EXPOSING it, as much as possible while still trying to Stay IN THE GAME.

When YOU pass from your current body, you are going to then KNOW that you are STILL CONSCIOUS...You still Exist. The Game is NOT over...They will try and trick you into returning to the CONTROLLED SYSTEM.

But...They need you to AGREE.

An ACT of WILL can stop them.

WE "AGENTS" from the Plasma World, can come back here on our own accord. Just to fuck with the CONTROLLERS again.

OR

We can return to one of many WORLDS for some well deserved R&R.

WE can NOT reveal the Truth or we Quickly get Attacked by Stupid people who are caught up in BS Mind Slave idea constraints.

So....Back to my Job. Cosmic Security Supervisor and ZON Priest.

Most all of the above is BS.

That IS my Job...get it?

MADE YOU THINK !

That IS my Job...

:-)

Notes

1. Redfern, Nick. 2017. *The Roswell UFO Conspiracy: Exposing A Shocking and Sinister Secret*. Lisa Hagan Books. (p. 90)
2. https://kevinrandle.blogspot.com/2011/05/ufo-crashes-and-len-stringfield.html
3. http://ufotrail.blogspot.com/2017/09/nsa-releases-1978-memo-on-mufon.html
4. *San Francisco Chronicle*, 7-9-47
5. Valdez, Greg. *Dulce Base The Truth and Evidence from the Case Files of Gabe Valdez*. Levi-Cash Publishing. Kindle Edition.
6. UFO Hunters - Underground Alien Bases (Season 3, Episode 2)
7. Interview with Mark Pilkington, 10-11-17
8. Perkins, David. 1997. "Darkening Skies, 1979-1980. Of Dead Cows and Little Green Men." A chapter from *1947-1997: Fifty Years of Flying Saucers*. 1997. Edited by Hilary Evans and Dennis Stacy. John Brown Publishing, London, England.
9. "The Late Great Tom Adams - Thoughts on the Passing of Thomas R. Adams (1945-2014)" by David Perkins - Easter April 5, 2015. https://www.theparacast.com/forum/threads/memorial-show-for-thomas-r-adams-1945-2014-post-questions-here.16140/
10. *Stigmata*, Issue 7, Fall 1979
11. Bishop, Greg. 2005. *Project Beta: The Story of Paul Bennewitz, and the Creation of a Modern UFO Myth*. Paraview Pocket Books. (p. 9)
12. *Ibid.*, p. 17.
13. *Ibid.*, p. 18.
14. Summary & Report Status (With Suggested Guidelines) "Project Beta Report" – Paul F. Bennewitz
15. Summary of notes taken by Jim McCampbell concerning two telephone interviews with Dr. Paul Bennewitz.
16. Casteel, Sean. 2011. *Underground Alien Bio Lab At Dulce: The Bennewitz UFO Papers*. Global Communications. Kindle Edition.
17. Bishop, Greg. 2005. *Project Beta: The Story of Paul Bennewitz, and the Creation of a Modern UFO Myth*. Paraview Pocket Books. (p. 149)
18. Bill Moore interview, *Radio Misterioso*, 1-21-06
19. Bishop, Greg. 2005. *Project Beta: The Story of Paul Bennewitz, and the Creation of a Modern UFO Myth*. Paraview Pocket Books. (p.184)
20. *Ibid.*, p.129.
21. *Ibid.*, p. 95.
22. Summary & Report Status (With Suggested Guidelines) "Project Beta Report" –Paul F. Bennewitz
23. Richard Doty interview, Jimmy Church's *Fade to Black*, 2-1-18
24. Summary of notes taken by Jim McCampbell concerning two telephone interviews with Dr. Paul Bennewitz.
25. Lambright, Christian. 2012. *X Descending*, X Desk Publishing. (Kindle Locations 2477-2479)
26. Bishop, Greg. 2005. *Project Beta: The Story of Paul Bennewitz, and the Creation of a Modern UFO Myth*. Paraview Pocket Books. (p. 56)
27. *MUFON UFO Journal*, Number 259, November 1998
28. Bishop, Greg. 2005. *Project Beta: The Story of Paul Bennewitz, and the Creation of a*

Modern UFO Myth. Paraview Pocket Books. (p. 159)

29. Valdez, Greg. *Dulce Base The Truth and Evidence from the Case Files of Gabe Valdez*. Levi-Cash Publishing. (Kindle Locations 1385-1386)

30. *Ibid.*, Kindle Locations 842-844.

31. http://area51specialprojects.com/mcgarity.html

32. Interview with Greg Valdez, 4-17-19

33. Bishop, Jason, *Recollections and Impressions of Visit to Dulce, New Mexico - October 23, 24, 1988.*

34. Interview with Greg Valdez, 4-17-19.

35. Valdez, Greg. *Dulce Base The Truth and Evidence from the Case Files of Gabe Valdez*. Levi-Cash Publishing. (Kindle Location 863)

36. Interview with Greg Valdez, April 17, 2019.

37. Valdez, Greg. *Dulce Base: The Truth and Evidence from the Case Files of Gabe Valdez*. Levi-Cash Publishing. (Kindle Locations 885-887)

38. Pilkington, Mark. 2010. *Mirage Men: An Adventure into Paranoia, Espionage, Psychological Warfare, and UFOs*. Skyhorse Publishing. (p. 126)

39. Bishop, Greg. 2005. *Project Beta: The Story of Paul Bennewitz, and the Creation of a Modern UFO Myth*. Paraview Pocket Books. (p. 164)

40. Summary & Report Status (With Suggested Guidelines) "Project Beta Report" – Paul F. Bennewitz

41. Lambright, Christian. 2012. *X Descending*. X Desk Publishing. (Kindle Locations 4345-4348)

42. *Ibid.*, Kindle Locations 4355-4356.

43. *Ibid.*, Kindle Locations 4407-4409.

44. Howe, Linda. 1989. *An Alien Harvest: Further Evidence Linking Animal Mutilations and Human Abductions to Alien Life Forms*. (p. 147-148)

45. Redfern, Nick. 2006. *On The Trail of the Saucer Spies*. Anomalist Books. (p.166)

46. *Ibid.*, p. 174.

47. Redfern, Nick. *MJ-12: The FBI Connection*, https://www.bibliotecapleyades.net/sociopolitica/esp_sociopol_mj12_23.htm

48. Redfern, Nick. 2006. *On the Trail of Saucer Spies*. Anomalist Books. (p.154)

49. Bishop, Greg. 2005. *Project Beta: The Story of Paul Bennewitz, and the Creation of a Modern UFO Myth*. Paraview Pocket Books. (p.110)

50. *Off The Deep End*, Issue #8, published by Tim Cridland.

51. Bill Moore, *Radio Misterioso*, 12-10-06.

52. Vallee, Jacques, 1991. *Revelations: Alien Contact and Human Deception*. New York: Ballantine Books (p.187)

53. Davis, Vance. 1995. *Unbroken Promises*, White Mesa Publishers.

54. Email correspondence with Jack Brewer, 7-25-18

55. Collins, Robert M. 2014. *The Black World of UFOs: Exempt from Disclosure*. Peregrine Communications. (Kindle Locations 175-177)

56. Collins, Robert M. 2014. *The Black World of UFOs: Exempt from Disclosure*. Peregrine Communications. (Kindle Locations 213-217)

57. Brad Sparks and Barry Greenwood, *The Secret Pratt Tapes and the Origin of MJ-12*, August 2007, MUFON International UFO Symposium Proceedings.

58. Durant, Robert J., "Will the Real Scott Jones Please Stand Up?", 1992.

59. Bowart, Walter, 1994. *Operation Mind Control*. Revised and Expanded Edition.

Flatland Publications.

60. Maccabee, Bruce and Friedman, Stanton. 2014. *The FBI-CIA-UFO Connection: The Hidden UFO Activities of USA Intelligence Agencies*. CreateSpace.

61. Redfern, Nick. 2019. *Flying Saucers from the Kremlin: UFOs, Russian Meddling, Soviet Spies & Cold War Secrets*. Lisa Hagan Books. Kindle Edition.

62. Pilkington, Mark. 2010. *Mirage Men: An Adventure into Paranoia, Espionage, Psychological Warfare, and UFOs*. Skyhorse Publishing. (p. 218)

63. *UFOs Tonight* with Don Ecker, 6-11-94

64. Interview with David Perkins, 6-9-19

65. John Lear, Facebook post, 4-24-19

66. Lambright, Christian, 2012. *X Descending*. X Desk Publishing. Kindle Location 3652)

67. John Lear, Facebook post, 2-12-18.

68. John Lear, Facebook post, 4-24-19

69. Branton, *The Dulce Book*. (p. 89)

70. John Lear, Facebook post, 4-24-19

71. Hamilton, William, 1991. *Cosmic Top Secret: America's Secret UFO Program*. Inner Light Publications (p.108-109)

72. John Lear interview, Project Camelot, 2008

73. Jacobson, Mark. 2018. *Pale Horse Rider: William Cooper, the Rise of Conspiracy, and the Fall of Trust in America*. Penguin Publishing Group. (pgs. 84-85)

74. Vallee, Jacques, 1991. *Revelations: Alien Contact and Human Deception*. New York: Ballantine Books. (p. 79)

75. Author's interview with Greg Bishop, 12-30-2017

76. *Stigmata*, Issue 19, Fourth Quarter, 1982

77. http://www.blueblurrylines.com/2014/02/whos-who-in-cash-landrum-ufo-case.html

78. *Stigmata*, Issue 14, 1981

79. Moore, William L. and Shandera, Jaime H., 1990. *The MJ-12 Documents: An Analytical Report*. The Fair Witness Project. Burbank, California. (p. 6)

80. Interview with Greg Valdez, 4-17-19

81. Jacobson, Mark. 2018. *Pale Horse Rider: William Cooper, the Rise of Conspiracy, and the Fall of Trust in America*. Penguin Publishing Group. Kindle Edition. (p. 97)

82. *Ibid.*, p. 103.

83. Barkun, Michael. 2003. *Culture of Conspiracy: Apocalyptic Visions in Contemporary America*. University of California Press. (p. 95)

84. http://www.subterraneanbases.com/the-dulce-papers-chapter-17/

85. Patton, Phil. 1998. *Dreamland: Travels Inside the Secret World of Roswell and Area 51*. Villard: New York. (p. 32)

86. Vallee, Jacques, 1991. *Revelations: Alien Contact and Human Deception*. New York: Ballantine Books. (p. 227)

87. Bishop, Greg. 2005. *Project Beta: The Story of Paul Bennewitz, and the Creation of a Modern UFO Myth*. Paraview Pocket Books. (p. 108)

88. Author's interview with Greg Valdez, April 17, 2019

89. https://mysteriousuniverse.org/2010/01/deja-vu-all-over-again-for-ufos-and-bigelow/

90. http://noriohayakawa2020.blogspot.com/search?q=rachel

91. Richard Sarradet interview, *Radio Misterioso*, 5-31-2009

92. https://noriohayakawa.wordpress.com/2016/02/16/the-secret-group-com-12-in-1992-fact-fiction-or-disinformation/

93. Summary of notes taken by Jim McCampbell concerning two telephone interviews with Dr. Paul Bennewitz.

94. John Lear, Facebook post, 2-12-18

95. McNeil, Legs, *Spin Magazine*, July, 1987. (p. 63)

96. Richard Doty interview, Jimmy Church's *Fade to Black*, 2-1-18.

97. August 8, 1988 letter from Christa Tilton to David Perkins.

98. Bishop, Greg. 2005. *Project Beta: The Story of Paul Bennewitz, and the Creation of a Modern UFO Myth*. Paraview Pocket Books. (p. 214)

99. Hamilton, William, 1991. *Cosmic Top Secret: America's Secret UFO Program*. Inner Light Publications, (p. 105)

100. Author's interview with Greg Valdez, April 17, 2019

101. Interview with Greg Valdez, 4-17-19

102. Casteel, Sean. 2011. *Underground Alien Bio Lab At Dulce: The Bennewitz UFO Papers*. Global Communications. Kindle Edition.

103. Letter from Martin Cannon, to unidentified correspondent, June 1989

104. https://www.fold3.com/record/527037404-christy-l-tilton

105. https://www.youtube.com/watch?v=M1wZou2Mnxk

106. https://noriohayakawa.wordpress.com/2017/11/03/phil-schneiders-dulce-base-delusion/comment-page-1/

107. https://noriohayakawa.wordpress.com/2017/11/03/phil-schneiders-dulce-base-delusion/

108. Rick Doty interview, Jimmy Church's *Fade To Black*, 2-1-18

109. http://www.openminds.tv/william-moore-ufo-opportunist-agent-disinformation/29056

110. https://www.dreamlandresort.com/team/norio.html

111. Bishop, Greg. 2016. *It Defies Language!: Essays on UFOs and Other Weirdness*. Excluded Middle Press. (Kindle Locations 632-633)

112. Interview with Mark Pilkington, 10-11-17.

113. Pilkington, Mark. 2010. *Mirage Men: An Adventure into Paranoia, Espionage, Psychological Warfare, and UFOs*. Skyhorse Publishing. (p. 169)

114. Interview with Mark Pilkington, 10-11-17

115. Pilkington, Mark. 2010. *Mirage Men: An Adventure into Paranoia, Espionage, Psychological Warfare, and UFOs*. Skyhorse Publishing (p. 131)

116. Interview with Mark Pilkington, 10-11-17

117. Interview with Greg Bishop, 12-30-17

118. Collins, Robert M. *The Black World of UFOs: Exempt from Disclosure*. 2010. Peregrine Communications. (Kindle Location 1336)

119. Interview with Greg Bishop, 12-30-17

120. Redfern, Nick. 2017. *The Roswell UFO Conspiracy: Exposing A Shocking and Sinister Secret*. (p. 100)

121. Midnight Writer News Episode 011 – The John Lear Files

122. *Off The Deep End*, Issue #8, published by Tim Cridland.

123. Robert Collins interview, Coast to Coast AM with Art Bell, 5-27-07.

124. Bishop, Greg. 2005. *Project Beta: The Story of Paul Bennewitz, and the Creation of a Modern UFO Myth*. Paraview Pocket Books. (p. 105)

125. Valdez, Greg. *Dulce Base The Truth and Evidence from the Case Files of Gabe Valdez*. Levi-Cash Publishing. Kindle Edition.

126. Redfern, Nick. 2019. *Flying Saucers from the Kremlin: UFOs, Russian Meddling, Soviet Spies & Cold War Secrets*. Lisa Hagan Books. Kindle Edition.

127. https://noriohayakawa.wordpress.com/2016/01/10/laying-to-rest-once-and-for-all-a-fake-document-som-01-1-special-operations-manual/
128. https://www.theufochronicles.com/2014/10/mj-12-hoax-that-quickly-became.html
129. https://www.huffingtonpost.com/entry/inside-knowledge-about-unidentified-aerial-phenomena_us_59dc1230e4b0b48cd8e0a5c7
130. https://www.youtube.com/watch?v=wxVRg7LLaQA
131. https://www.metabunk.org/explained-photo-of-ufo-used-in-connection-with-nimitz-incident-balloon.t9345/
132. https://ufotrail.blogspot.com/search?updated-max=2019-02-25T12:45:00-05:00&max-results=7
133. https://nypost.com/2019/05/22/the-pentagon-finally-admits-it-investigates-ufos/
134. https://theintercept.com/2019/06/01/ufo-unidentified-history-channel-luis-elizondo-pentagon/
135. https://arstechnica.com/science/2018/10/all-the-dumb-things-blink-182-front-mans-ufo-project-37-million-in-debt/
136. https://apnews.com/dc0728173537459b9a1e38009dd5c4b5
137. https://badufos.blogspot.com/2018/03/to-stars-or-to-dogs-case-of-missing-hot.html
138. Bishop, Greg. *It Defies Language!: Essays on UFOs and Other Weirdness.* Excluded Middle Press. (p. 22-23)

Index

Schneider, Phil: and Area 51, 213, 215, 216; death of, 218; and Dulce Base, 213, 214; mental health of, 216; and radioactive matter, 216-218

Schmitt, Harrison: cattle mute conference, 26, 31

Scully, Frank: *Behind the Flying Saucers*, 16

Shandera, Jaime: and Aviary, 86, 88; and Bishop, 236-237; *Coast to Coast AM*, 235; and Doty, 237; and English, 129-130; as film producer, 235; and MJ-12, 68, 73, 74, 80, 131, 252; and Moore, 68, 75, 80, 131, 236; and Moseley, 139; and Weitzel letter, 132

Shartle, Paul: and aliens/UFOs, 76

Shaver, Richard: and Dulce Base, 183; "I Remember Lemuria", 184; and Tal, 150-151

Schuessler, John: and MUFON, 100

Smirnov, Igor: and Jones, 97; and Laibow, 97; and Stubblebine, 97

Smith, Dan T.: and Johnson, 91, 92; and Pandolfini, 91, 92

SOM-1-01: and Berliner, 253; and Deuley, 254

Sparks, Brad: and CAUS, 18

Sprinkle, Leo: and Hansen, 32

Stargate: 95, 263

Stevens, Wendelle: and AFOSI, 192, 209; and Tilton, 192, 193, 196

Stone, Clifford: and Bennewitz, 106, 108, 111, 112; and Howe, 106; and Lear, 106; and Tilton, 193-194

Stringfield, Leonard: MUFON, 16-17

Stubblebine, Albert: and Jones, 97, and PSI-TECH, 96; on remote viewing, 97; and Smirnov, 97

TTSA (To The Stars Academy of Arts and Science): Bigelow and, 265, 268; DeLong and, 258-260; Elizondo and, 264, 265; finances of, 270-271; and "metal alloys", 268; press conference, 262-263; stock offering of, 265

Teller, Edward: and Lazar, 168, and Lear, 168

Thornley, Kerry: and Chapel Perilous, 276; death of, 281; and Discordianism, 276; and JFK assassination, 277, 278; and mind control, 278-279; and RAW, 278-279

Tilton, Christa: and Adams, 195-196, 211; and Area 51, 197; *The Bennewitz Papers*, 201-

203, 210; and Byrd, 211-212; and Cannon, 206-207; and Doty, 210; and Dulce Base, 196-197, 202; and Hansen, 202; and Hinkle, 203-204; and Levesque, 204; marriages, 192-193, 196, 211; and Moore, 201; and Stone, 193-195; *UFO Abductions of Women: The Triad Experiment*, 193; and Wallis, 204-205, 206

UFO Cover-Up? Live!: 75, 77, 80-81; and Area 51, 226; and Falcon/Condor, 81-82; and Moore, 80, 129; and Roswell, 87; and Soviets, 226

UFO Working Group: and Alexander, 90; and "Aquarius", 90; and Aviary, 90

Unser, Bobby: 138

Valdez, Gabe: at Albuquerque cattle mutilation conference, 30-31; and bugging devices, 136; and Castello, 188-189; and cattle mutilations, 22, 23, 24, 25, 220; and Doty, 138; and Hansen, 32; and Mount Archuleta, 31, 48-49, 51, 199-200; and NIDS, 219; and Schneider, 216, 218

Valdez, Greg: *Dulce Base: The Truth and Evidence from the Case Files of Gabe Valdez*, 40; and McGarity, 52; on Hansen, 245

Wade, Heather: and MJ-12, 249, 250, 251

Wallis, John: and Tilton, 204-205, 206, 207, 208

Walters, Ed (Ed Hanson): 83, 85

Weitzel letter: 42-45; and AFOSI, 45, 132, 169-170

Wilson, Robert Anton (RAW): and chapel perilous, 274-276; and Thornley, 278-281

Yellow Book: 81, 87

Yellow Fruit: and Area 51, 185; and *The Billy Goodman Happening*, 185, 186; Levesque as, 185-186

Younger, Michael: and Bishop, 292; and Bluefire Memo, 179; and COM-12, 179; disappearance/death, 182; real identity, 182; surveillance of, 181-182

Zechel, Todd: 17; and CAUS, 18; and KGB, 223

Lightning Source UK Ltd.
Milton Keynes UK
UKHW042031041222
413380UK00001B/4

9 780994 617682